THE
IRANIAN REVOLUTION
&
THE ISLAMIC REPUBLIC

THE
IRANIAN REVOLUTION
&
THE ISLAMIC REPUBLIC

NEW EDITION

Edited by
NIKKI R. KEDDIE
and ERIC HOOGLUND

SYRACUSE UNIVERSITY PRESS

The paper used in this publication meets the minimum requirements
of American National Standard for Information Sciences—Permanence
of Paper for Printed Library Materials, ANSI Z39.48-1984.∞™

Library of Congress Cataloging-in-Publication Data

The Iranian revolution & the Islamic Republic.

(Contemporary issues in the Middle East)
Revised papers originally presented to a Conference
on "The Iranian Revolution and the Islamic Republic:
New Assessments," held at the Woodrow Wilson
International Center for Scholars on May 21–22, 1982.
Includes bibliographies and index.
1. Iran—Politics and government—1979– —
Congresses. I. Keddie, Nikki R. II. Hooglund, Eric J.
(Eric James), 1944– . III. Series.
DS318.8.I72 1986   955'.054   86-17370
ISBN 0-8156-2387-9 (pbk.: alk. paper)

Manufactured in the United States of America

CONTENTS

PREFACE

THIS VOLUME is a completely revised and updated version of a volume published in 1982, under the same title, by the Middle East Institute and the Woodrow Wilson International Center for Scholars. It includes revised or rewritten versions of papers presented to a Conference on "The Iranian Revolution and the Islamic Republic: New Assessments," held at the Woodrow Wilson International Center for Scholars on May 21–22, 1982, along with edited transcripts of some of the discussion and a few additional papers given to the conference or written especially for the 1986 edition.

Some of the highlights of the papers herein are: analyses of the revolutionary clergy ruling Iran—their social origins, political lineups (based partly on these origins), and future sources of instability (Akhavi, Hooglund, Abrahamian); Iran's actual relations to the superpowers and what U.S. policy in Iran should be (Sick, Miller, Atkin, and Cottam); ideology and realities regarding women (Ferdows); critical approaches to the Iranian opposition (Najmabadi); and an eyewitness study of economic change in a rural area (Loeffler). Some important questions do not have whole papers devoted to them, such as the human rights situation, the Iran-Iraq war, and minority questions, but these topics are discussed in various papers.

Nikki R. Keddie did the basic editing of both editions, and Eric Hooglund did the transcription and editing of the oral remarks and the index. The editors would like to thank the Woodrow Wilson Center, especially Deputy Director Prosser Gifford, Louise Platt, Cynthia Ely, Elizabeth Dixon, Ella Edmond, and Andrea Pisani for their tremendous help in putting on the conference and with the original volume, as well as the word processing staff, especially Eloise Doan and also Donna Watson for typing the first edition. Special thanks are also due to Muriel Atkin and Jahangir Salehi, both of whom provided invaluable assistance in the tedious task of proof-reading the papers and transcribed remarks. Thanks for typing the second edition go to Irene Chow and Jane Bitar of UCLA Central Word Processing. We are also grateful to Ken Mayers, Jean-Luc Krawczyk, and Rudi Matthee who coordinated the preparation of the final transcript.

Part I of this edition is an entirely new section containing two papers (Hooglund and Karimi) based upon original research undertaken since the conference was held. Parts II through V follow the basic format of the 1982 edition. Some of the papers and some of the Discussant's Remarks include updates. Other papers (specifically Akhavi and Hooglund in Part II) have been completely revised in light of changes which have occurred since the spring of 1982.

The informal discussions transcribed herein include the most important and relevant contributions and have been edited for style and clarity only. When discussion speakers could not be identified from the tapes their remarks are simply listed as *Question* or *Comment*. The discussions and discussants' remarks remain as they were in the 1982 edition, with minor editing.

The editors would like finally to extend their thanks to all the speakers and discussants, to those who gave us additional papers, to the fine conference audience who contributed so much, and to the Middle East Institute who published the first edition.

We have used a simplified system of Persian transliteration, without diacritics. Arabic transliterations are used in chapters concerning the Arabs, and throughout for terms better known in Arabic than in Persian forms (chiefly Islamic terms). Words that have entered English are generally given their dictionary spellings, and names habitually transliterated by a system other than ours are left in their familiar forms. Foreign terms not in most English dictionaries are italicized only upon their first use in each chapter.

Los Angeles, California   Nikki R. Keddie
Washington, D.C.   Eric Hooglund
March 1986

CONTRIBUTORS and DISCUSSANTS

ERVAND ABRAHAMIAN is Professor of History, Baruch College, City University of New York. He is the author of *Iran Between Two Revolutions* (Princeton, 1982), and has published articles on Modern Iran in *Iranian Studies, IJMES, Middle East Studies, MERIP,* and *Past and Present.*

SHAHROUGH AKHAVI is Professor of Government and International Relations, University of South Carolina. He is the Author of *Religion and Politics in Contemporary Iran: Clergy-State Relations in the Pahlavi Period* (Albany, 1980) and of several articles on Iran and Egypt in a variety of books and journals. He is General Editor of the Middle East Series, State University of New York Press and Book Review Editor of *Iranian Studies.*

MURIEL ATKIN is Associate Professor of History, The George Washington University. She is the author of *Russia and Iran, 1780–1828* and of a number of articles on Russian and Soviet relations with Iran.

PATRICK CLAWSON, an economist working in Washington, has written several papers on the Iranian economy and has taught economics on the university level.

RICHARD W. COTTAM, University Professor of Political Science, University of Pittsburgh, served in the U.S. Embassy, Tehran, 1956–58. He is the author of *Nationalism in Iran, Competitive Interference and Twentieth Century Diplomacy, Foreign Policy Motivation,* and *The Rehabilitation of Power in International Relations* (with G. Gallucci).

ix

ADELE FERDOWS, Professor of Political Science at the University of Louisville has written both about Islamic extremism in Iran and about ideology and realities regarding women in contemporary Iran. Her work includes contributions to: *Women and the Family in Iran,* ed. by A. Fathi, 1983, and with Amir Ferdows, *Women and Revolution in Iran,* ed. by G. Nashat, 1982. She has articles in *IJMES,* May 1982, and *Oriente Moderno,* 1983.

ERIC HOOGLUND is Senior Analyst for the Iran Project of the National Security Archive. He has spent several years in Iran, including the revolutionary academic year 1978–79 teaching at the University of Shiraz. He has written numerous articles about Iranian social groups and politics and is the author of *Land and Revolution in Iran* (Texas, 1982) and co-author of *Triumph of the Turban: The Shi'i Clergy and Revolutionary Politics in Iran* (forthcoming).

SETAREH KARIMI is a development economist who has studied several third world countries, concentrating recently on Iran.

NIKKI KEDDIE is Professor of History, U.C.L.A., and has published numerous articles and books on Iran and the Middle East, the most recent of which are *Roots of Revolution: An Interpretive History of Modern Iran* (Yale, 1982), with M. Bonine, eds., *Modern Iran: The Dialectics of Continuity and Change* (Albany, 1981), ed., *Religion and Politics in Iran* (Yale, 1983), and, with Juan Cole, *Shi'ism and Social Protest* (Yale, 1986).

REINHOLD L. LOEFFLER is Professor of Anthropology at Western Michigan University. He has completed five years of research focussing on a year of field research in Boir Ahmad and Kuhgiluye, South Iran supported by Wenner-Gren, SSRC, and other research grants. He has published papers on various aspects of Boir Ahmad culture, and a manuscript for a book, *Peasant Religion of Iran,* is under consideration by the University of Texas Press.

WILLIAM GREEN MILLER served in Iran as a Foreign Service Officer 1959–64. He also served in the United States Senate as Foreign Policy and National Security advisor to Senator John Sherman Cooper from 1967–72, and as Staff Director of three Senate Committees before leaving in 1981 to become Associate Dean of the Fletcher School of Law and Diplomacy.

AFSANEH NAJMABADI (Azar Tabari) was the Nemazee Fellow (1984–85) at the Center for Middle Eastern Studies at Harvard University. She is co-author of *In the Shadow of Islam: the Women's Movement in Iran* (Zed Press, 1983), has written on the Iranian revolution for several journals, and is a member of the editorial groups of the journals *Khamsin* and *Nimeye digar*.

GARY SICK was the principal White House aide for Iran in the National Security Council staff during the Iranian revolution and the hostage crisis. He is the author of *All Fall Down: America's Encounter with the Iranian Revolution* (Random House, 1985). He is presently with the Ford Foundation, where he is responsible for programs relating to U.S. foreign policy.

Oral presentations were also given by Mangol Bayat and Shaul Bakhash, who contributed to the discussion within, as did Gregory Rose, Jahangir Salehi, Leonard Helfgott, and Claude van Engeland. Other contributors to the conference included Gene Garthwaite, William Millward, and Barry Rubin.

THE
IRANIAN REVOLUTION
&
THE ISLAMIC REPUBLIC

INTRODUCTION

Nikki R. Keddie

THE IRANIAN REVOLUTION of 1978–79 was a startling and important event. Its outbreak and course of development had scarcely been foreseen by members of the scholarly community or those in the U.S. government. It has introduced a number of relative or absolute novelties on the world scene, and its importance, both before and after its victory, is widely recognized. Nevertheless, there is a relatively small truly analytical literature on either the revolution or the Islamic Republic, and the American press has greatly reduced its coverage of events in Iran. In part this sparseness of coverage and analysis is owing to the difficulty for U.S. journalists and scholars of travel to Iran, but in addition it may owe something to the intractability of the material for Westerners, as Iran seems not to fit into the familiar Western historical, political, or ideological categories.

Largely in order to come to grips with some of the challenging intellectual and political problems raised by the Iranian Revolution and the Islamic Republic, a conference was held at the Woodrow Wilson International Center for Scholars in Washington, D.C. in May, 1982. As it was only possible to hold a short conference, a group of important topics was selected that lent themselves to panel presentation and discussion by people who had studied and in some cases had direct experience in dealing with them. Most of the papers presented are included in this volume, along with summaries of several oral presentations by panelists and of the most important discussions. The authors have revised, updated, and in some cases (for example, Akhavi, Atkin, Cottam, Najmabadi) completely rewritten their papers in the light of new developments for the 1986 edition. Also, this edition adds new papers on current topics like the Iran-Iraq War and its domestic implications, while omitting a few papers from the first edition on topics already well covered. In this introduction I will not try to summarize the papers—their length has already been limited to what is essential—but rather to provide a more general discussion of the Iranian Revolution and the Islamic Republic which may provide some background to the more specific studies enclosed.

Iran, whose long history provides many examples of messianic revolt punctuating longer periods of calm, can be a particularly deceptive country for foreigners. During quiet periods Iranians tend to be complaisant to foreigners and peaceful in their behavior. Yet in both traditional and modern times this peaceful exterior has been punctuated by numerous revolts. During the past one hundred fifty years there have been the militant and messianic Babi risings in the mid-nineteenth century; the smaller but successful movement against the all-inclusive Reuter concession of 1872; the successful revolt against a British tobacco monopoly concession of 1891–92; the temporarily successful Constitutional Revolution of 1905–11; the temporarily successful Mossadeq oil nationalization movement of 1951–53; smaller regional revolts after both world wars, and finally the Revolution of 1978–79. Few countries have such a history of large mass revolts not counting coups, and it seems clear that if complaisance makes up one part of Iranians' social character, when conditions seem to demand it these same Iranians are often aroused to mass revolt. Some observers have noted that both the largely Shi'i practice of *taqiyya*, or dissimulation of one's beliefs to ward off danger, and the many centuries of rule by oppressive governments, usually foreign, have taught Iranians to hide hostility towards religious and political oppressors, and this helps account for their frequent apparent acquiescence in the political status quo and in the power of foreigners in their country. On the other hand, once conditions reach a point that encourages revolt, the former amiability may be radically discarded, and both rulers and their foreign backers become subject to pent-up wrath. This process is not different in kind from what happens elsewhere during revolts, but it may be different in degree.

Most qualified observers are in general agreement about the factors behind Iran's 1978–79 revolution, and since these have been widely discussed they will only be briefly mentioned here. These factors include the way modernization was carried out by Muhammad Reza Shah especially in his last years. Although some stress the speed of "modernization," its *manner* seems at least as important. In essence, means were used that radically tore people from their accustomed ways of life and brought them brutally into unfamiliar ones, and that increased the economic, social, and cultural gaps between rich and poor. Land reform helped some, but in the end became largely a means for depriving many rural dwellers of jobs, or of enough land for subsistence, and, along with population growth, for encouraging a massive migration into overcrowded cities with inadequate jobs or amenities. The regime's economic policies favored a small wealthy group, often with close ties to the shah, and also encouraged large or multinational enterprises, while the traditional bazaar classes were increasingly cut out of the pie.

Iran's foreign policy was closely tied to the U.S. policy, and though some scholars argue that the shah was able to manipulate the U.S. as much as he was controlled by them, through such means as threatening to increase his relations with the U.S.S.R., for large numbers of Iranians close ties to the U.S. meant that the shah was seen simply as an American tool. Large-scale corruption touching the royal family and high governmental officials was also widely known and resented. Ironically, all these problems were worsened by the great OPEC oil price increase of 1973, of which the shah was the chief architect. The doubling of the Five Year Plan budget in 1974, insisted on by the shah, brought increasing problems of inflation, bottlenecks at roads and ports, shortages of needed material, and all the signs of a greatly overheated economy. Cutbacks in 1975–76 suddenly eliminated the construction jobs that had supported rural-urban migrants. Thus began the (Davies) "J-curve" situation typical of revolutions, in which a period of economic growth is followed by a sudden period of sharp decline. The 1977 reduction in government funds to the clergy under the prime minister Amuzegar (possibly ordered by the shah) gave a further push to discontent, this time on the part of the increasingly popular clergy.

It is possible to date the beginnings of the 1978–79 revolution to attacks on the holy city of Qom, where demonstrations opposed a scurrilous January 1978 article against Khomeini, in exile in Iraq since his 1963–64 oppositional activities, by the semi-official newspapers *Ettela'at*. It was not, however, known at the time that people were witnessing the beginning of a revolution and not just another demonstration. Even when other mass demonstrations followed at traditional forty-day mourning intervals, it was not clear to most people before September how serious the situation was. Thus, when it is stressed that U.S. intelligence miscalled the situation, which is true, it should not be inferred that many Iranians or other foreign ministries were much better informed. It is true that Israel and France received better reports from some representatives than the U.S. government did, but it is not true, as is sometimes stated, that these reports predicted with accuracy the scope of the revolution or the imminent fall of the shah, and neither Israel nor France acted according to an expectation of the shah's impending fall. And, as late as the summer of 1978 most Iranian intellectuals seen by foreigners, including myself, were in a state of near-euphoria, sure that the demonstrations, now that they had succeeded in eliciting promises of liberalism and democracy from the shah, were now essentially over and Iran could develop on a liberal and constitutional basis.

It would seem that American failures in Iran were not so much failures in intelligence as failures in policy, especially as it is unlikely that the U.S. government could or would have seriously changed the course of events in 1978–79 even had it had better intelligence. Changes in U.S. policy would have had to be longer-term and more far-reaching to have had a significant effect on strong Iranian feeling against control of their country by American and other Western political and economic interests. America's dependence on Iranian and Persian Gulf oil, its promotion of huge sales of arms and other goods to Iran in order to compensate for oil imports and help meet U.S. balance of payments and trade problems, and U.S. desire to use Iran as a strategic bastion against the Soviet Union and to support U.S. aims in the Gulf and in the Middle East, led to growing U.S. reliance on the shah and his regime. It is unlikely that the U.S. would have modified this significantly even had our intelligence been better. Even after the fall of the shah, the U.S. retained similar policies toward other autocratic or unpopular but pro-American governments, including those of Sadat and various monarchies.

U.S. policy, particularly in later phases when the shah had a blank check in ordering arms and when huge arms orders further unbalanced the Iranian economy, led naturally to Iranian blame of the U.S. for much of the growing autocracy, corruption, and economic disarray. The close ties of the shah to the U.S. led to the U.S. being widely blamed for problems in Iran, and to the revolution's becoming nearly as anti-American government as it was anti-shah. Anti-U.S. slogans were prominent in the great mass demonstrations from September 1978 through January 1979, and this attitude continued strong after the revolutionaries took power in February 1979. (Further discussion of U.S. policy before and since the revolution is found in the contributions by Miller, Sick, and Cottam.)

Mass movements against an alliance of local despots and their foreign supporters are fairly frequent in the third world, but the Iranian revolution was special both in the role played by a large section of the orthodox clergy supported by Islamic ideology and in its successful use of increasingly massive urban demonstrations to bring down a well-armed regime.

The role of the clergy and of Islamic ideology have been discussed elsewhere, and here it is worth stressing just a few points. First, Iran, which officially followed the minority Shi'i branch of Islam since the beginning of the Safavid dynasty in 1501, had a Shi'i clergy and doctrine that increasingly stressed the independent power of the most qualified clergy, the *mujtahids* and ayatollahs, to give independent judgment on all matters covered by holy law, which would include many that the West would call political as well as religious questions. Although the ulama under the early Safavids were largely state-employed or sponsored, their economic independence grew with time, not only via donations of inalienable property, but through their independent control, which continued even under the Pahlavis, of the chief religious taxes and donations. This control was one of several things that distinguished them from the Sunni ulama who were in a majority in the Muslim world. From the early nineteenth century on, certain ulama became leaders of increasingly powerful movements against Western infidel incursions and Iranian government policy. Thus, ulama helped bring about a war against Russia in 1826, the cancellation of the all-encompassing economic concession held by Baron de Reuter, a British subject, in 1872–73, the successful protest against a British tobacco monopoly in 1891–92, and were leaders in the constitutional revolution of 1905–1911, and in mass demonstrations against the government in 1963 as well as in the revolution of 1978–79. Over time the ulama's ideology and position became increasingly differentiated from those of the state, which was seen both as Western-controlled and oppressive.

Some of the special and surprising features of the 1978–79 revolution may be understood via a comparison of some aspects of that revolution with that of 1905–11, but the partial similarity of that revolution to that of 1978–79 should not blind us to major and singificant differences between the two. There follows a brief venture into comparative twentieth-century history, which may shed light on recent events.

Iran is one of the few countries in the world to have had two major popular twentieth century revolutions that succeeded in changing the form of government—the revolution of 1905–11 and that of 1978–79. A comparison of their similarities and differences can be instructive for understanding the political and social history and continuing development of modern Iran.

To note some similarities: both revolutions were carried out by coalitions consisting largely of ulama, bazaaris, and intellectuals, although in the 1978–79 revolution the participation in addition of the urban masses, including the poorest among them, was much greater. Both revolutions incorporated in their coalitions groups which had different

ultimate aims, although the central aims in both cases were to end despotism and the overwhelming influence on the government of major
Western powers. In the constitutional revolution as in the recent one, most
of the secular intellectuals and professionals wanted a Western-type liberal
democratic government, with an elected parliament and executive, and
guarantees for freedom of speech, assembly, and press. In 1978–79 many
in both the intellectual and middle-class groups would have been glad to
reinstate the essentially democratic constitution of 1906–07, in which the
king was supposed to be a figurehead like the kings of England or
Belgium. In the 1906 revolution a small minority of intellectuals as well as
a few workers and others also had leftist or socialist aims, and this group
had grown greatly by 1978–79. In the later revolution, there were sizeable
leftist or socialist groups, which differed about what tactics to follow.
They agreed that the most important question for Iran was the reorgan-
ization of its social and economic structure so as to create social or
national ownership of the means of production, a further redistribution of
land in favor of the peasants, and worker participation in the management
of industries.

In both revolutions the ulama provided important ideological
leadership, but in both revolutions there were also splits among the ulama:
in the 1906 revolution chiefly between ulama who favored and helped lead
the revolution, like Sayyid Abdollah Behbahani and Sayyid Mohammad
Tabataba'i on the one hand, and opponents of either the entire constitutional movement or of its non-shari'a nature, like Shaikh Fazlollah Nuri.
In the recent Revolution divisions occurred first between those ulama who
avoided political action and those who favored it, and later between those
who accepted Khomeini's interpretation of Islamic government and those
who rejected it on various theoretical and practical grounds. In both
revolutions ulama were important, but in neither were they united. Bazaaris were especially important in the first revolution, as at that time they
made up most of Iran's middle class and could mobilize most of its
artisans, which they did very effectively on several occasions, notably the
great *bast* at the British legation in 1906. In 1978 bazaaris also contributed much time and effort, but by that time the modernized middle class
was just as important in the revolution and in society. Both middle classes
tended to become disillusioned after 1979, more than after 1906, in part
because the Islamic government took measures limiting freedom of trade,
industry, the press, and so forth.

Other similarities between the two revolutions were the establishment in both of new constitutions based on new principles of government,
the breakup of the coalitions that brought them to power as parts of those
coalitions were either repressed by the government or came to see that

their aims were not those of the center, the mobilization of more wide-spread mass movements in both revolutions than had been politicized before, and the disillusionment of many people once it became clear to them that their utopian expectations of the revolution were not at all being realized.

In addition to a few major similarities of the two revolutions, there were also important contrasts. One obvious contrast concerns the total nature of the Islamic Revolution: as compared to 1906–07 much larger masses of the people were mobilized, and the existing dynasty was not just made subject to a constitution, but was overthrown. Very few members of the old regime, as compared to 1906, were allowed to stay in government but rather the whole top governing cadre was changed; the revolution took measures to favor the popular classes over the elite, reversing the past in some measure; and a single ideology was increasingly promulgated and ulama took increasing control. None of these things happened after the constitutional revolution, which was less massive, less idological, and lacked a charismatic leader.

To a Western observer at least, one major difference between the two revolutions appears as a paradox: during the first revolution, at a time when very few Iranians had Westernized educations or knew much about the West, a very Western-style form of government and constitution were installed and were even accepted by ulama leaders of the movement. In 1978–79, by contrast, when Iranians were far more Westernized by education and culture then before, there was a reaction against things Western and an installation of a constitutional system that claimed to be inspired by the practices of the Prophet and early Islam. How may we explain this apparent contradition?

The main explanation lies in the chief enemy that the revolutionists saw themselves as fighting in each case, and their consequent turn toward an ideology contrary to that of this chief enemy. In both revolutions, as noted, both despotism and foreign influence were seen as enemies, but they were seen as having very different kinds of importance. In 1906 the chief enemy was seen as the arbitrary Qajar shahs, who had deliberately left Iran backward and not allowed it to strengthen itself via modern education or encouragement of economic development. The foreign powers, chiefly Britain and Russia, who manipulated the Qajars were seen as a secondary problem that could be handled if the dynasty were made subject to parliamentary control and its policies changed. Even many ulama accepted the need for a Western-style constitution in these terms.

The 1978–79 revolution, by contrast, came after fifty years of intensive and mainly despotic modernization from the top, which was increasingly seen as subject to Western—first British then American—

control or influence. Westernization, although one may say that it had only been tried in a partial and distorted form, was seen as something that tore people from their cultural roots and increased the wealth of the rich at the expense of the poor. Largely because the ulama had far greater ties to the masses than did the leftists, who were persecuted, leftist solutions to social injustice did not become widely understood or popular, while those of ulama like Ayatollahs Khomeini and Taleqani did spread. Hence, the time was right for a new mass response to a new central enemy: no longer was it believed that Western ways could overcome a traditional shah, as in 1906; now instead the Islamic tradition, widely accepted and not royal, was adapted to fight a Westernizing shah who was seen as a willing tool of the U.S. Hence, the difference in central ideologies of the two revolutions resulted largely from the differences in the political and cultural scene which changed the main perceived enemy from a traditional shah to the West and Westernization.

A second reason for the great difference in dominant ideologies between the two revolutions is the different social classes involved in the two. The first revolution was largely limited to the ulama (many of whom were, however, increasingly opposed to it), the small group of secular intellectuals, and the bazaar. The 1978–79 revolution, however, mobilized by the end nearly all the urban social classes and some rural ones. Very important were workers and also the "subproletariat" without regular factory jobs, made up chiefly of the huge stream of rural migrants to the cities. These popular classes, who made up the largest group in the 1978–79 revolution, had few ties to Western ideologies, whether liberal or socialist. While some workers were led by leftists and others followed the left-Islamic Mojahedin-e Khalq, the majority of this group responded to the more familiar idiom of a radicalized ulama-led Islam which was both tied to their own culture and promised solutions for their problems. Hence, the very popular nature of the revolution resulted in its increasing Islamization.

Finally, the charismatic leadership and uncompromising stand of Khomeini should not be ignored as a factor in changing people's thinking. During the revolution he knew when to stand firm against the regime when others favored constitutional compromises, and he has often been able to sense the mood of the masses and the possibilities of a situation better than anyone else.

To take a final point of both similarity and contrast between the revolutions: in both, as in many world revolutions, the original revolution-ary coalition largely broke down once power was taken and the dif-ferences between different opponents of the old regime came to the fore. In contrast, however, the first revolution's political groups rarely resorted to

violent suppression of adversaries, except when Mohammad Ali Shah
seized power by a coup and he and his supporters were overthrown. The
current revolution is now far more absolutist in its ideology and its
treatment of dissident members of the revolutionary coalition than the
first ever was. This difference reflects the difference between militant
populist Islam today and the constitutionalism of 1907. Possibly too,
ideological and socio-economic dissent from the dominant ideology are
greater today than they were in the past, despite attempts to suppress
them.

    More than ever in the past and more than in any other Muslim
ruling group to date, Islam has been interpreted as a populist ideology of
mass politics by Khomeini and his followers. Since orthodox clergy have
rarely led populist revolutionary movements, this development seems
strange, not only in the West but to many Muslims as well. Yet by now it
should be clear that many different ideologies may serve to inspire masses
of ordinary people to fight to better their lives.

    For many centuries utopian religious messianism, generally out-
side the mainstream of orthodoxy, was a channel for the popular classes,
in particular to express their active desire for an economically just, better,
and more egalitarian way of life. Such messianic mass movements are
found repeatedly in all the major prophetic and monotheistic religions,
including Islam, where the standard tag for the messianic Mahdi was "he
who will fill the earth with justice and equity as it is now filled with
injustice and oppression." Rigorous orthodoxy was also at times, particularly since the beginnings of more modern economic systems, a vehicle
for mass desires for a better world; Savanarola in Florence and Calvin and
Calvinists, especially in Geneva, are good examples. Liberal constitutional democracy has also inspired mass movements to achieve the good
society, whether in the French and American revolutions and their nine-
teenth-century aftermaths, or in constitutional movements in the twentieth-century third world, including Iran.

    In recent decades mass revolution has been associated particularly
with Marxist doctrines of class struggle and socialism or communism, as
in Russia, China, Cuba, Vietnam, and other countries. Very recently,
however, there has been a resurgence of religious populism, whether in its
chiefly Latin American Catholic form, or in the populist sides of the
"Islamic Revival" of recent years. In part this "revival" involves the Islamic
masses now entering politics, but in part it is also a rejection of the
ideologies of a West seen as hostile and oppressive. No longer do the
middle and upper classes that tend to emulate the West have a monopoly
of power. As the new popular classes enter the political arena they are far
more inclined to voice their desires in familiar Islamic terms (and tradi-

tions of social justice, equity, and independence may be found in Islam) than in unfamiliar, and even ill-regarded, Western ones. It is a special feature of Khomeini that he was able to stress parts of Islam that appealed to the "deprived" against the rich, and to the oppressed Muslim against the oppressing Great Satan from the West. In appeals by Khomeini and those around him we find clear echoes of many of the Western ideological systems they reject—in their parliamentary, constitutionalist, ministerial regime; in their appeal to the masses against economic oppression and their widespread adoption of nationalizations and other socialist measures; and in the third worldist and partly nationalist emphasis on the greatest possible self-sufficiency. Even traditional messianism is present, as it is in most modern revolutions, both in semi-messianic feelings and titles surrounding Khomeini and in the common revolutionary belief that all problems will be solved if only the ideology and its practices are followed. Eric Hooglund's second paper within notes the popular class origins of many of the revolutionary clergy, who reflect the viewpoints of their own class background.

Although a number of ideologies may support similar mass desires for a better life, economically and culturally, this does not mean that the practical results of different ideologies are the same. Ideologies are not simply invented by revolutionary leaders, but have a certain irreducible minimum of pre-exisiting content which the leader and his followers will not abandon, so that a communist revolution, for example, will look different in basic ways from a revolution with Islamic ideology.

Movements and governments, whether revolutionary or not, which strongly stress their Islamic nature, tend to move in the direction of punishments and practices found in the Quran or in the sayings and practices attributed to Muhammad and to early Muslim leaders. This has brought, for example, movements or gestures toward the restoration of early Islamic punishments in states ranging from those in Arabia, through Pakistan and Sudan, to Iran, and even Libya (where, however, Qadhafi has become decreasingly "Islamic" and the legislated punishments are not carried out). Similarly, in a whole range of countries that want to stress their "Islamic" nature, practices traditionally characteristic of urban middle-and upper-class Muslim women before Westernization are now imposed on all women—veiling and sexual segregation of various kinds are the most notable. (For Iran, ideological aspects of the position of women are discussed by Ferdows.) The reemphasis on Quranic law brings with it legal polygyny, easy divorce for men but not for women, and so forth. In part this has more to do with literalist Islam than with anti-woman feelings per se. It is also true, however, that the masses and bazaar classes have been less tied to Westerners and Western ways than have the new middle and upper classes, and the former classes have come to the fore dramatically in the Iranian and Algerian revolutions, and to a considerable degree also elsewhere. These classes are most hostile to Western control, and hence most likely to be appealed to by the anti-Western nature of Khomeini's ideology, which allows both for radical and anti-imperialist ideas and for traditional Islamic identification. These classes tend to identify with traditional rather than "modern" practices regarding women.

Many Iranians had become disillusioned with western governmental forms and with similarly "Western" Marxism and nationalism. At a minimum these did not have the appeal of Khomeini's radical Islam, which in fact incorporated many features of parliamentarism, nationalism, socialism, and a "Third Worldist" reaction against the West as the great exploiter of oppressed peoples, while at the same time retaining the Islamic identity that was still crucial to most Iranians. It is perhaps this radical and unacknowledged syncretic mixture of traditional and revolutionary ideas, more than the "fundamentalism" that is so often attributed to the Khomeini school, which accounts in large part for Khomeini's great success with masses of Iranians. Najmabadi's paper suggests that the current identification of Islam with politics is so pervasive that few Iranians will soon return to secular views.

The period since the revolutionary victory of February 11, 1979 has sometimes been divided both by Iranians and Westerners into three "revolutions." The first, from victory till the taking of the American hostages on November 4, 1979, was characterized by a coalition government dominated by secular, or relatively secular, liberals, while at the same time an originally secret Revolutionary Council dominated by clericals, and Khomeini himself, often made the real decisions. This could be called "dual government" or a period like that of Kerensky's government before the Bolshevik revolution. The second was a period of increased radicalization culminating in the dismissal of the first elected president, Bani Sadr, in June, 1981, after he and the strong left Islamic movement, the Mojahedin-e Khalq, turned against a government more and more monopolized by the clerical radicals of the Islamic Republican Party and by Khomeini. The third revolution encompassed this final break with religious liberals and leftists, and has continued until now (although there are signs of moves toward normalization of foreign relations with several countries and possibly of a somewhat decreased reign of terror). Arbitrary executions and jailings continue, however.

The above pattern of growing radicalization as the revolution progressively turns against and devours its own children is one found in most of the great world revolutions which break almost totally with old regimes and bring new groups and classes, as well as new ideologies, to power. Crane Brinton has provided the classic comparison of stages in the English, French, American, and Russian revolutions in his *Anatomy of Revolution,* of which the relevance to Iran has been noted by James Bill and several other writers. Since Brinton's time the Chinese and Cuban revolutions, at least, would provide further examples. In Brinton's scheme one would expect a deradicalization or "Thermidor" to occur, followed perhaps by a military ruler or Bonaparte who preserves many of the revolution's gains while introducing more order and less radicalism. Some such trend may be beginning in Iran, although many feel that a serious deradicalization is unlikely to occur until after Khomeini's death, when it could come either from within or outside the regime.

Few careful observers give much chance of rule to the variety of exile groups abroad, whose leadership now centers in Paris, and whose ideology ranges from pre-revolutionary monarchist to varieties of leftism. Among these groups only those exiles of the left Islamic Mojahedin-e Khalq, followers of Mas'ud Rajavi, are known to have a strong organization within Iran. This group was responsible for the counter-terror against IRP leaders that followed attacks on the Mojahedin and Bani Sadr in June, 1981, and this guerrilla warfare continued for a time, although on a smaller scale. The Mojahedin may have an important future role, more because of their continued activity in Iran than their statements outside it. The other exiles, however, if history and logic hold any lessons, are unlikely to play a major role in any future change of government in Iran, although some may be called in to participate in a less dramatic way if things do change. It is, however, also quite possible that a "Thermidorian" trend will come from within the regime.

A feature most notable in the radical "Third Revolution" stage is the growth of discord and factionalism within the IRP, discussed by Akhavi and Abrahamian. It should be noted here that some of the literature on this subject does not deal with the groups discussed within as clear fractional groups but uses the term *maktabi* as a broad term to mean fundamentalist politicians loyal to the new regime and to Khomeini, while only the Hojjatiyeh is considered a membership group, begun some years ago as an anti-Baha'i organization, but later extending its idological positions to other matters. IRP discord is not confined to named and stable groups.

Serious practical and ideological rifts exist within the IRP on a number of key points, among which are: (1) land reform, where the socially radical want to carry out further division of land, some of which has already been legislated, while clerical conservatives, including some of the elderly and influential "Great ayatollahs" never enamoured of Khomeini say that private property is sacred to Islam; (2) succession to Khomeini, who favored the succession, ratified in 1985, as single *faqih* of his disciple Ayatollah Montazeri, but met some resistance to this, especially from those who wanted one or more better trained and more experienced clerics to get the post; (3) implementation of the monopoly of foreign trade law, opposed by many bazaaris and by non-radical clerics. Dissension has sometimes taken the form of vetoes by the conservative Council of Guardians of laws passed by the more populist parliament.

In addition, there are disagreements regarding policy toward the Soviet Union. Although, as Muriel Atkin has noted, the absolute economic position of the U.S.S.R. is smaller than under the shah, given the absence of a U.S. role and the weakness of ties to the West, the Soviet economic role is relatively greater, (even though economic relations with Third World countries have deliberately been raised far more). By 1982, possibly in part because of leaders who opposed the level of ties to the Soviet Union, relations had become strained on several points, including continued Iranian attacks on Soviet policy in Afghanistan and growing attacks on the pro-Soviet Tudeh Party and Fedayan majority, which tried to get on with the Iranian government but were decreasingly allowed to function freely. Also important was Iran's continuation of the war with Iraq, including invasion of Iraqi territory, while the Soviets want Iran to accept Iraq's *status quo ante* terms, which would have spared the Soviets growing embarrassment at seeing two "friendly countries" that were both getting some aid from the Soviets or their allies engaged in war. By late summer, 1982, some Soviet analyses became critical of the Iranian regime and implicitly friendly to the anti-regime Mojahedin. As noted in Atkin's analysis, the arrest and trial of Tudeh Party leaders brought a further deterioration of relations. Relations with the Soviets continue, however.

The Iran-Iraq war, which was discussed, although not as a principal topic, at several points in the conference, has an importance beyond the embarrassment it created for both superpowers. It demonstrated the profound nature of Iran's revolution in which (much as during the French, Russian, and other major revolutions) foreign powers vastly underestimated the ability of a regime they saw as "in disarray" to resist foreign attack. As with other revolutions, the Iranian one, for all its internal disagreements, showed an amazing ability to pull together, to innovate militarily (and the use of young human minesweepers and other martyrs is a small part of this innovation), and to show a combination of self-sacrifice, patriotic unity, and miliary ability that confounded most outside observers (though not most academic Iran specialists, who expected Iran to expel Iraqi invaders). Like revolutionary France, Russia, and even Cromwell's England, the Iranians have chosen to pursue their enemies abroad (a choice common to many non-revolutionary regimes, including the Allies in both world wars). At the same time, however, Iran is keeping options open for a negotiated settlement, and contradictory statements have been made by different leaders as to Iran's terms. Many now believe that a settlement is possible after the death of Khomeini, who at least until a new position was hinted early in 1986, seemed determined to topple Saddam Hussein and his regime.

Despite the expulsion of the Iraqis there is widespread discontent in Iran, as noted by Loeffler and others, although nobody has been able convincingly to measure its extent and significance. Food shortages, unemployment, the decline in production, and galloping inflation are felt by nearly everyone, even though the government favors the poor and tries to assure that nobody starves. Jailings, beatings, and executions continue, if at a somewhat reduced rate, and most are understandably afraid to speak or act politically in disapproved ways. Women who have tasted newer ways dislike being sent back to veiling, segregation, and reduced job opportunities. Ethnic minorities like the Baluchis, the Qashqa'i, and especially the Kurds continue to engage in armed struggles for autonomy, and their role will continue to be a problem for future governments, which may fear a break-off by some minorities. Many trained persons have left, and universities remain closed. While the level of executions and steps leadng to forced conversion of Baha'is has dropped since it first escalated three years ago, nobody knows if this is permanent. Despite all this, the government's relative egalitarianism and measures for the poor, as well as its Islamic claims, have kept it popular among many of the masses of the population. The Islamic Republic has, for all its manifold problems, shown itself already to be more resilient and enduring than many in the West expected, and it represents a novel phenomenon whose scope and importance extend well beyond Iran.

I

Iran in the 1980s

IRAN 1980–85:
POLITICAL and ECONOMIC TRENDS

Eric Hooglund

THE MAJOR PREOCCUPATION of the government and people of Iran during the past five years has been the war with Iraq.[1] This conflict has affected both countries adversely. In Iran there have been several hundred thousand casualties, including at least one hundred and fifty thousand deaths.[2] Industrial, commercial, residential, and infrastructural property valued at several billions of dollars has been destroyed. An estimated one and a half million civilians have been uprooted from the war zone, primarily the southwestern portion of Khuzistan province. In addition to these consequences, the war has forced the clerical authorities in Tehran to divert resources away from socio-economic development and into military expenditures.

While the human and material costs have been heavy, the war's impact has not been entirely negative; in an important sense the war has served as a catalyst to help the post-revolutionary theocratic regime to consolidate its power. The new political elite, the Shi'i clergy and their lay allies, have used the Iraqi invasion and subsequent war to mobilize popular acquiesence to the new governmental institutions. Also, from an economic perspective, the war's continuance has not seriously impeded Iran's ability to export oil, and consequently revenues were maintained at an acceptable level until the 1985–86 price falls. This has meant that Tehran until 1986 had a reliable source of income in the form of hard currency, and officials utilized this income both to prosecute the war and to co-opt the masses with various subsidies and incentives. It is the objective of this chapter to review these political and economic developments since the beginning of the war.

When Iraq launched its invasion in the autumn of 1980, the activists of the 1978–79 popular revolution were preoccupied with resolving the question of who should be the legitimate inheritors of political power. By 1980, five broad ideological orientations were in contention for dominance. The most important grouped together advocates of a theocratic government. They had succeeded in drafting a new republican constitution, approved in a popular referendum in December 1979, that invested ultimate authority in a supreme religious jurist, or *faqih*. This constitution gave the Shi'i clergy effective political power. Not all of the clergy supported the concept of clerical political activism, but Ayatollah Khomeini did and his endorsement provided the constitution with an aura of legitimacy. The promoters of theocracy had formed the Islamic Republican Party (IRP), which developed into an effective political organization comprising clerics—primarily junior men who were preachers rather than scholars—and lay political activists who envisaged a government guided by Islamic principles as interpreted by men with training in Shi'i religious law. The leaders of the IRP had acquired experience in mobilizing large crowds for demonstrations during the revolution and utilized their skills to marshal popular support for the new constitution and other IRP policies.[3]

A second ideological current was secularist—those who believed that the clergy should not be involved in government. Supporters of this view ranged from conservative but influential *ulama* such as the Grand Ayatollahs Shariatmadari and Qommi and Ayatollahs Mahallati and Zanjani to liberal political activists like Hedayat Matin-Daftari. The secularists were convinced that the revolution had been both necessary and positive but they were apprehensive about the objectives of the IRP. They opposed the new constitution because of its articles relating to the role of the clergy and out of concern that civil liberties and human rights were not adequately guaranteed. The secularists were divided into several political parties, all operating more or less clandestinely by the summer of 1980.

Leftist ideologies represented a third force in post-revolutionary Iran. Marxist ideas had been influential among Iran's educated youth since the early 1940s. Several political parties which were avowedly Marxist, or consciously borrowed Marxist concepts, openly recruited for new members after the revolution. The oldest of these parties was the Tudeh, originally established in 1941. The Tudeh had decided to work within the new constitutional arrangements because party leaders believed that the clerical leaders, especially those allied with the IRP, were objectively opposed to imperialism and comprador capitalism. The Tudeh's tolerant attitude toward the evolving theocracy may have been one reason for its inability to inspire widespread popular interest in its programs. A Marxist party with more appeal, at least among the educated youth, was the

Fedayan-e Khalq. This party was deeply divided, however, over the issue of whether to cooperate with or to oppose the new clerical government. In June 1980, it had split into a majority faction willing to support the Tudeh position and a minority faction opposed to clerical rule.

None of the Marxist parties attracted as much attention of the public, especially the youth, as did the Mojahedin-e Khalq. The Mojahedin identified itself as a populist Islamic party incorporating many Marxist ideas into its own ideology and recognizing Marxism as a progressive force.[4] The Mojahedin were the main organized opposition to the IRP by mid-1980. There had already been violent confrontations between supporters of the two rival parties in numerous cities and towns, and it is likely that the outbreak of the war with Iraq only postponed the bloody showdown between them.

A fourth ideological force, for regional autonomy, was based primarily among Iran's ethnic minorities—the Arabs, Azerbaijani Turks, Baluchis, Kurds, Qashqa'i Turks, and Turkmen. Supporters of greater freedom from central government control had been active among all these groups after the revolution. Among the Kurds, especially, who number approximately two to two and a half million and live in the western mountains adjacent to Iraqi and Turkish Kurdish areas, there was widespread resentment of Tehran. Local Kurdish activists assumed control of their cities and towns in the spring of 1979 and expelled non-Kurdish government officials. In response, the Provisional Government dispatched the Revolutionary Guards to Kurdistan to suppress the incipient rebellion. Thus the war in Kurdistan was already in its thirteenth month when the war with Iraq broke out. Two Kurdish political parties, the Democratic Party of Kurdistan and the Komeleh, had organized fighting forces to oppose the Revolutionary Guards. In September 1980, the Kurdish fighters controlled most of rural Kurdistan, with the Revolutionary Guards confined to the provincial capital of Sanandaj and a few other towns.[5]

A final ideological trend was monarchist. The popular nature of the revolution, plus the revelations of royal excesses under the shah published almost daily in the press in 1979–80, had widely discredited the idea of a monarchial restoration. The many formerly powerful Iranians whose only hope lay in a restoration were mostly in exile, and had not succeeded either in organizing support within Iran or in uniting around a single personality or party outside of the country.

By mid-1980, the proponents of theocracy stood as the most powerful political force in the country, but they did not constitute a cohesive group. Their rivalries began to surface after the first Majlis under the new constitution had been elected and set about to choose a government. One key division revolved around alternative conceptions regarding the role of the clergy. Abol Hasan Bani Sadr, elected president of the republic in January 1980, advocated a more indirect political role for the clergy, while the Islamic Republican Party, led by Ayatollah Mohammad Beheshti, wanted clerics to fill important executive positions.

The war both intensified this dispute and served to delay its resolution. Initially, Bani Sadr tried to use the war to demonstrate the necessity for filling government positions with technocrats rather than untrained clerics. His efforts only solidified the hostility of the IRP leaders; in June 1981, they succeeded in getting the Majlis to impeach and remove him from the presidency. Since that time, the IRP has dealt ruthlessly with its opposition and presented itself as the authoritative interpreter of Ayatollah Khomeini's ideas. Even though Khomeini has never become a formal member of the party, his consistent support of IRP policies has contributed significantly to the party's perceived legitimacy.

The elimination of Bani Sadr was relatively easy because he failed to develop any effective political organization to articulate and support his views. The situation was different with respect to another source of opposition to direct clerical participation in government. The religious society known as the Hojjatiyeh followers became increasingly concerned after 1980 as the number of clerics in high policy-making positions expanded. The Hojjatiyeh professed that, in the absence of the Shi'i Twelfth Imam, the exercise of political rule was usurpation. They contended that the clergy must confine its role to that of providing religious guidance to the community of believers, and leave politics to laymen whose ignorance of religious doctrine made them more suitable to usurp the legitimate rights of the Hidden Imam. The Hojjatiyeh's criticisms of clerical politicians coincided with the development of opposition, primarily from business interests, to IRP efforts to assert greater government control of the economy. In order to forestall the emergence of the Hojjatiyeh as a catalyzing opposition force, the IRP launched a campaign against the society's "deviant" religious views during the summer and fall of 1983. Even Khomeini suggested indirectly but publicly that the positions of the Hojjatiyeh were incorrect and harmful. Subsequently the Hojjatiyeh decided to suspend its activities, presumably in order to avoid confrontations with IRP-organized street gangs.

Apart from dissent within the ranks of the supporters of theocracy, the IRP has confronted ideological opposition to the Islamic Republic. This has not diminished since 1980, but its effectiveness has been adversely affected by the war. The most serious challenge to the IRP had been posed by the Mojahedin. In June 1981, the Mojahedin seized upon the impeachment of Bani Sadr to initiate a campaign of armed rebellion against the IRP-dominated government. The Mojahedin engaged in shootouts with the Revolutionary Guards all over the country and claimed responsibility for the assassinations of many national and locally prominent clerics. In addition, the Mojahedin were suspected of planting the bomb at IRP headquarters in June 1981 which killed Beheshti and more than seventy party leaders, and a bomb two months later which took the lives of the new president, Mohammd Ali Rajai, and Prime Minister Javad Bahonar. The government responded to the Mojahedin challenge with mass arrests and summary executions. An estimated seven thousand seven hundred persons, mostly young people, are believed to have been killed in 1981–82.[6]

The severity of the government's reaction effectively eliminated as a serious internal opposition the Mojahedin as well as the Marxist Peykar and Fedayan (minority) parties which had joined it in the armed struggle. While the Mojahedin do continue to operate underground cells in the country, and periodically claim responsibility for isolated bombings in Tehran and other cities, their primary role today is largely that of an external opposition force.

The reasons why the Mojahedin failed to secure popular support in their efforts to overthrow the clerical government in 1981–82 are very complex. Clearly one important factor was the war with Iraq. During the height of the Mojahedin uprising, Iraq still occupied approximately one third of Khuzistan province, including the important city of Khorramshahr; the city of Abadan was besieged and in danger of being captured; and the cities of Ahvaz and Dizful were in range of Iraqi artillery guns. Thus, the Mojahedin's assault upon the government coincided with a grim phase of the war. This made it easy for the IRP to portray the Mojahedin as traitors and agents of foreign enemies at a time when popular anger against Iraq was high. The later willingness of the Mojahedin leader, Mas'ud Rajavi, to hold discussions with Iraqi officials provided Tehran with further propaganda against the Mojahedin.

Rajavi had escaped to France with Bani Sadr in July, 1981. Subsequently the two men formed the National Resistance Council (NRC) to unite the external opposition to the IRP government. Predictably, given Bani Sadr's lack of an effective organization to advance his own philosophy, the Mojahedin dominated the NRC, continuing their own publishing activities and recruiting among Iranian students in Europe and the US, while Bani Sadr was gradually reduced to a figurehead. The two men finally split in the spring of 1984, ostensibly over differences regarding the proper stance to adopt towards Iraq.[7]

The Marxist parties have not fared any better than the Mojahedin. The Tudeh and the Fedayan (majority) both agreed to continue supporting the government at the time of the Mojahedin uprising, and stuck to this position throughout the conflict. Only in the fall of 1982, long after the Mojahedin had been suppressed, did the Tudeh express cautious criticism of government policies, specifically the decision to take the war into Iraq. IRP anger over this, coupled with irritation over warming Soviet-Iraqi relations, triggered the IRP attack on the Tudeh. Many IRP leaders had always believed that Tudeh cadres were nothing more than spies for the Soviet Union, and had never favored tolerating the Tudeh for expedient domestic or international policy reasons. In February 1983, the Tudeh secretary-general and more than two dozen other party leaders were arrested. In May, the Tudeh leaders were presented on television confessing that they were spies for the USSR. The party was disbanded by the government, more than one thousand additional members were arrested, and all other Tudeh Party members were ordered to turn themselves in to the authorities.[8] In view of the conscious efforts of the Tudeh to work within the constitutional system and support the government, the severity of the IRP-ordered crackdown was unanticipated.

The Kurdish struggle for regional autonomy also has been affected by the war with Iraq. Despite the fighting in the south, the government has launched several new offensives in the Kurdish areas since 1980. The Revolutionary Guards have captured all the principal towns and have contained the fighting to rural, mountainous areas. The government's relative success can be attributed to two factors. One is the inability of the Kurds to enlist support from non-Kurdish parts of Iran. While the Kurds have received some aid from the Mojahedin and two smaller Marxist parties, the country's Persian-speaking majority, as well as the largest ethnic minority, the Azerbaijani Turks, tend to be unsympathetic to the Kurdish cause.

A second reason for Tehran's relative success against the Kurds has been the latter's inability to exploit the war between Iran and Iraq for their own political advantage. Baghdad naturally has been interested in the struggle of the Iranian Kurds and other ethnic minorities for greater autonomy, and early in the war even provided small amounts of aid. However, Iranian Kurdistan borders Iraqi Kurdistan, an area that has not been under the effective control of the government in Baghdad since the end of 1982. The Iraqi Kurds have grievances against their own government, and, like the Iranian Kurds, desire more political and cultural freedom. One of the principal Iraqi Kurdish leaders, Mas'ud Barzani, who heads the Iraqi Kurdish Democratic Party, has allied his forces with the Islamic Republic. Barzani has been fighting against Iraqi troops in Iraqi Kurdistan almost since the inception of the Gulf war, with the notable exception of a ten-month ceasefire in 1984. Throughout 1985 Barzani's Kurds, relying upon critical support from Iran in the form of military equipment, medical supplies, food provisions, and logisitics, staged a series of offensives that drove Iraq's civilian and military personnel out of an area extending an average of twelve miles west of the border and up to forty-five miles from north to south. These Kurdish victories were an important factor enabling the Iranian army to launch its February, 1986 offensive in the mountains overlooking the strategic town of Sulaymaniyah in northern Iraq.[9]

However much Tehran may perceive the Iraqi Kurdish Democratic Party as an ally, its Iranian counterpart is still considered an enemy. Thus, the army and Revolutionary Guards have kept constant military pressure on Iran's Kurds. By 1984 the forces of the Islamic Republic effectively controlled most of the Kurdish areas of western Iran, including the strategically important border passes. Considering that the Iraqi side of the border was under the control of Iraqi Kurds loyal to Iran, those Kurds who were still trying to resist the Iranian government were for all practical purposes cut off from any potential aid out of Baghdad. In addition, since Iraq was defending a long border south of Kurdistan and attempting to contain Iranian forces that had invaded pockets of Iraqi territory, it seemed highly unlikely Iraq would undertake any offensives in the north that could have at least an indirect effect of alleviating the pressure on Iran's Kurds. Thus the Iranian Kurds—unlike the Iraqi Kurds—have not benefitted from their enemy's enemy. Nevertheless, the IRP has exploited the appearance of Iraqi collaboration with the Kurds as "proof" that the Kurdish fighters are traitors to Iran. Few Iranians outside of the Kurdish areas question such charges.

The other two ideological orientations opposing the IRP vision of Iran have been largely impotent since the war with Iraq began. The secularists have neither a strong political party nor an effective leader. The secular leaders tend to reject armed struggle as an acceptable means for achieving political change. During the first two years of the war, most secularists—who also tend to be Iranian nationalists—deemed it inappropriate to oppose the government even in peaceful ways and stressed the need to maintain national unity in the face of foreign invasion and occupation. By 1984 this hesitation had eroded owing to Iranian military advances, and some secular leaders have been willing to voice criticisms. Many of the secular political activists, however, now live in exile in Europe and the United States and thus are unable to provide leadership to an internal opposition movement.

Supporters of a monarchical restoration have no organized movement within Iran. All existing pro-monarchy groups are based outside of the country, and any internal strength they may have has yet to be tested.[10] Monarchists claimed credit for a spontaneous demonstration in Tehran in the summer of 1983, on the anniversary of the granting of the first constitution in 1906. It is unclear whether the demonstrators were motivated more by a desire for a secular constitution rather than the Islamic one now in force, or for a return to a "constitutional monarchy." At any rate, there is little evidence of sympathy in Iran for any of the monarchist groups operating outside. This may be attributed partly to the division among the monarchists, although the groups are much less divided than previously. More importantly, perhaps, some leading monarchists have openly collaborated with Iraq since 1980.

The IRP has been generally successful, then, in exploiting the war against all its opposition.[11] At the same time, it has demonstrated its ability to defend Iran from foreign aggression. In the process of mobilizing national solidarity for the war effort, the party has also been conscious of the necessity to build and strengthen the institutions which will perpetuate clerical rule.

Thus the war has been used not simply to discredit opponents but also to broaden support for the theocracy. In practice, this has meant a thorough desecularization of society.[12] The legal system has been "Islamicized" with new criminal, civil, commercial, and moral codes prepared by Shi'i jurists. The educational system has been purged of teachers and students suspected of not being sufficiently Islamic, and textbooks continue to be revised to conform with religiously acceptable interpretations. All of the government ministries, the military, the Revolutionary Guards, the police, and other security forces now have special offices headed by clergymen who are responsible for ensuring that personnel comport themselves according to Islamic standards of acceptable behavior and demonstrate sufficient knowledge of Islamic doctrine and rituals. Participation in regular communal prayers and abstinence from alcoholic beverages, drugs, and illicit sex are considered essential for proving one's Islamic worthiness. Strict dress codes are also enforced for both men and women. Men, for example, must wear long pants and long-sleeved shirts which are buttoned up to the collar bone when they appear in public. Women are expected to observe *hejab,* which has been interpreted to mean all of the hair and all of the flesh other than the face and hands must be covered.

The emphasis on developing Islamic norms has already affected non-Muslim minorities, who are expected not to engage in practices which might offend Muslims. Thus, Christians and Jews must observe the prohibition on the consumption of alcoholic beverages and maintain the segregation of the sexes at social functions. The largest religious minority, the Baha'is, have actually been subjected to officially sanctioned persecution. At least two hundred Baha'is had been executed, and an estimated 767 were in prison by the end of 1985. Baha'is are forbidden to hold government jobs or attend public schools. The ruling clerics justify such harsh measures against the Baha'is on grounds that the adherents are apostates, a reference to the fact that the religion originated among Shi'i Muslims in Iran in the mid-nineteenth century.

The IRP's success to date in maintaining its dominant political position has been facilitated by its control over the security forces. The war has been the primary factor in the expansion of both the regular and the irregular armed forces. By the end of 1985, the total number of men serving as fighters for the Islamic Republic was estimated at half a million; approximately 185,000 were in the professional military—the army, air force, and navy; about 250,000 were in the Revolutionary Guards; and at least 100,000 rotating "volunteers" were kept at combat readiness in the Basij-e Mostazafin (Mobilization of the Oppressed). Besides the IRP, these forces constituted the primary organized—and armed—group within Iran and consequently were the focus of attention by both those who feared and those who hoped that they could serve as a potential source for a coup d'état against the government. The army in particular has been perceived as the most likely locus of any serious challenge to the regime. In fact, since 1980 the government has announced that it has foiled several coup plots by army officers. For example, there were two separate conspiracies in the summer of 1980 involving more than 600 officers. In 1982, several score officers were implicated in an alleged plot to assassinate Khomeini, and at least seventy were executed. In 1983, five air force officers were charged with a plot to bomb Khomeini's home.

Despite the involvement of some officers in these anti-government conspiracies, several significant facts make it improbable that a successful coup d'etat would originate within the army. First, the army has been purged of career officers whose loyalty to the present constitutional structure is suspect. Second, most of the current officer corps have advanced from junior ranks since 1979, and done so on the strength of their demonstrated loyalty to the IRP. Third, except for the career officers, the army is composed of young draftees thoroughly indoctrinated in the new religious and political values. Fourth, the IRP itself exercises direct ideological—and political—control over the army through a special office within the ministry of defense which assigns its own representatives— invariably Shi'i preachers—at all levels to monitor soldiers and ensure that they perform Islamic rituals and behave properly. Fifth, the army as an institution has demonstrated its fealty to the regime in power since February 1979, when the army command decided not to oppose the revolutionaries who had taken over the government.

The creation of new government institutions and an effective security apparatus has preoccupied the IRP, but the stability of the regime also depends upon its ability to meet the material needs of the population. In this respect, the impact of the Gulf war upon the Iranian economy has been quite significant. Initially, the war severely affected the economy. Khorramshahr, Iran's main port of entry for imports, was devastated and captured by Iraq; its largest refinery on Abadan Island was damaged too extensively to operate; a flood of more than a million refugees from the war zone placed a heavy strain on services. In 1980 Iran was still embroiled in the hostage affair and was just beginning to experience the effects of economic sanctions which the U.S. and its European allies had imposed.[13] These sanctions, combined with the destruction of cargo in the customs warehouses of Khorramshahr, produced a shortage of foodstuffs and other consumer necessities. The government introduced a rationing system for many products, including meat, rice, dairy products, gasoline, and heating oil. Operated out of the mosques, the system was reasonably effecient in ensuring that minimal supplies of essentials reached the majority of the urban population.

The resolution of the hostage crisis led to the lifting of international sanctions early in 1981. Smaller ports such as Lengeh, Bushehr, and Bandar Abbas, all farther down the Gulf and removed from the war zone, were expanded to handle more ships,[14] while a brisk transshipment trade developed between Dubai in the United Arab Emirates (UAE) and ports along the Iranian coast. An increasing volume of imports was brought into the country via the overland route from Europe through Turkey. Smaller refineries were expanded to compensate for the lost production from Abadan and all petroleum exporting was centered on Kharg Island. As a consequence, Iran was able to reverse the initial setbacks caused by the war within two years. By the middle of 1982, in fact, the increased production and export of oil was earning the government more than one and a half billion dollars monthly, and in 1983 oil revenues reached a record twenty-six billion dollars for the year.[15]

Oil revenues began to decline in 1984, and by the summer of 1985 they were averaging only $1 billion per month—about the same amount it cost to prosecute the war with Iraq. Nevertheless, the regime was able to maintain a minimal level of socioeconomic services and investment. Oil revenues have continued to provide the principal source of foreign exchange needed to finance imports of weapons, food, and other goods.

While the industrial sector does not appear to be producing at its pre-revolutionary levels, output in most factories reportedly has recovered from the low levels of 1979–81. The government itself has made major investments in key industries such as steel, copper, and petroleum. There has also been an expansion of factories producing war-related goods.[16]

The high unemployment experienced by urban workers in the 1979–81 period has also been reduced, although the unemployment rate among adult male heads of household may still be as high as ten percent. Unemployment among youth is also lower than in the 1979–81 period, although this can partially be accounted for by the fact that an estimated nine hundred thousand youths have been removed from the labor force temporarily or permanently due to the war.[17]

Agriculture has not fared any better under the Islamic Republic than under the ancien régime.[18] Food purchases continue to represent a heavy burden on the import bill. Since 1983, food imports have cost an estimated four billion dollars annually. The combination of domestic production and foreign food has still been inadequate to satisfy completely consumer demand. Therefore, the government has maintained a food rationing system since the beginning of the war with Iraq. Meat, rice and dairy products are the most important foods that are subject to rationing. There have been complaints about the rationing system: that the best quality foods get siphoned off into the black market; that hours must be spent each day in long lines; that local shops frequently run out of rationed products before all persons holding ration cards can make their purchases; and that an increasing variety of non-food consumer items have been added to the rationing list.[19] Despite these problems, however, the rationing system has worked tolerably well; its main beneficiaries have been the urban poor who have been able to obtain low-cost, essential foods that otherwise may have been hoarded by the middle and upper classes.

The ability of the Iranian economy to provide both guns and butter under the impact of a major war has not gone unnoticed by the enemy. Since February, 1984, Iraq has made concerted efforts to decisively disrupt Iran's petroleum export capacity, and thus the primary source of revenues sustaining its economy. Baghdad initiated a policy of striking tankers in the Gulf loaded with Iranian oil. The attacks on shipping— including Iranian retaliation against tankers carrying oil from the Arab countries of the Persian Gulf—caused insurance rates on ships calling at Gulf ports to increase significantly. Iran met this challenge by discounting its oil so that its international price remained competitive and revenues thus continued to accrue. During 1985 Iraq intensified its aerial bombardment of Iran's oil export capabilities: several of the jetties on Kharg Island were severely damaged; tankers used to shuttle oil between Kharg and Sirri Island, located farther down the Gulf coast and out of range of Iraqi aircraft and missiles, were attacked with greater frequency; and the important pumping station on the Gulf coast near Ganaveh was hit.

By the winter of 1986 Iraq's bombing campaign had failed to halt

Iran's oil exports. Nevertheless, the overall damage inflicted interfered with Tehran's ability to sell the volume of oil it considered necessary to meet budget requirements. The combination of oil export decreases and oil price declines that has been experienced since the autumn of 1984 resulted in budget shortfalls for the fiscal years ending in March 1985 and March 1986. Consequently, the government has been forced to reduce spending for many non-military programs, and this contraction has had negative repercussions for the economy.[20]

In assessing the overall impact of five years of war, it seems that the process of mobilizing the populace for war has clearly facilitated the IRP's project to desecularize Iran. As long as the country is perceived to be in danger, there seems to be general acquiescence to government policies. The government has been able to capitalize upon the image of Iran as a victim of aggression. Even the virtual reign of terror against the Mojahedin in the last half of 1981 failed to provoke a widespread protest. During the first eighteen months of the war, in particular, when Iraqi troops were still in occupation of part of Khuzistan, and Iranian forces were unable to make any substantive military gains, there was a general tendency among the population to avoid criticism of the handling of the war. Even Bani Sadr's efforts to politicize the war, as part of his own campaign against the IRP leaders during the first part of 1981, failed to arouse any discernible indignation against politicians whom the then president was accusing of impeding the war efforts by their alleged technical incompetence. On the contrary, his criticism of the government's war policies was one of the factors which led to his impeachment and downfall.

There seems to have been a gradual change in popular attitudes toward the war, though, since the end of 1982. Iranian military successes, beginning in early 1982 and culminating in the liberation of Khorramshahr and the expulsion of Iraqi forces from most of Iranian territory by the fall, have tended to alter perceptions of the war. The Iranian offensives into Iraq, undertaken at the cost of heavy casualties and achieving through the end of 1985 only minimal territorial gains, have been controversial. There has not been, however, any public debate about war objectives. Khomeini's own position since June of 1982, that there can be no peace with Iraq until the government of Saddam Hussein is overthrown, has had the effect of discouraging open discussion. Nevertheless, the broadening of Iran's announced terms for ending the war, from liberating Iran of foreign forces to liberating Iraq of the Ba'th government, reportedly has aroused concern among the political elite and military commanders as well as among the general population.[21] There have been credible reports of serious disputes over war policies within the leadership cadres of the IRP and even at the top levels of the government.[22] In spite of these concerns, however, it seems likely that there will be no decision in favor of negotiating a termination of hostilities as long as Khomeini himself remains determined to have the present leaders in Baghdad replaced by Iraqi supporters of an Islamic Republic. It is also reasonable to assume that Khomeini's death may provide an opportunity for moderating this policy.

Among the population as a whole, concern over the war has manifested itself as a diffuse form of war-weariness. There is no evidence to suggest that expressions of frustration with the prolonged fighting have crystallized into opposition to the government's policies. Indeed, the war is still generally perceived as a wrong inflicted upon the country, and the government has been able to recruit young men to join the armed forces without encountering major resistance. Nevertheless, Iranians who have travelled outside their country since 1983 report that there is pervasive impatience and a growing concern about the increasing casualties. It would probably be premature to characterize this general uneasiness as opposition to the war.[23] The sense of grievance against Iraq is still strong. It was reinforced in May and June, 1984, and again in March and April, 1985 when Iraqi missiles and aerial bombs caused several hundred civilian casualties in south Tehran and more than a dozen cities and towns of western Iran.

The clergy and their lay supporters in the IRP have demonstrated since 1979 that they are capable of ruling Iran. They have had to carry out their programs under the burden of a major war that has caused hundreds of thousands of casualties and has resulted in billions of dollars of property destruction. The IRP has proven adroit in exploiting the war to suppress opposition and to mobilize a significant proportion of the population behind efforts to create a theocracy. The charismatic authority of Ayatollah Khomeini, the patriotic fervor of the people, and the government's ability to provide both guns and butter have all been important factors that have aided the IRP. By the end of 1985 it was clear that the theocratic government had made considerable progress toward consolidating itself. Nevertheless, critical tests of its self-proclaimed popularity and legitimacy still lay in the future.

NOTES

1. This is a revised version of my article, "The Gulf War and the Islamic Republic," published in *MERIP Reports,* Nos. 125/126 (July–September, 1984) pp. 31–37. Permission from *MERIP Reports* to use that article is gratefully acknowledged.

2. The Iranian government has yet to publish any comprehensive statistics on war casualties. Nevertheless, the names of those killed and missing in action are periodically printed in the press. The total number of names tabulated from these lists between September 22, 1980, and June 30, 1984, is 129,000. At least twenty thousand additional men have been killed in battles since the summer of 1984.

3. For an excellent analysis of politics and the role of the clergy during the first two years after the revolution see, Shaul Bakhash, *The Reign of the Ayatollahs: Iran and the Islamic Revolution* (New York: Basic Books, 1984), PP. 52–165.

4. For more detail about the Mojahedin's attitudes toward Marxism, see Ervand Abrahamiam, *Iran Between Two Revolutions* (Princeton: Princeton University Press, 1982), pp. 492–493; and Suroosh Irfani, *Revolutionary Islam in Iran* (London: Zed Press, 1983), p. 109.

5. For an overview of the situation in Iranian Kurdish areas in 1979–80, see "The 'Open Wound' of Kurdistan," *The Middle East,* July 1980, pp. 17–20.

6. For a detailed report on those who died violently during the reign of terror from June 1981 until December 1982, see *Mojahed,* September 8, 1983.

7. Rajavi's meeting with Iraq's foreign minister, Tariq Aziz, in March 1984 was cited by Bani Sadr as the primary reason for his break with Rajavi. See *Iran Times,* April 20, 1984, p. 1.

8. See *Iran Times,* May 6 and 13, 1983.

9. A detailed analysis of the political-military alliance between Iraqi Kurds and Iran is presented in Gwynne Roberts, "Kurdish Gains Put Pressure on Iraq," *Financial Times,* January 7, 1986.

10. Monarchist groups in exile are reviewed in Richard Chesnoff, "Iran/Paris: The Iranian Exiles," *The New York Times Magazine,* February 12, 1984.

11. For further detail and first-hand accounts of the opposition movements, see interviews and articles in "Khomeini and the Opposition," *MERIP Reports* No. 104 (March–April 1982) and "Iran Since the Revolution," *MERIP Reports* No. 113 (March–April 1983).

12. For an informative analysis of the "Islamicization" of society, see Jean-Loup Herbert, "La force mobilisatrice d'une spiritualité," in *Le Monde Diplomatique,* April 1984, pp. 17–18.

13. For an analysis of the effect of sanctions on the Iranian economy, see Philip Shehadi, "Economic Sanctions and Iranian Trade," *MERIP Reports* No. 98 (July–August 1981), pp. 15–16).

14. Bandar Abbas's development as a major shipping port is described in *The Middle East,* May 1984, p. 51.

15. *Le Monde Diplomatique,* April 1984, p. 14.

16. The problems of Industry since the revolution are discussed in Bakhash, *The Reign of the Ayatollahs,* pp. 178–185.

17. Officially, conscription is universal for all males aged 19 to 24, but deferments seem to have been fairly easy to obtain for educational purposes up through the end of 1983. Since then the draft has become much less selective, although it still seems that military service falls disproportionately upon the lower class and rural youth.

18. For an evaluation of agricultural production since the revolution, see "Striving towards more efficient agriculture," *Arabia: The Islamic World Review,* July 1983, pp. 29–31.

19. *Los Angeles Times,* April 12, 1984, p. I-B4; *Financial Times* (London), June 5, 1984, p. 20; and *Washington Post,* January 9, 1986, p. A25.

20. For an analysis of the war on Iran's economy, see Chris Kutschera, "The New Entrepreneurs," *The Middle East,* March 1986, pp. 7–9.

21. The army in particular has been critical of the human wave tactics used by the Revolutionary Guards in their offensives against Iraqi positions. See *Financial Times,* June 5, 1984, p. 20.

22. *The Middle East,* April 1984, p. 16.

23. It is significant, however, that Mehdi Bazargan, Iran's first post-revolution prime minister, announced in June 1985 that he would campaign for the presidency on an anti-war platform. The Council of Guardians ruled him ineligible as a candidate, and subsequently his party, the Iran Freedom Movement, called upon its supporters to boycott the presidential elections that were held in August.

ECONOMIC POLICIES and STRUCTURAL CHANGES SINCE the REVOLUTION

Setareh Karimi

IT IS SEVEN YEARS since the Islamic Republic was established in Iran, an event which has had profound impact on its economy. Accounts of the economic changes that have occurred since the revolution either have described the multitude of economic crises the country has faced or have dealt with the expansion of government ownership and control in the economy.[1] There has been little discussion of the other economic policies of the regime. Of course, in the past seven years the government has continued to make huge budgetary allocations, to set many prices, to fix foreign exchange and tariff rates, to issue industrial permits, and to allocate credit. How have such policies differed from those of the previous regime and how consistent have they been with the stated long-term goals of self-reliance and equity? With the data available it is now possible to make a preliminary assessment of the economic policies and performance of the regime. The scope of this chapter is clearly limited; many important areas of economic policy are not covered and those which are considered are not analyzed in depth. Yet, even such a limited examination of the data and the policies sheds light on the similarities as well as the differences between the pre- and post-revolutionary economic structure and policies. It also shows how the government lacks effective programs to bring about some of the structural changes it considers desirable.

The chapter is divided into four sections. The first section examines some of the main macroeconomic trends as well as redistribution policies. In section two trade patterns and policies are analyzed. Industrial and agricultural policies are discussed in sections three and four respectively.

MACROECONOMIC ASPECTS

Some of the main macroeconomic data of Iran are provided in Table 1. The overall trends in the economy are well known. Gross national product has declined (practically every sector has suffered a fall in output), and all categories of expenditure—private consumption, government expenditure on goods and services, and capital formation—have decreased. There was an upturn in 1982 which appears to have continued in 1983. In 1983 real per capita income was 25 percent below its 1977 level. Inflation has been rampant and unemployment widespread. There has been a tendency to blame the poor performance on disruptions caused by the revolution, the trade sanctions following the hostage crisis, the economic burden of the war, general economic insecurity, and inept management of the economy. Certainly, all these factors have affected economic activity adversely, but the main causes of the decline have been the reduction in oil production after the revolution and the concomitant cutbacks in government expenditure, especially its development component.

In 1977 about one-third of the gross domestic product, three-fourths of government revenues and nine-tenths of foreign exchange earnings came from the oil sector. Clearly, this sector had a pivotal role in the economy. Oil exports, however, were relatively unaffected by revolutionary turmoil or war damage. Rather, government production and pricing policy and conditions in the international oil market influenced their level. After the revolution there was a clear consensus that oil exports should be lowered, with some factions arguing for larger reductions than others. No one, however, wanted to push them to the low level actually reached in 1980 and 1981. Oil production decreased from 5600 thousand barrels per day (bpd) in 1977 to 1473 thousand bpd in 1980, while oil exports fell from 4800 thousand bpd to 761 bpd in the same period. A discussion of the factors responsible for this sharp fall in exports is beyond the scope of this chapter, but its impact on the economy was significant.[2] To appreciate the magnitude of this impact it is worth noting that the value of the decline in oil production between 1979 and 1980 was two and one half times the value of the entire output of the industrial sector in 1979. The economic recovery in 1982 was obviously due mainly to the upturn in oil exports. In that year the oil industry's share of the gross national product was 16.7 percent, down from 33 percent in 1977. This lower share might be taken as evidence of the regime's success in bringing about basic structural changes in the economy, making it less reliant on oil. Because the sector's output is valued using an artificially low foreign exchange rate, the "real" decline in its share of the GNP was considerably smaller. In some respects, the economy is even more dependent on the oil sector today.

Those who advocated cuts in oil exports maintained that the country could not productively absorb the revenues. They believed that oil income was being squandered not only on armaments but also on useless projects and luxury consumption. The reduction in the government budget, mainly in its development spending, was not made in response to the fall in revenues but was an autonomous decision supported even by the moderates. Political agitation and revolutionary zeal, however, might have been instrumental in the cancellation of particular projects. The decline in investment expenditure affected the construction industry directly and had repercussions in the rest of the economy. Short-run disclocations, though not always fully anticipated, were considered as the inevitable cost of attaining the goal of self-reliance and economic independence. For example, in 1979, the government could have reduced the inflation rate through more liberal import and foreign exchange policies instead of running a $6.0 billion surplus in the foreign exchange account. Such policies, however, were inconsistent with the regime's long-term objectives as well as being contrary to the existing revolutionary sentiments. Thus, at least in the early period, the cutbacks in certain types of consumption and investment were considered desirable.

Even prior to the revolution the economy was badly in need of a stabilization policy. The revolution was, of course, a surgical method of adjustment. It must also be noted that the country has shouldered the burden by itself. It is unique among the large oil exporters with large populations; Iran alone has not resorted to foreign borrowing. Indeed, the regime has paid off much of the debt incurred by the shah (admittedly using some of the assets accumulated then). This policy has been very much in line with the goal of self-reliance.

Although Iran has not burdened its future generations with foreign loans, they have not been entirely spared the costs of the adjustment. Capital formation has fallen both absolutely and as a share of the GNP. To the extent that the decline has involved the extravagant projects of the shah, its impact on future productivity will be limited. Other types of investments, however, have also been affected. For instance, private investment in machinery in 1980 was less than 20 percent of its 1977 level, while that of the government was nearly halved. Since 1982 the investment rate has recovered somewhat, but it is unlikely to reach its pre-revolutionary level of 30 percent of GNP, an unusually high rate for the Iranian economy, achieved only at the height of the oil boom.

Changes in the other components of national expenditure, private consumption and government expenditure on goods and services, are of obvious interest. Surprisingly, despite the tremendous cost of the war, real government expenditure on goods and services (public administration, defense, and social services), has fallen, a fact which is also confirmed by the budget data (once allowance is made for inflation). The fall in government expenditure on goods and services has not resulted in a corresponding cut in social services, at least not for the poorer groups. Even though the regime is prosecuting a costly war, the budgetary expenditure associated with the war effort and the military has not risen unduly. In 1983 this expenditure was about 1,000 billion rials which in real terms may be smaller than the 600 million rials spent in 1978. The foreign exchange component of military expenditure probably has declined because arms purchases have dropped and expensive foreign military training contracts have been cancelled.

Private consumption has decreased, at its lowest point being 20 percent below its 1977 level (a per capita drop of 27 percent). A politically sensitive item, private consumption did not decline proportionately as much as the other components of gross national expenditure between 1979 and 1981, but neither did it rise as much after the recovery began. Moreover, the distribution of private consumption among households has been modified markedly, implying that all segments of the population have not been equally affected by the decline. Indeed, if the official statistics are to be trusted, certain groups appear to be enjoying higher consumption levels than they did before the revolution.

Because the changes that have occurred in the distribution of private consumption reflect the priorities of the regime, an examination of that pattern is of particular importance. A detailed and systematic analysis is not possible but certain suggestive trends can be discerned. First, there has been a shift in favor of rural households, whose average consumption increased after the revolution but has remained fairly constant since 1979. Within this sector there was a worsening of the distribution in 1979 which was more than reversed by 1982. Second, in urban areas, the 40 percent of households with the lowest expenditure have experienced an improvement in their share of total expenditure to the extent that their real expenditure has consistently risen since 1979, albeit only slightly. The middle 40 percent of urban households suffered a reduction in their living standards in 1980 and probably also in 1981, but enjoyed a somewhat higher expenditure in 1982 than in 1977. Third, as the above figures imply, the top 20 percent of households bore the brunt of the decline in private consumption.[3] Within this group, high-salaried employees of the government and the private sector have suffered the greatest decline through both salary reductions and the erosion of their purchasing power due to inflation. Of course, certain individuals and groups, taking advantage of their political connections or the opportunities created by the proliferation of black markets, have made substantial gains. Their number however, is, perforce limited. On the whole, the poorest groups have maintained or slightly improved their consumption standards while the better-off segments of the population have experienced sizable losses.

Among the mechanisms employed by the government to influence the course of the developments described above, two deserve special mention here. These are inflation and the system of rationing and controls introduced since the revolution. Because the country has lacked an effective taxation system and because the government has avoided making some hard political decisions, competing demands for resources have been reconciled through inflation. Despite the attempts to blame anti-revolutionary hoarders and avaricious middlemen, it is clear that government deficits (shown in Table 1) were the main cause of the rise in prices. In the worst year, the reported deficit was 13 percent of the gross national product. In reality, the situation was worse because losses of the newly nationalized firms are not included in the figures. The deficits have been financed chiefly through the central bank, resulting in the rapid expansion of the money supply. The increase in the consumer price index (reported in Table 6) may not appear unusually high in comparison with the rate of inflation in many other developing nations. Its impact is severely felt, however, because there is no indexing of wages and salaries in Iran.

The government has sought to soften the impact of inflation on lower income groups through the rationing of many basic goods and the imposition of price controls on a wide variety of products. It has supplemented this policy with a restructuring of the food subsidy program of the previous regime so as to help the poor. Subsidies on such luxury items as red meat, sugar used in confectionery, and edible oil for use outside the home have been eliminated. The elimination of luxury subsidies, together with the rationing of most subsidized foods, has lowered the real cost of the subsidy program from its pre-revolutionary level (see Table 1).[4] The government has thus succeeded where many other developing countries have failed. Surely, its willingness to spread the resultant economic hardship more evenly has been a factor in enabling the government to contain subsidy expenditures without unduly alienating the poorer classes.

TRADE PATTERN AND POLICY

Despite the constitutional provision for a government monopoly in foreign trade, its nationalization is still controversial. This controversy is part

TABLE 1

BASIC MACROECONOMIC DATA

(billions of rials)

	1977	1978	1979	1980	1981	1982	1983	1984
Gross National Product (constant 1974 prices)	4005.6	3287.8	3127.8	2669.6	2728.3	3112.5	3534.4	
Private Consumption (constant 1974 prices)	1829.1	1745.0	1525.9	1459.7	1548.3	1642.9	1805.5	
Government Purchases of Goods and Services (constant 1974 prices)	799.2	797.3	636.7	580.4	606.9	583.6	572.1	
Capital Formation (constant 1974 prices)	1074.7	928.3	575.8	553.8	562.8	618.5	859.6	
GOVERNMENT BUDGET								
Current Government Expenditure	1223.0	1550.7	1537.7	1683.7	2032.4	2252.6	2564.0	2494.8
Government Development Expenditure	921.6	657.1	523.3	568.1	674.7	914.8	1163.5	883.0
Government Expenditure on Subsidy Program	71.7	30.5	79.2	37.3	81.3	110.0	106.3	121.5
Government Budget Deficit	388.5	508.5	269.2	903.1	1004.2	775.8	954.3	732.6

SOURCE: Central Bank of Iran, *Economic Report and Balance Sheet*
The Plan and Budget Ministry *Economic Report: 1984*

of the doctrinal debate on the nature and extent of private enterprise in the Islamic Republic, but has little bearing on the more basic issues of foreign trade policy, particularly the level and composition of trade. The desire to foster greater economic independence and self-sufficiency through limiting the role of foreign trade in the economy and changing its commodity composition and geographical pattern has been widely shared within the regime. This goal reflects the belief that self-reliance is a prerequisite for the pursuance of an independent foreign policy. It is also based on the view that the shah's high oil exports and open-door import policies wasted Iran's oil resources, ruined its agriculture, made its industry dependent on foreign technology and raw materials, and promoted Western consumption patterns. Except for some disagreement on the appropriate level of oil exports and on the role that the Eastern bloc countries could play in reducing Iran's dependence on the West, there has been little dispute or even discussion within the regime on other aspects of a desirable trade policy.

I have already alluded to the changes that have occurred in the level of exports and imports. The economy is considerably less open, export of goods and services constituting about 15 percent of the GNP in 1983, compared with over 38 percent in 1977. The import ratio has undergone a corresponding reduction. The change in the level of trade has been accompanied by a shift in its geographical composition shown in Table 2. The observed pattern reflects both policy decisions and structural constraints. First, clearly, foreign policy and strategic objectives have influenced the choice of trading partners. The U.S. has lost its dominant position while the developing countries and the centrally planned economies have boosted their share. This shift has outlasted the hostage crisis and the rerouting of American goods through third countries. A major factor in the decline of imports from the U.S. has been the rise in food purchases from countries such as Thailand, Argentina, Brazil, and Australia. The rise in the developing countries' share is mostly due to the expansion of trade with Turkey and Pakistan which owe their newly acquired favored position to strategic considerations.

Second, developments in the structure of world trade have also affected the geographical composition of Iran's trade. For example, the non-OPEC share of industrial nations' oil imports has been rising. Mexico would have replaced some of the U.S.' imports of Iranian oil even in the absence of the revolution. Also, Iran's imports of manufactured goods from any newly industrialized nations would have risen in any case.

Third, some of the short-term changes were attainable partly because the volume of trade contracted drastically. Had the pre-revolutionary level persisted, neither the Eastern bloc countries nor the develop-

TABLE 2

GEOGRAPHICAL COMPOSITION OF IRAN'S MERCHANDISE TRADE

(percent)

	1977	1979	1980	1981	1982	1983	1984
EXPORTS							
Industrial Countries	82.6	79.4	64.6	60.0	65.3	67.4	66.1
United States	17.3	21.2	3.1	0.6	3.4	5.6	4.3
Other Major Industrial Countries (Japan, U.K., Germany, Italy, France)	42.3	42.2	46.7	38.3	41.2	41.1	40.0
Developing Countries	15.5	18.0	27.9	29.9	27.0	27.0	28.2
Centrally Planned Economies	2.1	1.9	6.4	11.1	7.6	5.4	5.7
IMPORTS							
Industrial Countries	84.8	72.7	65.8	67.2	58.5	65.8	65.2
United States	16.0	13.4	0.1	2.5	1.2	1.1	1.2
Other Major Industrial Countries (Japan, U.K., Germany, Italy, France)	52.1	44.0	45.0	45.1	38.3	47.0	43.3
Developing Countries	9.1	12.7	19.6	15.5	20.8	21.1	22.2
Centrally Planned Economies	6.0	12.9	14.9	16.5	20.6	12.7	12.4

SOURCE: International Monetary Fund, *Direction of Trade Statistics*, 1984 and 1985 Yearbooks

ing nations would have been in a position to accommodate shifts of such magnitude. Therefore, it is not so much the rise of trade with these countries as it is the reduction of trade with the industrial nations that have produced the new pattern.

Fourth, within the industrial countries there has been a redirection of trade towards the smaller nations such as Sweden, Spain, and Austria. A contributing factor to this development has been the cancellation of many supply contracts with foreign firms, which has expanded the source of parts and materials for the domestic manufacturing industry. Although all long-term trends may not be discernible, Iran's trade is clearly much more diversified now. This is a healthy development, which in all likelihood will continue. The country may not have progressed far along the road to self-sufficiency but now it is less dependent on any single country.

The commodity composition of imports can be studied only at an aggregate level here. The data presented in Table 3 indicate that the regime has failed to attain its goals. On the import side, the share of capital goods has fallen while that of consumer goods has risen. This change mirrors the shift in domestic expenditure discussed above. As domestic investment has recovered, so have the imports of capital goods. The regime stopped the importation of many luxury consumer goods upon coming into power; more were banned after the start of the war. Nevertheless, the growth of food, pharmaceuticals, and fuel imports (after the destruction of refining capacity), has limited the government's ability to reduce imports of consumer goods. Note that a major increase in capital goods and intermediate goods' share may not be considered desirable since it would make the productive sectors more dependent on foreign inputs. The rise in food and agricultural imports has been particularly embarassing for the government. Even this high level of food import may increase further, because in 1982 world agricultural prices were generally low.

On the export side, the already high dependence on oil has risen further to the extent that in 1982 it accounted for nearly 99 percent of merchandise exports. Immediately after the revolution, the value of non-oil exports had risen because exports of carpets went up in 1979 and 1980. Capital flight and higher customs valuations of exports due to stricter exchange controls probably account for much of this increase. Whatever the cause of their early rise, non-oil exports have fallen sharply since 1981. In 1982 the volume of such exports was less than one quarter of its 1977 level. The government has repeatedly stressed the need to reduce reliance on oil exports. Indeed, the first post-revolutionary plan envisaged an annual rate of growth of 48.7 percent for non-oil exports, a

TABLE 3

COMMODITY COMPOSITION OF TRADE

(percent)

	1977	1978	1979	1980	1981	1982	1983
IMPORTS							
Consumer Goods	18.6	20.6	26.4	26.7	23.2	22.6	16.1
Intermediate Goods	54.2	51.6	54.4	57.3	60.9	57.9	59.9
Capital Goods	27.2	28.0	19.2	16.0	15.9	19.5	24.0
Total	100.0	100.0	100.0	100.0	100.0	100.0	100.0
Food and Agricultural Products	15.9	11.4	19.4	15.2	18.2	19.9	15.4
EXPORTS							
Oil's Share of Total Merchandise Exports	97.2	97.7	97.8	95.0	96.8	98.1	98.3

SOURCE: The Central Bank, *Economic Report and Balance Sheets*, various years.

goal which is totally unrealistic, considering past accomplishments and existing policies.

Several factors account for this dismal performance in non-oil exports. First, in view of the changing economic structure and high domestic inflation, the rial is highly overvalued. Fearing further inflation, the regime has been reluctant to devalue the currency. Second, due to its understandable concern over capital flight, the government has introduced such strict foreign exchange controls that they are counterproductive. Third, the extreme divergence between the official and the black market rate for foreign exchange has encouraged smuggling, which in turn has replaced legitimate exports. Fourth, declining production and high domestic demand have limited the supply of exports. As long as measures are not adopted to correct these distortions that limit non-oil exports, Iran will not be able to reduce its dependence on oil.

INDUSTRIAL POLICIES AND·PERFORMANCE

In the industrial sector the most visible change since the revolution has been the near total takeover of large-scale enterprises by the government and public bodies, notably Bonyad-e Mostazafin and Shahid. By 1982, 87 percent of manufacturing firms employing over five hundred workers were government owned or controlled. The corresponding figure for companies with more than one thousand employees was 95.4 percent.[5] Nearly one thousand public enterprises accounted for 70 percent of the labor force and 75 percent of the value added in industrial establishments with 10 or more employees. These ratios are bound to grow as existing projects come into production. The extent of nationalization has been greater than what was originally intended under the "Industrial Protection and Development Law" enacted a few months after the revolution. A number of firms which were to become partially owned by the nationalized banks (according to the ratio of their loans to the assets of the firms) have come under total government control because it has claimed they had negative net worth. In addition, approximately three hundred firms have been taken over by various revolutionary organizations, usually after their owners were expropriated by revolutionary courts.

Whatever the reason, it is clear that the entire industrial bourgeoisie of Iran, despite claims to the contrary by some leftist opposition groups, has been eliminated. Recently, discussions have taken place proposing the return of some companies to the original owners. Considering the vested interest of the bureaucracy and the huge losses many firms have suffered in the past several years, it is unlikely that a significant number will be handed back.

The Islamic Republic naturally has not been favorably disposed towards foreign investment in industry. Except for the takeover of American investments, however, there has been no legislation to nationalize joint-venture firms. The majority of such companies, nevertheless, have come under government control according to provisions of the nationalization law. In general, the government has made it difficult to repatriate profits, royalty payments, and technical assistance fees, forcing some foreign firms to abandon their investments or to sell out. In the case of the largest foreign investment in the country, the Iran-Japan petrochemical complex, the government insisted, unsuccessfully, that the project be completed as originally planned. Altogether, the regime has followed a low-key and pragmatic policy towards existing foreign participation in industry. Formerly ubiquitous foreign brand names have been changed, saving Iran the royalty payments. In the most important instance of such reforms, generic labeling has been introduced in the pharmaceutical industry. Many supply and technical-assistance contracts have been renegotiated. Despite occasional revolutionary excesses, such measures appear quite sensible.

Institutions have been created to operate the newly nationalized establishments in much the same way as the rest of the bureaucracy is run. The firms are not required to make profits nor are they asked to meet any production targets. The regime has constantly condemned the profit motive and material incentives. Yet there has been little discussion of how moral incentives are to be applied in the operation of public enterprises. No recognizably Islamic principle for organizing industrial production has emerged. Until now the state-owned sector has been incurring huge losses which the nationalized banks have underwritten.

Drastic changes in the pattern of ownership and other disruptions caused by the revolution and the war have had a profound effect on industrial output and productivity. Figures in Table 4 show that the output of large manufacturing firms (with over fifty employees) did not regain its pre-revolutionary level until 1982 and that labor productivity (output divided by employment) is still below its 1977 level. Many firms are still operating under full capacity. One reason for the large fall in labor productivity after the revolution was the government's reluctance (for obvious political reasons) to allow industrial employment to decline in the face of falling output. Indeed, it forced many firms to give permanent employment to their seasonal workers, and in the summer of 1980 legislated a 5 percent increase in the number of employees in all manufacturing firms with fifty or more workers.

Despite lower labor productivity, until 1983 real wages and salaries were higher than before the revolution. Following the wave of strikes in the fall of 1978, wages rose. The largest rise, however, was not due to strikes; it came in 1979, when unemployment was becoming widespread in the rest of the economy. This increase was due more to an administrative blunder than to the power of organized labor. In 1979, the government had issued a directive to raise the largely inoperative minimum wage. In order to keep existing wage differentials, other wages and salaries were raised by the same amount. By the time the implications of this policy were understood, it was too late to rescind the directive. Since then, the government has allowed inflation to erode the unintended gain to the point that average earnings in 1983 were below what they were in 1977 (see Table 4). In addition, salary ceilings have been imposed and wage differentials have been narrowed by allowing smaller raises for higher-paid workers than for the lower-paid. The average figures, therefore, overestimate the decline from their post-revolutionary height in the earnings of those in the bottom of the pay scale. Probably this group still remains better off than before the revolution.

Its nationalization policy notwithstanding, the government has time and again announced its intention to redirect "wandering" private capital from trade and speculation to industry. As a clear sign of its success in doing so, it has pointed to the increase in the number of provisional industrial permits granted. A closer examination of the data (presented in Table 4) reveals, however, that this "accomplishment" is somewhat illusory. The numer of establishment permits, which is a better indicator of investment plans, and the number of operation permits, which reflects actual investment, do not show a dramatic change. The number of such permits has been rising, but the value of investment and the number of jobs created imply that the new units are little more than small workshops. Their aggregate impact is also marginal. In 1982 the number of jobs created in the units that began operation was less than 2 percent of the workforce of industrial establishments with ten or more employees; investment in such firms was less than one-fifth of the government development expenditure for the sector. In any case, because many small manufacturing units operated without a license prior to the revolution, the increase in the number of permits does not necessarily represent a surge in investment. It may simply reflect a greater need since the revolution for such permits in order to obtain scarce machinery and material.

Small-scale industry has not received much assistance or more than rhetorical attention from the government. Several developments, however, have reversed the decline it experienced immediately after the revolution because of the cutback in demand. The ban on some imports

TABLE 4

THE INDUSTRIAL SECTOR STATISTICS

	1977	1978	1979	1980	1981	1982	1983
Index of Production (large establishments) 1974 = 100	150.6	129.1	129.7	121.5	137.5	157.6	195.2
Index of Employment (large establishments) 1974 = 100	120.4	126.3	132.8	137.5	141.9	149.4	159.5
Index of Real Wages and Benefits per Employee, 1974 = 100	130.3	146.4	202.2	187.4	161.7	143.7	132.0
No. of Provisional Permits Issued	857	322	652	1977	2709	3337	4502
No. of Permits Issued for Establishing New Units	731	435	708	877	1670	1678	2065
Expected Level of Investment in Such Units (billions of rials)	59.5	16.1	17.6	18.2	31.5	49.2	58.7
Expected No. of Employees		6758	9366	13852	15881	19920	23936
No. of Permits Issued for Operating New Units	232	109	144	208	540	834	743
Value of Investment in Such Units (billions of rials)	57.6	13.8	10.8	21.2	12.5	19.8	21.1
No. of Employees		6420	3582	4515	5746	9191	8139
Government Development Expenditure for Industry (billions of rials)	102.6	89.7	69.9	70.6	77.2	118.6	159.8

SOURCE: Central Bank of Iran, *Economic Report and Balance Sheets*, Ministry of Industry, *New Industrial Permits*: Third Quarter of 1983, The Plan and Budget Ministry, *Statistical Quarterly: # 5 June 1984*.

and the shortages of others have created profitable opportunities for domestic industry. In the absence of competition from the government-controlled large-scale firms, many small workshops have taken advantage of these opportunities. Such units abound in the apparel, chemical, plastics, and metal product industries, although it is impossible to estimate their relative importance. Even the somewhat larger private firms have benefitted from the existence of a seller's market. Between 1979 and 1982 employment in all firms with ten or more employees increased by 30 percent. Those with more than fifty employees registered an 18 percent rise, implying that those in the ten to fifty employee category experienced a much higher rate of growth. The dynamism of the smaller private firms is unlikely to continue for long, because they are becoming more entangled in the growing web of government controls and are denied access to various imputs. Government officials do not particularly appreciate the ingenuity and enterprise of this sector and consider much of its activity wasteful.[6]

The development budget for industry reveals much about the government's industrial policy. First, the total allocation to industry reflects its favored position. Despite the cuts made after the revolution, industry's share in the development budget has been consistently higher than it was before the revolution. Second, the allocation of this budget among the different industries follows roughly the pattern established by the previous regime, with petrochemicals and basic metals getting a lion's share (about seventy percent). Third, the continued emphasis on these and other heavy industries reflects the government's stress on self-sufficiency. That petrochemicals and basic metals are "sunset" industries (declining on a world scale), make little contribution to employment, and have little export potential does not seem to be of much concern to the government. Given the present investment projects, it appears that at least for the next decade Iran's industrial sector will be characterized by a dual structure, much as it was in the previous regime. A few thousand large firms in the modern sector will coexist with several hundred thousand small units, with few linkages between the two sectors. Of course, there will be a basic difference; nearly all of the modern sector will be state-owned.

AGRICULTURAL POLICIES

Land reform still remains an unresolved issue within the regime but there is little disagreement on the need to accord high priority to the development of the rural sector. This "rural bias" supposedly reflects both the regime's concern for the welfare of the most deprived segment of the society and its avowed objective of achieving self-sufficiency in basic foods. In July 1982 the government declared that agriculture was to be the "axis" of development, a goal which was later incorporated formally in the now-defunct first development plan. Has the regime backed its words with deeds? What have been the concrete measures adopted and how successfully have they promoted rural development?

In a period when most other sectors of the economy have experienced cutbacks in development funds, credits, and imported inputs, the agricultural sector has fared relatively well. Table 5 shows the flow of certain resources to the sector. Inputs of fertilizer and machinery have risen markedly. Both are highly subsidized because the government sells them below cost, but also because, being imported inputs, implicit subsidies are provided through the undervalued exchange rate. The fertilizer subsidy is the second largest item in the government subsidy program, having risen from 5.6 billion rials in 1977 to 41.0 billion rials in 1983. Responding to the fall in the relative price of machinery and fertilizers, farmers have increased their use, though not necessarily in the production of basic food grains. This policy may have raised some rural incomes but it has hardly contributed to the goals of self-sufficiency or rural employment creation.

The data on financial allocations to agriculture through development outlays and agricultural credit present a somewhat mixed picture. Only in 1979 and 1983 did agriculture's share of development expenditure rise substantially above its level in 1977, and once the figures are corrected for inflation, it is clear that real expenditures have fallen, especially in the period 1980 to 1982. Agricultural credit has expanded rapidly, probably outstripping the rise in prices of agricultural inputs. It should be stressed that credit allocation has been changed in favor of smaller holdings. Before the revolution about one-third of all agricultural credit was being handled by the Agricultural Development Bank of Iran, which catered to a limited number of large commercial farms. Such credit was drastically curtailed after the revolution, when the bank was merged with the Agricultural Bank. The number of farmers receiving institutional credit has nearly doubled, to over 600,000.

The regime has sought to encourage production also through higher prices for a number of crops, notably wheat, whose price has risen three and one-half times since the revolution. Government-guaranteed minimum prices have been periodically revised upwards, but it appears that, with some exceptions, they have not kept pace with inflation. For

TABLE 5

RESUORCES ALLOCATED TO THE AGRICULTURAL SECTOR

	1977	1978	1979	1980	1981	1982	1983
Chemical Fertilizers (*1000 tons*)	772	582	900	1097	1279	1641	1931
Tractor Sales (*units*)	10142	7482	11599	12771	14863	18977	32000
Agricultural Credit (*billions of rials*)	77.0	58.3	96.5	123.5	149.6	184.3	221.0
Government Development Expenditure for Agriculture (*billions of rials*)	42.1	53.9	55.9	26.7	35.3	48.7	91.9

SOURCE: Central Bank of Iran, *Economic Report and Balance Sheets*, Iran Statistical Center, *Annual Statistical Handbook*, The Plan and Budget Ministry, *Economic Report*; 1982 and first half of 1983.

TABLE 6

WHOLESALE AND CONSUMER PRICE INDEX

1974 = 100

	1977	1978	1979	1980	1981	1982	1983	1984
Index of Consumer Prices	160.2	176.2	196.3	242.5	297.9	355.2	418.1	462.1
Index of Wholesale Prices	136.9	149.9	179.6	243.3	279.7	318.1	358.0	385.2
Index of Wholesale Food Prices	139.1	158.8	205.0	276.6	344.0	396.6	470.7	518.4

SOURCE: Central Bank of Iran, *Economic Report and Balance Sheets*.

non-government transactions, however, market prices are generally higher. Because food imports are limited to the basic rationed commodities (except in the case of wheat), free market prices of many agricultural products have risen. The data presented in Table 6 indicate that with the index of wholesale food prices rising faster than the overall index, agriculture's terms of trade may be improving. Changes in relative prices among farm products have made certain crops, particularly vegetables and summer crops, more profitable, prompting many farmers to switch crops. This trend has been of much concern to the government, which has tried to discourage such shifts by withholding inputs and credit. In some instances, it has resorted to plowing under fields planted with these crops. Such a policy, though understandable in view of the government's desire to attain self-sufficiency in the basic grains, is not consistent with its aims of raising rural income and stemming migration to the cities.

According to official data the agricultural sector has performed rather well, averaging an annual growth rate of 5.3 percent between 1971 and 1983. These figures are highly suspect.[7] One should not, however, point to growing food imports as a sign of declining agricultural output (an argument often used against the previous regime). There are now one and one-half times as many people to be fed in the urban areas as there were in 1976. Moreover, the rationing program has extended the food subsidies into rural areas, encouraging higher food consumption. Government purchase of wheat from farmers has fallen below its pre-revolutionary level and sugar beet and cotton production have declined. These may be due to the shift to other crops, stimulated partly by relative price changes and partly by the breakup of large farms (which favored wheat and cotton), rather than to a fall in farm output. The increased use of agricultural inputs and the relatively stable level of rural household expenditure, despite falling non-agricultural rural employment opportunities (see below) appear to indicate agricultural growth, although not at the rate claimed by the government.

It is safe to say that productivity has not registered any noticeable gains and, indeed, may have declined. Rural households appear to be enjoying somewhat higher living standards since the revolution. This improvement is reflected in household expenditure data and in the wider ownership of consumer durables and the greater availability of electricity and piped water (see Table 7). This may be a continuation of a trend already visible at the end of the previous regime, but there has certainly been a marked increase in rural development projects, primarily access roads, electrification, and provision of piped water. Higher agricultural prices, subsidized inputs, and more and better distributed credit have helped raise rural living standards despite the substantial reduction in

TABLE 7
RURAL LIVING STANDARDS

	1979	1983
% of Households with:		
Refrigerators	14.5	32.2
Televisions	8.1	21.6
Piped Water	19.9	40.5
Electricity	27.7	51.6
Average Household Expenditure Per Month (1974 rials)	12245	12192

SOURCE: Central Statistics Center, *Annual Statistical Handbook.*

wage employment resulting from the cutbacks in national development projects.[8] Different segments of the rural population have not benefitted equally from these changes. As we mentioned above, the distribution of rural household expenditure became more unequal in 1979. Because larger farms were in a better position to take advantage of the new opportunities and because landless peasants were more affected by the decline in wage income, such a deterioration is entirely plausible. The data for 1982, however, indicate that the distribution of rural household expenditure improved to the extent that it is less unequal than in 1977.

Although urban-rural differentials are smaller now than they were before the revolution, they are on the rise again because of the levelling off in rural expenditures. Migration to urban areas continues unabated. Food imports keep increasing. The cost of subsidies had been contained for a while, but now the subsidies need more funding. All of these difficulties strongly suggest that the regime has not tackled the fundamental problems of rural development. Correcting the excesses of the previous regime, though commendable, is not enough by itself. Programs for agricultural research, for the introduction of high-yield varieties, for water and soil management, for the modernization of the livestock sector—in short, programs to promote technological change and innovation—have received scant attention since the revolution. In their absence and without a comprehensive framework, allocating more funds and physical inputs to the sector will become progressively more expensive and is unlikely to provide a long-term solution. Furthermore, the rapid spread of the bureaucratic controls over agricultural imputs and outputs will be an added obstacle to the development of the sector.[9]

CONCLUSIONS

Clearly the economic record of the Islamic Republic is a mixed one. It has succeeded in correcting many of the excesses of the previous regime, but it has failed so far to correct some of the basic imbalances in the economy. The government has implemented a number of effective policies, but it has also mismanaged the economy. It has been criticizing the shortcomings of pre-revolutionary policies but has not been forthcoming with many positive solutions. Of course, with the war drawing so many resources from the rest of the economy, it may be asking too much to expect the regime to undertake a major development effort. Yet, it does not appear that the programs that have been adopted have been appropriate to the country's long-term needs.

Many of the economic problems that the regime faces are essentially those which plagued its predecessor. In particular, it has not managed to break out of the vicious cycle of dependence on the oil sector. The existence of oil revenue and exports confers on the government the luxury of ignoring economic efficiency in the other productive sectors. This neglect, however, further reinforces the dependence on the oil sector. The "waste" in the economy is probably considerably lower than previously and its nature has been changed. On the other hand, faced with a stagnant market for oil, the regime cannot afford to ignore the long-term structural problems.

Although the economic structure of the Islamic Republic has many features in common with that of pre-revolutionary Iran there are also important differences. The government has clearly done best in distributing income and wealth. Social justice as a principle of "Islamic economics" has been the easiest to follow, partly because the previous regime's record was so poor in this respect. Without growth, however, further redistribution will be difficult to achieve. Iran is also more economically independent even if it has not achieved more self-sufficiency. Both greater equality and greater independence will be positive factors for the country's future development should other favorable conditions obtain. Once the war ends, the probable reduction in military expenditures will also represent a significant departure from the policies of the previous regime.

The Islamic Republic may be a novel phenomenon, but the Islamic Republic has shown little novelty in its economic policies. There are many parallels to be found in other populist regimes in the third world such as Nasser's Egypt, Algeria, Tanzania, and Burma. Those who favor the Republic may point to its record in achieving greater economic equality, while those who oppose it can stress its economic difficulties. In the final analysis, however, the Islamic Republic probably will be judged more for its non-economic acts and ideology than for its economic accomplishments or failures.

EPILOGUE (April 1986)

Events in the past year, especially the recent large drop in the price of oil, have highlighted the shortcomings of the regime's economic policies. The government's failure to effect basic structural change in the economy, its disregard for efficiency, and its neglect of the unemployment problem have left the country vunerable to the "reverse oil shock." Moreover, the expansion of the public sector and the mushrooming of government controls have greatly increased the rigidities in the economic system. Yet, the factions that have gained ascendency in the political arena advocate still more state control. The recession which began over a year ago is now turning into a major crisis as the shortage of imports leads to widespread factory shutdowns and drastic cutbacks in development expenditures. The already severe unemployment problem is assuming alarming proportions. Further curtailment of consumption and investment will be extremely painful but more belt tightening is unavoidable. The regime can try to make it more palatable to its supporters by renewing its attempts to redistribute income and wealth. In the immediate future, the prospects are for greater austerity, some redistribution, and more controls. None of these policies can address the long term economic problems whose resolution requires a fundamental realignment of the political forces in the country.

NOTES

*The data presented in this paper are normally for the Iranian solar year which extends from 21 March to 20 March of the Gregorian year. For simplicity the nearest Gregorian year to the Iranian year is used here.

1. See Patrick Clawson, "Iran's Economy: Between Crisis and Collapse" MERIP Report, no. 98, July–August 1981, pp. 11–15. Shaul Bakhash, The Reign of the Ayatollahs: Iran and the Islamic Revolution (New York: Basic Books, 1984), chapters 7 & 8 provide a lucid account of the nationalizations and land reform. See also M.H. Pesaran, "Dependent Capitalism in Pre-and Post-Revolutionary Iran," IJMES, vol. 14, #4, November 1982, pp. 501–522.

2. For an account of the causes of the fall in oil exports see Shaul Bakhash, The Politics of Oil and Revolution in Iran, The Brookings Institution, Washington D.C., 1982.

3. The data on the distribution of household expenditure can be found in Iran Statistical Center, *Indices of Inequality of Income Distribution in Iran,* Internal Report #63, Tehran, 1983 (in Persian).

4. Here real cost refers to the budgetary allocation deflated by the consumer price index. The economic cost of the subsidy program is higher because imported foods are implicitly subsidized through the increasingly undervalued exchange rate.

5. See *Statistics of Large Manufacturing Establishments Under Public Sector Management, 1982,* Iran Statistical Center, Tehran, 1984 (in Persian).

6. See *Report on Two Years' Operation of the Ministry of Industry,* Ministry of Industry, Tehran, September 1983, p. 11.

7. Even government authorities have expressed skepticism about the reliability of the agricultural data. See The Plan and Budget, *Economic Report: 1982 and first half of 1983,* Tehran, 1983, chapter 12. See also the article by R. Loeffler in this volume.

9. Purchases of various farm imputs are closely controlled by a number of government bodies such as Jehad-e Sazandegi, Ministry of Agriculture and Land Councils. As an extreme example of this kind of control the case of poultry farming is worth noting. For each cyle of raising chickens a farmer has to contact 14 different organizations to obtain his inputs. See Barzegar, *Weekly Journal of Agriculture and Livestock Breeding,* 6 Esfand 1362 (February 1983).

II

The Revolutionary Clergy

CLERICAL POLITICS in IRAN SINCE 1979

Shahrough Akhavi

PRELIMINARY OBSERVATIONS

THE ISLAMIC REPUBLIC OF IRAN has witnessed the following institutional milestones since the return of Ayatollah Khomeini in February 1979: (1) In March 1979 a referendum was held in which the Iranian people approved of a change in the political structure of the state from a hereditary monarchy to an Islamic Republic. (2) In August 1979 elections were held for a Council of Experts (originally to have been a Constituent Assembly) to prepare a draft of the Constitution. (3) In November 1979 a national plebiscite was held in which the people gave their approval to the final version of the Constitution, which featured the central role of the *faqih* (supreme clergyman) in the new social order. (4) In January 1980 elections took place for the office of President of the Republic, leading to the assumption of office by a non-cleric, Abol Hasan Bani Sadr. (5) In March and May 1980 parliamentary elections took place, and the majority of the seats eventually went to the Islamic Republican Party (IRP), associated with Khomeini through its chief architects, Ayatollah Sayyid Mohammad Beheshti and Hasan Ayat. (6) In June 1981 Bani Sadr was removed from office after a parliamentary commission found him culpable of a variety of alleged derelictions, including "unconstitutional behavior." This led to escalating urban violence, assassination of regime figures (including Beheshti, Ayat, the successor of Bani Sadr and his Prime Minister), and a reign of terror against regime opponents, notably the Mojahedin-e Khalq. (7) In December 1982, elections took place for a Council of Experts whose membership would be empowered to choose Khomeini's successor, thereby apparently consolidating regime rule. (8) Beginning in April 1983 and continuing through that year, a series of mass arrests took place of *Tudeh* (pro-Moscow Communist) Party members and leaders, indicating again the ability of the regime to tighten its grip on political rule. (9) In May 1984 elections were held for the second Majlis (parliament), the hallmark of which was the failure of the non-clerical nationalists (such as the members of the National Front or the Freedom Movement) to gain re-election. (10) In November 1985 it was inadvertently announced that Ayatollah Hosein Ali Montazeri had been formally elected by the Council of Experts to be Ayatollah Khomeini's successor.

Curiously, despite the cumulative effect these developments have had in tending to strengthen the hand of those clerics loyal to Khomeini's ideological vision, their rule is characterized by major discontinuities. Of course, this has to be expected in any revolutionary situation. It would be too much to expect consistency down the line when the very nature of social change in the last seven years in Iran is characterized by massive dislocations. Withal, one cannot help but be struck by the fact that *velayat-e faqih*—Khomeini's prescription for clerical executive power and rule—has not been more consistently defined or implemented.

Instead, the regime's success is better gauged in terms of its ability to hang on tenaciously to its gains and to deny the broad array of opposition groups the ability to penetrate the system and exercise influence. To the extent that the Khomeini clerics have reached agreement on whom to exclude from power, they have succeeded in ruling. But when one examines public policy, it soon becomes clear that the discontinuities are very significant indeed.

Among the public policy areas in which the regime is in trouble are agriculture generally, industrial policy, policy on property rights, trade, finance, national minorities, defense, labor, education, refugees, food, housing. Additionally, one must not forget that the succession problem has been addressed but not resolved, despite Montazeri's formal election.

The point is not, of course, that the Khomeini clerics have failed consistently down the line in all of these areas. Rather, it is maintained that consistency in formulating and implementing *policy* is missing. This means that while discrete instances exist of the successful application of decisions, planning and carrying out such decisions in the context of a broad vision and program has not taken place.

INSTITUTIONAL STRUCTURES

The institutional structures of the new state order continue to evolve. Ayatollah Khomeini seemed to suggest, in December 1982, that the revolution had succeeded enough to warrant talking about a new phase of Iranian politics. The time had come to emphasize discipline over ardor, to stress state building and support for the new state structures. An eight-point decree was issued in Khomeini's name, and its general thrust was that it was time to rationalize the gains of the revolution and to argue the supremacy of authority and stability values over revolutionary advocacy and passion. However, perhaps because he himself had refused to commit himself heart and soul to this new line, the crystallization of jurisdictions, hierarchies, and responsibilities has not occured. Khomeini probably wanted to let the masses know that he did not support arbitrary detentions, searches, seizures, etc. It is unlikely, however, that he meant to launch a period of state bureaucratization. Nonetheless, a certain group of clerics who now hold power seem to be desirous of expanding state power and with it, inevitably, their own positions within the new state order.

Figure 1 is an attempt schematically to represent the state structure of the Islamic Republic as of late 1985. If one compares this structure with that of the state apparatus in the late Pahlavi period,[1] the most striking difference is the significance of the judicial institutions since 1979. A second difference is the presence of paramilitary and "militant" organizations, such as the *pasdaran* (revolutionary guards), the revolutionary committees and the amorphous urban groups known as the *hezbollah* (those of the party of God). But the Khomeini clerics have tried to incorporate the guards and the committees into ministries, creating a Ministry of Pasdaran Affairs for the former and absorbing the latter into the Ministry of Interior. A third and perhaps final major difference is the greater autonomy that the leaders of some of these organizations enjoy vis-à-vis their counterparts under the monarchy. While all lines seemingly lead to and emanate from the faqih, it is virtually certain that there is a good deal of room for local decision-making.

CLERICAL FACTIONALISM

The nature of these organizations, of course, tell us something about politics and power in the revolutionary period. But do we know anything about the political leanings of the individuals filling these positions? Political discourse in Iran suggests that two factions are currently contending for power. One group is allegedly known as *maktabi imami*, while the other is called *hojjati*. The growing consensus among scholars is that these are false labels, especially maktabi. Others argue that an identifiable group called hojjati exists and that it began in the late 1950s as a loosely

FIGURE 1

STATE STRUCTURES of the ISLAMIC REPUBLIC of IRAN

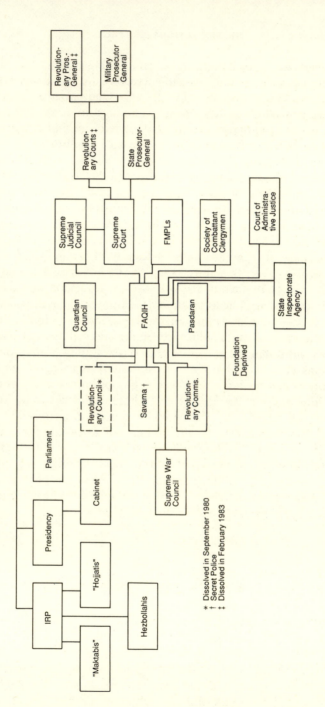

* Dissolved in September 1980
† Secret Police
‡ Dissolved in February 1983

According to the Deputy Prime Minister for Revolutionary Institutions, Sayyid Isma'il Da'udi, twelve revolutionary organizations exist (*IT*, 31 Urdibihisht 1361 H. Sh./21 May 1982): (1) Pasdaran; (2) Reconstruction Jihad; (3) Revolutionary Courts; (4) Revolutionary Committees; (5) Imam Khomeini Relief Agency; (6) Martyrs' Foundation; (7) Islamic Revolution Housing Foundation; (8) Foundation for Deprived; (9) War Veterans Foundation; (10) Islamic Propaganda Organization; (11) Literacy Movement; (12) Guilds Affairs Committee.

knit organization of anti-Baha'i clerics. But these scholars, too, prefer to view the cleavages among the clergy today not in terms of clearcut factions but of tendencies. Additionally, they warn that maktabi is a label that is self-appropriated by those who want to show their supreme loyalty to Khomeini while denying the claims of their rivals to the same.

Nonetheless, whatever term one wishes to use, it is still possible to identify power conflicts and also to seek to identify individuals in the leadership with one or another position. Since 1979, a variety of clerics have resisted the idea of velayat-e faqih. It is fair to say that these individuals perceive Khomeini's interpretation of this concept to be a clerical rule. They base themselves on criticism of Khomeini's writings and statements since 1970, the unmistakeable thrust of which is that the clerics should exercise executive power. They prefer the looser *vesayat-e foqaha,* which they interpret as general supervision by the clergy over affairs. This was the original intent of article two of the supplementary fundamental laws of 1906–1907. At the most, these clerics are willing to concede the principle of velayat-e faqih in times of exceptional turmoil but contend that it lapses when a government is installed, a parliament is elected and a new state order comes into being. The following individuals can be placed in this group:

1. Ayatollah Mahmud Taleqani (d. 1979)
2. Ayatollah Morteza Motahhari (d. 1979)
3. Ayatollah Abol Fazl Zanjani (d. 1983?)
4. Ayatollah Hasan Lahuti (d. 1981)
5. Ayatollah Mohammad Kazem Shariatmadari (d. 1986)
6. Ayatollah Abdullah Shirazi (d. 1984)
7. Ayatollah Mohammad Reza Golpayegani
8. Ayatollah Hasan Tabatabai Qommi
9. Ayatollah Allamah Nuri
10. Ayatollah Naser Makarem Shirazi
11. Shaikh Ali Tehrani
12. Ayatollah Sadeq Ruhani
13. Ayatollah Mohammad Reza Mahdavi Kani?

The regime has oriented itself in a variety of ways to these individuals. Taleqani and Motahhari had already written essays supporting the notion of a council of mujtahids empowered to issue binding authoritative opinions.[2] Both were extremely popular with their constituencies, but their early deaths removed whatever longlasting impact they might have made on the future course of developments. It is possible that Motahhari had amended his earlier opposition to a single clerical leader ruling the Shi'ite community in favor of Khomeini's leadership. But it is hardly likely that Taleqani had become converted to this view.[3]

The next two individuals were vocal in 1979 and 1980 in protesting excessive centralization of power, but their voices were soon silenced by the Khomeini clerics. The former, in any case, had been a pro-Mosaddeq clergyman, and this affiliation was bound to cost him as the new regime unleashed a flood of criticism against Mosaddeq and his followers. Lahuti had early been entrusted by the regime to organize the pasdaran but rapidly fell into disfavor as a consequence of critical comments about the course of events in Iran.

The next four, all grand mujtahids, have been silenced as a consequence of trial, incarceration or harrassment. Shirazi's death had reduced the circle of eminent mujtahids from eight (if we include Khomeini) to seven. Of the seven, only Khomeini and Marashi Najafi would seem to be solid advocates of velayat-e faqih. Two others, Ayatollah Abol Qasim Kho'i of Najaf and Ayatollah Ahmad Musavi Khvansari of Tehran, have been quietists and their opinion is difficult to judge.

Of the next three individuals on the list, Nuri, too, has been out of the political arena despite the fact that he was an important mobilizer of urban protest in 1978–79 in Tehran. Perhaps he became overly identified in the regime's mind with Sadeq Qotbzadeh (executed by the regime in 1983), whose temporary arrest in the fall of 1980 for criticizing media censorship led to bazaar protests and shutdowns. Makarem Shirazi appears to have been totally silent since his opposition to velayat-e faqih during the deliberations of the Council of Experts in the summer of 1979. Tehrani, in the meantime, after several incidents of direct criticism of the regime from his base in Mashhad, has entered self-imposed exile in Iraq, whence he has been giving press interviews broadly condemning Khomeini's rule. Ruhani has publicly spoken out against confiscatory land legislation, arguing that if land is illegally appropriated, then it must be returned to its owners. "Otherwise, even if an individual has committed a thousand crimes, his property goes to his heirs."[4] Although this does not suggest explicit criticism of velayat-e faqih, it is an attack on those implementing decisions in its name.

More remarkably, however, Ayatollah Ruhani has made the following scathing comments at the Mohammadiyeh Mosque in Qom in late November 1985:

> My duty today is to say that I see Islam in danger, that the *marja'iyat* [principle of exemplary leadership by the most eminent clerics] to be in danger. Last night's speech and press conference indicates that the high ranking clergy sat among themselves in a closed room and bore witness

that the majority of the people gave the leadership after Mr. Khomeini to Zayd [i.e., Ayatollah Montazeri] and that they have elevated this Zayd to the level of *marja'*. This is a lie. The election of the marja' of the Shi'ites is not in the hands of the common people to make. These actions will drag Islamic government to destruction. I hereby declare that I oppose this sort of election of the leader of our country . . . They say that the people elected these persons [members of the Council of Experts]. This is a lie. The people did not elect anyone, nor did they give their vote to anyone. Even supposing this *was* the case—which it is not—this contradicts the principle of Islamic government. I declare that this government is un-Islamic, that it has given itself an Islamic name but is clearly against the provisions of the Quran. It acts against Islam and is even worse than communist governments.[5]

The last person on this list is Ayatollah Mahdavi Kani, whose name is followed by a question mark. Mahdavi Kani has served on the Guardian Council, and he has also at various times been in charge of the revolutionary committees, Minister of the Interior and interim Prime Minister. His practice has been to stay outside the IRP, and he has thus acquired a certain reputation for independent-mindedness.[6]

One may compare the thirteen clergymen listed above to the following supporters of velayat-e faqih, whether in its form of single clerical leadership or a committee of clerics ruling a political system in which clerics hold executive power:

      1. Ayatollah Mohammad Hosein Beheshti (d. 1981), architect of IRP, Supreme Court Chief Justice.

      2. Ayatollah Hosein Ali Montazeri, elected successor to Khomeini, leader of the Friday Mosque Prayer Leaders (FMPL) network.

      3. Ayatollah Abol Karim Musavi Ardabili, Chief Justice of the Supreme Court; member of the Supreme Judicial Council; Provisional FMPL in Tehran.

      4. Ayatollah Ali Meshkini, FMPL (Friday Mosque Prayer Leader) in Qom; chairman of the Central Committee of the Council of Experts.

      5. Ayatollah Abol Rahim Rabani Shirazi (d. 1982), member of the Council of Guardians.

      6. Ayatollah Yusuf Sane'i, former State Prosecutor-General, former member of the Council of Guardians; Member of the Supreme Judicial Council.

      7. Hojjat al-Islam Javad Bahonar (d. 1981), Prime Minister.

      8. Hojjat al-Islam Mohammadi Gilani, member of the Council of Guardians, formerly Revolutionary Prosecutor-General for Tehran.

9. Hojjat al-Islam Mohammad Rayshahri, Minister of Information and Intelligence, formerly Revolutionary Prosecutor-General of the Armed Forces.

10. Hojjat al-Islam Ali Akbar Nateq Nuri, former Minister of the Interior.

11. Hojjat al-Islam Ali Qoddusi (d. 1981), Revolutionary Prosecutor-General.

12. Hojjat al-Islam Ali Khamenehi, President of the Republic; Chairman, Supreme Defense Council; Secretary-General, IRP; Provisional FMPL (Friday Mosque Prayer Leader) in Tehran.

13. Hojjat al-Islam Ali Akbar Hashemi Rafsanjani, Speaker of Parliament; Imam's Representative to the Supreme Defense Council; Member of the Central Committee of the Council of Experts; Provisional Friday Mosque Prayer Leader in Tehran; Member of the Central Committee of the IRP.

14. Ayatollah Ahmad Jennati, Member of the Council of Guardians.

15. Ayatollah Lotfollah Safi, Member of the Council of Guardians.

16. Ayatollah Abol Qasim Khazali, Member of the Council of Guardians.

17. Hojjat al-Islam Mohammad Emami Kashani, Member of the Council of Guardians; Provisional Friday Mosque Prayer Leader in Tehran; Director, Adminsitrative Justice Tribunal.

18. Hojjat al-Islam Mohammad Momen, Member of the Council of Guardians.

19. Hojjat al-Islam Mohammad Musavi Bojnurdi, Member of the Supreme Judicial Council.

20. Hojjat al-Islam Abol Fazl Mir Mohammadi, Member of the Supreme Judicial Council.

21. Hojjat al-Islam Morteza Moqtadai, Member of the Supreme Judicial Council.

22. Ayatollah Mohammad Mehdi Rabani Amlashi (d. 1985), former Deputy Speaker of Parliament; Member of the Central Committee of the Council of Experts; Member of the Central Committee of the IRP; formerly State Prosecutor-General.

23. Ayatollah Mohsen Malakuti, Friday Mosque Prayer Leader in Tabriz.

24. Ayatollah Jalal al-Din Taheri, Friday Mosque Prayer Leader in Isfahan.

25. Ayatollah Hosein Khademi, dean, Isfahan theological seminaries.

26. Ayatollah Abbas Vaez Tabasi, Friday Mosque Prayer Leader in Mashhad; Member of the Central Committee of the IRP.

27. Ayatollah Haeri Shirazi, Friday Mosque Prayer Leader (FMPL) in Shiraz.

28. Hojjat al-Islam Movahhedi Kermani, Member of the Central Committee of the IRP; Imam's Representative in the National Police.

29. Hojjat al-Islam Muhammad Khatami, Minister of Islamic Guidance.

30. Hojjat al-Islam Musavi Kho'iniha, State Prosecutor-General.

Among these individuals, one supposes, the great majority are in favor of institutionalizing clerical power in the organizations that they head. A smaller group among these persons, led by Ayatollah Montazeri, favors a separation between revolutionary organs and state agencies. Montazeri has become known for numerous speeches in which he has lamented bureaucratization and a lapse of revolutionary fervor. In late 1983 he complained that "we are still unsuccessful in our adminstrative revolution" due to "satanical elements," "excessive protocol," "futile expenditures," and "certain non-Islamic laws in banks. . . ." The Islamic Republic needs cadres and leaders to exercise "a certain moral courage and administrative audacity which unfortunately we have lacked so far." Directing his ire at the budget proposed for March 1984–March 1985, he noted "vast sums . . . [are] earmarked for non-productive affairs, for instance superfluous salary-receiving personnel." And he suggested that the proposal to convert the Reconstruction Crusade into a ministry would convert a revolutionary organ into a bureaucratic one.[7]

Montazeri has also urged Rafsanjani and Khamenehi to pay more attention to the IRP, a revolutionary organ whose influence, he implied, was being eroded. The kinds of revolutionaries we need, he seemed to be saying, are not careerists, opportunists, in a word, bureaucrats. "Some people want others to obey them like dumb animals, and if they express an opinion, they will be rejected, even if they are believing, wise and revolutionary. On the contrary, believing, independent and brave people should find their way to the religious seminaries, the government and the Majlis so that if the Prime Minister, the Majlis Speaker or the President said something contrary to their opinion, they have the courage and strength to express their views."[8]

Astonishingly, in a statement released to the press, Montazeri warned: "There is a famous saying in the world that revolutions devour their children. Today, I feel the same thing is happening in our society . . . a gradual and creeping coup is under way . . . free and independent individuals who are committed to Islam . . . are wise and capable . . . are in danger of being eliminated . . . Today, I feel that weak and obedient individuals are more attracted to the government, to the Majlis . . . even to the religious seminaries."[9]

Montazeri has also called for close consultations between officers of the military and pasdaran, on the one hand, and the rank and file soldiers. Again, this stance supports the more revolutionary and anti-bureaucratic tendencies. Rank becomes an impediment to revolutionary work, in this view. The day will come, he noted, when the Friday Mosque Prayer Leaders will be the actual governors of Iran's provinces. It will be crucial for them, therefore, to imitate Imam Ali's rule and never publicly humiliate others. In fact, Prayer Leaders should regularly interact with their clerical colleagues, whatever leadership roles have been assigned to them. After all, other clergymen "might have an influence among the people and may wish to serve. They should be consulted."[10] The clergy must refrain from "self-indulgence, luxury and extravagance in everyday life" and avoid "undue love and pursuit of material comfort."[11]

Ayatollah Khomeini has joined in warning against bureaucratization. For example, in 1982 he vetoed the idea urged by Supreme Court Justice Ayatollah Ardabili and the State Prosecutor-General at that time, Ayatollah Rabani Amlashi to merge the revolutionary courts into those of the Ministry of Justice.[12] And in the summer of 1983, in granting an audience to the newly appointed Minister of Pasdaran Affairs, he warned against the bureaucratization in that organization.[13]

Ranged against this tendency is another that emphasizes authority values and stability. Of course, no cleric will defend "self-indulgence" and "luxury." But to the extent that these words are criticisms of the expansion of state power through control of offices in the administrative apparatus, they have not gone unchallenged. Rafsanjani, for example, has warned that the parliament rostrum is a "dangerous place," and it would be wrong to let just anyone speak from it. As he put it, "a person might do something whereby a poisonous climate of opinion might be created . . . In the Majlis above all we want a good and pious person."[14]

Ayatollah Sane'i has suggested that the sort of good and pious person the leadership is looking for will inevitably accept the current course of the regime: "If one supports the laws of the Quran and of Islam, the Constitution and the system of the Islamic Republic, one cannot refrain from supporting the government, the Majlis and the Supreme Judicial Council."[15] On another occasion, Sane'i claimed: "no conflict exists among the responsible officials [who] . . . originate from the theological seminaries and are the adepts of the Imam of the Age (that is,

Khomeini)."[16] Ayatollah Khomeini himself has demanded an end to criticism of the regime on numerous occasions, variously belittling such critics as "satans" or "simpletons."[17] Other times, he concedes the legitimacy of differences of views but cryptically suggests that they are "within the nation, not among individuals." In any case, he has warned that those responsible for publicly airing their conflicts will be accountable to God for harming Islam.[18]

Reinforcing this notion of divine punishment which will be visited upon those who differ with the wishes of the regime, President Khamenehi has equated discipline with revolutionary values: rather than being a "satanical" issue, discipline is a "divine" one, he argued.[19] In fact, Khamenehi's desire to achieve monolithic unity and conformity was to advocate the introduction of the hezbollah elements into the universities.[20] (The hezbollah have been viewed by many as enforcers of the regime's writ and considered not revolutionary but in fact street gangs intimidating those holding views considered "heterodox.")

Perhaps the outstanding difference between those urging centralization and state control, on the one hand, and those insisting on revolutionary initiative may be seen in speeches made by Prime Minister Mir Hosein Musavi and Montazeri within days of one another in late 1981. In his maiden speech to parliament on 2 November 1981, Musavi insisted on the importance of re-establishing state control over affairs. Only a few days later, Montazeri characteristically remarked that regional ulama know about developments much more than do officials of the ministries in Tehran who are out of touch with matters outside the capital.[21]

Apart from a cleavage based on "permanent revolution" versus greater attention to bureaucratization, state-building, and institutionalization of rule, it is possible to see clerical politics in terms of a socioeconomic cleavage. This division is based on whether or not the state should directly intervene in the economy and society. In the absence of direct evidence, positions have to be inferred from public statements. Following that procedure, it seems that Rafsanjani, Khamenehi, Ardabili, Sane'i, Meshkini, and Montazeri favor a strong public sector. They therefore seemingly advocate the principle of expropriation of property in order to redistribute it to the advantage of the destitute; they support the nationalization of trade and banking, although differences may exist among them as to the utility of including internal commerce. On the other hand, it is fairly certain that divisions exist among the above-named individuals over the relative importance to be attached to industrial versus agricultural development. The classic pattern of LDC industrialization has been to use the agricultural sector as a source of revenue (through taxation and [forced] savings) and as a market for the consumption of goods. Hopefully, backward linkages would then be constructed so that the countryside could develop by increasingly creating a demand for capital goods needed for agricultural growth. Montazeri and some of his allies have been critical of the Islamic Republic's record thus far in the rural areas. He has attacked Rafsanjani and Khamenehi for paying too much attention to the urban and industrial sectors.[22] Consequently, despite the fact that the socio-economic dimension tends to unite leading clerics, they still have opposing views on certain specific policies.

Probably ranged against the Rafsanjani, Khamenehi, Ardabili, Sane'i, Meshkini, Montazeri group is one led by Mahdavi Kani. Among his allies are presumably those who sit on the Guardian Council: Gilani, Jennati, Safi, Khazali, Emami Kashani, Momen. Additionally, powerful individuals, such as former Interior Minister Nateq Nuri, are likely affiliated with this factional tendency. Their preference is to protect private property ownership, whether in land, in trade or finance. In identifying these individuals, attention has been given to their speeches, their behavior (in the case of Nateq Nuri) or their incumbencies. However, it must be admitted that much guesswork informs the identification of the individuals in the Mahdavi Kani faction.

It is clear that despite the factionalism that exists between contending clerical groups, the regime is managing to maintain social control. The opposition has been unable to prevent regime consolidation under conditions which thus far have been extremely unfavorable to it. Such opposition movements, to cite one observer, "all have their Kronstadts and Mahabads, their dismantled workers' councils and their more democratic Mensheviks."[23] On the other hand, the "organizational weapon" by which the Khomeini vision and practice has been implemented is certainly not the political party. Even if one accepts the assertion that the IRP was created in 1977, it was hardly an important mobilizer and articulator in the revolution. That task was and continues to be best accomplished by the network of FMPL's-revolutionary committees-bazaaris that served Ayatollah Khomeini so well.

The following cases will suggest some of the flavor of clerical politics since the revolution. Faced with the Guardian Council's rejection of legislation affecting land tenure, the Rafsanjani faction importuned Khomeini for direct intervention to reverse the veto. According to Rafsanjani, Khomeini agreed to devolve some of his authority as faqih upon the parliament. The theoretical justification for this attempt at overriding the constitutionally sanctioned right of the Guardian Council to reject parliamentary statutes if these are deemed inimical to Shiite Islam has centered on the relationship between what has been termed the "Primary" and "secondary" principles of the doctrine. Rafsanjani argued that in certain cases the secondary precepts supervene over the primary ones. In a speech, the Speaker of parliament invoked "societal necessity" (zaruratha-ye jami'eh), and "collective interests" (masaleh-e kolli)in times of difficulty ('osr), with a view to avoiding "sin" (haraj). Khomeini supposedly agreed to divest some of his authority on parliament provided that the deputies wanted this, the divestiture would be provisional, and it would be revoked "as soon as circumstances had changed."[24]

However, nothing more was heard about this attempt to circum-vent the Guardian Council until February 1983. In a public speech to the entire nation, Khomeini insisted that "there is no connection between the secondary decrees (that is, principles) and the implementation of velayat-e faqih . . ."[25] This must be seen as a clear rebuff to Rafsanjani and his supporters, who may be seen in this case to have wanted to curtail the power of the rival faction.

Another case involves the extremely complicated issue of property expropriation. The staunchly pro-Khomeini cleric, Ayatollah Ardabili, in February 1982 complained about extortion and irrational confiscations of land by local authorities attempting to apply paragraph three of the land law issued by the Revolutionary Council in April 1980. The principle of this paragraph was that seven-member committees would be established in the countryside. These were to permit the landlords in the regions to retain from two to three times the acreage normally tilled by the ordinary peasant through custom ('orf) and then to redistribute the remainder of the land to the common cultivators.

Ardabili noted that local committees were hastily being set up and indiscriminantly parcelling out properties without any regard to appropriate procedures. He did not condemn the principle of land re-distribution, of course (since his clerical faction supports the principle of confiscation), but he suggested that its implementation had to wait until its "shortcomings" were rectified. In the meantime, pamphlets issued by the IRP and the (still legal) Tudeh Party (pro-Moscow) contained petitions signed by peasants urging the application of the land bill. However, Ayatollah Khomeini had himself intervened in this matter in November 1980 and suspended the law's provisions. At this point, Ayatollah Khazali, a member of the Guardian Council and presumably an opponent of land confiscation, publicly stated that the law had been misapplied in the past and in any case had been deferred by "another, sacred official (that is, Khomeini)."[26] In fact, the Guardian Council has frequently intervened to overturn legislation not only dealing with land but other forms of property, including trade, housing and finance.

Khomeini's reaction has been mixed. At one point, he lashed out at parliamentary deputies for passing legislation they knew would be rejected by the Guardian Council. Therefore, he argued, the inevitable impasses that have emerged over social and economic matters are due to the Majlis's own insensitivities. "If the Guardian Council says something is against Islam, then it is against Islam," he admonished.[27]

On the other hand, in September 1984 he attacked the Guardian Council for "interfering too much" in affairs. "You must conduct yourselves in such a way that it not come to pass that you are opposed to parliament . . . You must keep in mind that if discussion and conversation turn into argument and you confront one another, this will cause weakness and eventually the Council of Guardians will disappear."[28] Equally intriguing are Khomeini's varying responses to the role of the bazaar in society. He has variously attacked the bazaar for price-gouging and "economic terrorism" (in 1979 and 1980), lamented that the regime and the bazaar were out of step with one another (as in the spring of 1981 when the bazaars shut down especially in Tehran and Qom over hezbollah attacks against President Bani Sadr at Tehran University); and in the summer of 1984 he warned government leaders to let the bazaar have a decision-making role. "If you do not let all the people take part in trade, industry and so on, then you shall not be successful." And again: "it is not right to think that the bazaar is corrupt from top to bottom . . . If the government permits the bazaaris (to take an active role in matters affecting them), then those who have not invested capital may do so and people who imagine that the government is not doing anything for the people will become aware that this is not so."[29]

Clearly the bazaar's support for the regime is critical in view of the links between it and the clergy in the past. The government has had to be careful in proceeding to establish an economic base in which cooperative and public sectors co-exist with the traditional private sector. In a lengthy speech in parliament in mid-1983 the Prime Minister defended the revolutionary nature of the bazaar while warning against the penetration into it of counterrevolutionaries. He thereupon demanded a purge of such elements and strongly attacked criticisms of the cooperatives that the regime had established. Some fear the abolition of traditional distribution methods, he noted, but "we believe in what is appropriate for the nation rather than use of this or that particular method of distribution." In reaction to this speech, 118 of the 270 parliamentary deputies are alleged to have sent the Prime Minister a letter of support for his arguments.[30] This seems like a sizeable number, but looked at another way, what seems more impressive is the apparent unwillingness of the majority of the MPs to join this effort. It may be that this roughly fifty-fifty split is generally representative of the cleavage among the clerical elites on a variety of socio-economic issues.

CONCLUSIONS

Some analysts argue that the true test of the institutionalization of the revolution will come upon Khomeini's death. If power is peacefully and in an orderly way transferred to (a) mutually agreed successor(s), then the regime can have greater confidence in the durability of the Islamic Republic. Earlier I argued that clerical power depended, among other things, on the loyalty of the pasdaran. However, pasdaran factionalism has made this difficult. Probably the most notorious episode of fragmentation among the pasdaran occurred in Isfahan in 1983. Factions of the revolutionary guards corps affiliated around rival clerics there, namely Ayatollahs Taheri and Khademi. Armed clashes resulted, and Ayatollah Montazeri interceded on behalf of Taheri, the Friday Mosque Prayer Leader. Ultimately, a new commander of pasdaran units for Isfahan was appointed.

In fact, the evidence for pasdaran factionalism comes from regime figures, as well as the exiled groups opposing the Islamic republic. It seems that it would be critical for the regime to ensure the integrity of the linkages between the Friday Mosque Prayer Leader network (which is presumably under the control of Montazeri, Rafsanjani, Meshkini, Ardabili, and Khamenehi), the pasdaran and the bazaar/"maiduni"[32] elements. The most likely succession scenario is a committee composed of the above individuals in which Montazeri becomes *primus inter pares*. Montazeri's designation as Khomeini's successor by the Council of Experts in 1985 does not, in my view, suggest that he will be the unique leader of the country after Khomeini's departure. Of course, much will depend on external events, including the behavior of the superpowers and the evolution of the Iran-Iraq war. But if the Islamic Republic is to survive the departure of Ayatollah Khomeini, it will need to prevent the formation of private armies loyal to particular Friday Mosque Prayer Leaders of reputation and power. One thing is virtually certain, however: the political, social and economic cleavages outlined in this paper will continue to exercise a powerful pull on the course of future events. Although a natural tendency, after Khomeini, will be for the clerics to unite in the face of immediate adversity, it is unlikely that such unity will endure for longer than the short term.

NOTES

1. Khorsrow Fatemi, "Leadership by Distrust," *Middle East Journal*, XXXVI, 1 (Winter 1982), pp. 50–51.

2. *Bashi dar bareh-ye Marjaiyat va Ruhaniyat*, 2nd ed. (Tehran: Sherkat-e Sahhami-ye Enteshar, 1341 H.Sh.), pp. 165–98, 201–11, 233–49.

3. Taleqani, for example, was overwhelmingly elected from Tehran to serve on the Council of Experts, the task of which was to write a draft constitution. On the critical vote on article five, which refers to the faqih as the representative of the Hidden Imam in the Islamic Republic until the latter's return, Taleqani cast a negative vote. On this see the important book by Bahram Afrasiyabi and Said Dehqan, *Taleqani va Tarikh*, 2nd ed. (Tehran: Entesharat-e Nilufar, 1360 H. Sh.), p. 538.

4. Shaul Bakhash, *The Reign of the Ayatollahs* (New York: Basic Books, 1984), p. 205.

5. Cited in *Qiyam* (Paris), 21 Azar 1364 H. Sh./12 December 1985, no. 4 (new series), consecutive numbering 129, p. 6. This exile publication supports the line of former Prime Minister Shahpur Bakhtiar.

6. The regime clerics might harbor some misgivings about Mahdavi Kani because of this. His sudden stepping down from candidacy to run for President in the fall of 1981 and his relinquishing of his leadership role over the revolutionary committees on 9 August 1982 suggest efforts to isolate him.

7. Foreign Broadcast Information Service [hereafter, FBIS]–SAS–83–238, 9 December 1983.

8. FBIS–SAS–83–241, 14 December 1983.

9. *Ibid.*

10. *Ibid.*

11. FBIS–SAS–83–234, 5 December 1983.

12. *Iran Times* [hereafter, IT], 7 Khordad 1361 H. Sh./28 May 1982. This paper is published once weekly in Washington, D.C. Normally, it contains sixteen pages, fourteen of which are in Persian and two in English. All references to IT pertain to Persian language articles.

14. For example, in his audience to the newly appointed Minister of Pasdaran Affairs and other officials of this corps, Khomeini warned against bureaucratization within this heretofore revolutionary organ *(nehad-e enqelabi)*. FBIS–SAB–83–156, 11 August 1983.

14. FBIS–SAS–83–242, 15 December 1983.

15. IT, 2 Shahrivar 1363 H. Sh./24 August 1984.

16. IT, 6 Aban 1362 H. Sh./28 October 1983.

17. IT, 26 Mordad 1363 H. Sh./17 August 1984; FBIS–SAS–83–100, 23 May 1983; FBIS–SAS–83–195, 6 October 1983.

18. FBIS–SAS–84–106, 31 May 1984.

19. FBIS–SAS–83–142, 22 July 1983.

20. IT, 6 Aban 1362 H. Sh./28 October 1983.

21. IT, 29 Aban 1360 H. Sh./20 November 1981.

22. FBIS–SAS–83–234, 5 December 1983.

23. Kurt Greussing, Berlin Institute for Comparative Social Research, Free University of Berlin, West Berlin, FRG, personal communication to me.

24. IT, 1 Aban 1360, 23 October 1981.

25. FBIS–SAS–83–032, 15 February 1983. This is particularly noteworthy, since Rafsanjani triumphantly had declared a few days earlier that Khomeini had indeed agreed to activate his powers as faqih and devolve them upon the parliament in regard to matters unresolved between it and the Guardian Council if ⅔ (cf. ½ in 1981) of the MPs desired this. IT, 22 Bahman 1361 H. Sh../11 February 1983.

26. On this entire episode, see IT, 30 Bahman 1360 H. Sh./19 February 1982.

27. IT, 22 Bahman 1361 H. Sh./11 February 1983.

28. IT, 16 Shahrivar 1363 H. Sh./7 September 1984.

29. IT, 9 Shahrivar 1363 H. Sh./31 August 1984.

30. FBIS–SAS–83–134, 12 July 1983. Perhaps the chief opponent to the growing involvement of the state in the economy is Ayatollah Mahdavi Kani. In the fall of 1982, for example, he vigorously attacked the parliamentary bill to nationalize foreign trade as an "annulment of people's property ownership" and ridiculed the idea that the government could regulate the flow of some "200,000 different types of goods" in imports alone. IT, 19 Azar 1361 H. Sh./10 December 1982.

31. FBIS–SAS–83–251, 29 December 1983; FBIS–SAS–84–002, 4 January 1984.

32. The following episodes all illustrate this point. In the fall, 1981, Khomeini told members of the pasdaran and revolutionary committees to stop their conflicts and adhere to chains of command. All are brothers and "there is no higher or lower" in Iran. However, he said, order is necessary, since without it "your brotherliness will come into conflict." IT, 16 Mehr 1361 H. Sh./8 October 1982.

In the spring of 1982, the pasdaran journal, *Payam-e Enqelab,* published an article by Khomeini's representative in the guards corps urging pasdaran officers to stop resigning because that was against the wishes of clerical rule. FBIS–SAS–084, 29 April 1983.

Also in the spring, 1983, President Khamanehi lectured pasdaran contingents on the need for discipline among the units: "Order must extend further into the guards." FBIS–SAS–83–101, 24 May 1983. Not long thereafter, Ayatollah Montazeri complained about "the danger of discord among forces" that he said was being "forcefully felt today." FBIS–SAS–83–125, 28 June 1983.

In July 1983, the commander of the pasdaran, Mohsen Rezai, unleashed an attack in the pages of *Payam-e Enqelab* against Ayatollah Mahdavi Kani for this criticism of what he perceived to be careerist tendencies among some pasdaran officers who wanted to become generals. FBIS-SAS-83-146, 28 July 1983.

Towards the end of the year, Ayatollah Khomeini addressed pasdaran officials in the following terms: "You gentlemen ought to be careful . . . not always [to] . . . direct criticism at those at the top. We should come down, right down here . . . be careful not to fall victim to pride." FBIS–SAS–83–216, 7 November 1983. And President Khamenehi stressed to pasdaran in Shiraz about a month later that indiscipline was intolerable: "Differences of opinion may exist but should not become the cause of disputes." The pasdaran must remain "pure" and "monolithic", FBIS–SAS–83–241, 14 December 1983.

It will be noted that all of these statements came after the regime began to transform the pasdaran into organized military units for the first time by creating armor, artillery and infantry units among them; and after the parliament enacted a law to create a Ministry of Pasdaran Affairs in order to rationalize procedures in the corps. See IT, 21 Khordad 1361 H. Sh./11 June 1982.

SOCIAL ORIGINS of the REVOLUTIONARY CLERGY

Eric Hooglund

THE SHI'I ISLAMIC CLERGY has emerged as the dominant group in the revolutionary political elite of Iran.[1] Not only did many of them play a prominent role in mobilizing mass support for the revolution during 1978–79, but since the establishment of the institutions of the present government mollas have been recruited as personnel to fill various decision-making positions at both the national and local level. Yet, despite the clergy's importance as a political force, there has been inadequate research done to date on this group.[2] Thus, several significant questions relating to their origins, values, and attitudes on a variety of politically salient issues have remained unaddressed. As a result it has been difficult to make critical assessments of current politics, at least in terms of how politics are conducted within the clergy and among the clergy and their lay supporters.

In this chapter I propose to underake a preliminary investigation of the origins and certain attitudes of the clergy. The empirical data are based upon interviews which I conducted with different levels of clerics in Shiraz during the spring and summer of 1979. It is important to emphasize that my interviews were not structured or systematic. Much of the information was collected accidentally, that is, as a result of meeting mollas without prior arrangement in a variety of social settings. Each evening I would record the substance of any conversations in a journal. It was only two years later that I had an opportunity to re-examine my journal and organize the wealth of information recorded. Since my own data revealed apparently significant patterns, beginning in the fall of 1981 I requested colleagues in Tehran and Shiraz who had access to members of the clergy to obtain answers to numerous questions relating to clerical social origins and political attitudes. I am very grateful for their cooperation, since I have been able to fill many lacunae in my data.[3] In addition, I have supplemented my data with information culled from various Persian newspapers.

In any discussion of the clergy it is important to emphasize that mollas do not constitute a monolithic group in Iran. The most important division is a hierarchic one. At the very top are the *mujtahids*. Mujtahids are preeminent religious scholars whose learning qualifies them to interpret religious laws for Shi'i Muslims. Since the end of the 18th century, Shi'i doctrine has accepted the principle that every believer must choose a mujtahid as a personal guide in all matters pertaining to faith. A Shi'i must always be guided by a living mujtahid. Since mujtahids are considered to be fallible, the rulings of a living mujtahid take precedence over those of one who has died.[4] Older religious scholars who have attained the status of a mujtahid are often accorded the title of ayatollah. There is no authoritative figure for the number of ayatollahs in contemporary Iran, but it is generally accepted and there were about one hundred of them in 1980. Ayatollah Khomeini and five other mujtahids were considered so superior to other ayatollahs in terms of their erudition and personal following that they were referred to as the *ayatollah ozma,* or grand ayatollahs.

In its broadest definition the clergy in Iran includes an estimated 150,000 to 180,000 persons. Thus, the ayatollahs constitute only a tiny elite. They are scholars, experts in Islamic theology and law, who have devoted their careers to studying and teaching. In contrast to the mujtahids are the great body of mollas whose primary occupation is preaching in the mosques. The 1966 Census, the most recent one for which occupational data have been published, enumerated only 12,445 persons as employed full-time in religious professions.[5] Although the statistical data did not indicate the basis upon which gainful employment in religion was determined, we can assume that most such persons were mollas who had completed a course of study in one of the urban theological colleges *(madrasehs)* and derived all their livelihood from performing religious services. At the time of the revolution, the numbers of such mollas may have expanded to fourteen thousand or fifteen thousand. There probably has been considerable inflation in their numbers since 1979 due to the fact that the enhanced status of mollas in society has made it attractive for persons who had been only part-time practitioners, or had dropped out of the clergy entirely, to return to the profession.

A third category of the clergy is composed of the seminary students, or *tullab* (pl.). All of the major cities, as well as most of the smaller ones, have seminaries, or madrasehs. The main seminary center is Qom, whose colleges enroll approximately sixteen thousand students. Another five thousand tullab are enrolled in the seminaries of various other cities, especially the madrasehs of Mashhad, Isfahan, Tabriz, and Shiraz. Madraseh courses of study usually are a minimum five years to prepare tullab to be preachers, and there are different levels of more advanced study.[6] The tullab have been very important agents of the revolutionary government for the mobilization of support in urban slums and rural areas since the revolution.

The major section of the clergy, an estimated 100,000 persons, are not professional clerics in the same sense as the mujtahids, mollas, and tullab; rather, they are people who have had only limited or no formal training in a madraseh, but who perform a variety of religious functions ranging from services officially sanctioned by the clerical hierarchy to activities which, if popular, are frowned upon, or even condemned, by Shi'i scholars. These nonprofessional "mollas," both male and female, are an important link between official and popular religion, especially for a majority of the population, which lives at a subsistence level whether in the cities or rural areas. Since the revolution many of them have acquired political roles as local organizers for the "real" mollas and use their contacts with the population to help disseminate the ideas of the Islamic Republican Party. Even though they are not professionally trained, these people perceive themselves, and in turn are perceived by the public at large, as part of the clergy.

The group of clergy about whom little is known, but who nevertheless play a prominent role in Iranian politics, is the preachers; that is, the mollas and the madraseh students studying to be mollas. These are the primary interpreters of the ideas of Ayatollah Khomeini and the official line of the IRP to the public, or at least that part of the public which attends mosque services on a regular basis. Preachers do not confine their sermons to any specific day or time. Rather, since the revolution they have tended to use any prayer services or religious ceremonies as occasions for preaching. In most mosques it has become common for daily sermons, usually following the communal evening prayers, to be given. Such sermons inevitably are heavily political in content, with religious symbols being used to reinforce whatever messages they are intended to convey.

Preaching and leading prayers are no longer the primary duties of mollas. Their political role now is of even greater importance. Throughout Iran mollas participate in various political organizations. They serve as members of the Revolutionary Committees (komitehs); they are active in the local branches of the IRP; and in large cities they have formed their own political action committees. These organizations form interlocking networks which help to assure the clergy's domination of politics at all levels of government. For example, the Revolutionary Committees supervise local government; the IRP recruits lay persons, who share the clerical vision of politics, to help manage the country; and the political action committees serve as forums in which the clergy can discuss and debate issues privately.

Since the clergy have succeeded in assuming such a significant role in Iranian politics, it is essential to try to examine their social origins in order to gain some insight into the attitudes they may adopt and the policies they may espouse. This writer knows of no study which has done this on a national level. However, it would be instructive to review relevant data for mollas in one city since patterns found in one local setting may be applicable more generally. Thus, I propose to take data from the city of Shiraz as a case study.[7]

At the time of the 1978–79 revolution, Shiraz was Iran's fifth largest city with a population of approximately 450,000. Shiraz was not considered to be a major religious center, but it did have an important shrine which attracted pilgrims, and there were several madrasehs in the city. The Shi'i hierarchy was headed by two mujtahids, both of whom enjoyed a national reputation, at least in religious circles. There were an estimated 250 professional mollas occupied full-time as preachers, shrine administrators, or staff assistants to the two mujtahids, both of whom ran extensive religious organizations consisting of madrasehs and various types of charitable and welfare institutions. An estimated 180 students were studying in the madrasehs. At a conservative estimate, at least one thousand persons in the city and nearby villages were nonprofessional religious personnel who maintained some sort of affiliation with the religious establishment in Shiraz.

The most complete data which I gathered was on the tullab of the two principal madrasehs. Since most of these had become preachers by 1982, even before having completed a standard course of study, they are an appropriate group to examine. I have complete data on fourteen tullab and incomplete data on twenty-nine more. For comparative purposes the discussion will be limited to the fourteen cases for which complete data is available. The fourteen are all males who in 1979 ranged in age from nineteen to twenty-three. In terms of their social background the following patterns are observable.

1. Origins: All fourteen were from Fars province; 50 percent were from rural areas: seven said they came from villages; four were from small towns and only three were from the city of Shiraz. This rural predominance is also reflected in the incomplete data; ten of twenty-one whose origins were identified came from villages.

2. Education: All fourteen had at least six years of primary education before coming to the madraseh. In all cases this had been in a government (that is, secular) school. Seven of the students had completed the ninth grade, again in a government school. Two others had gone as far as the twelfth grade but had not received a high school diploma. Two did have high school diplomas. One of them readily acknowledged that he had come to the madraseh because he had failed to get into a secular college.[8] Among the fourteen only two had had any prior religious training: one was tutored privately by a molla for "about a year," and another studied in a *maktab* (religious school) for a year.

3. Family background: Six tullab said that their fathers were farmers. In all cases they insisted that their fathers were not landlords. One acknowledged that his father owned about eight hectares (about twenty acres); there is no data for the others. Three students said that their fathers were shopkeepers; in two cases the shops were in town bazaars, and in one case in a village. Two tullab said that their fathers were *kargars*, or workers. One each had fathers that were a molla, shoemaker, and tailor.

4. Social Attitudes: All fourteen approved of strict *hejab* (veiling) for women. All supported some education for girls. Six said that primary education was sufficient for girls. Three expressed uncertainty as to what education beyond primary school would be appropriate. Three others said girls could go to high school until their families decided they should get married. Two tullab said that girls should be permitted to get as much education as their natural intelligence allowed, including college, although they insisted that for the majority of girls high school was sufficient. All expressed strong disapproval of women working outside the home, and they expressed a general hope that an Islamic regime would end this. When pressed about the need for women to serve as teachers and work in hospitals, they agreed that perhaps there was a need, but they said they would not want their own wives to work outside of the home after they were married (four were actually married).

5. Political Attitudes: All fourteen tullab expressed support for Khomeini in the strongest terms. They said that he was their imam. They hastened to explain that imam meant leader and did not mean the same as when used as a title for the twelve imams. They believed that Khomeini was going to set up an Islamic government and once that was accomplished all injustice *(zulm)* and corruption would be banished from Iran. They were fearful of the *kommunists,* a blanket term they used for the Tudeh, Peykar, Fedayan, and even secular non-Marxist parties. They expressed ambivalence about the Mojahedin. None seemed to understand why Khomeini and the Mojahedin were cool to each other (note that these data were gathered prior to the final break in relations in June 1981) but insisted that Khomeini must be right in his suspicions.

6. Clerical Politics: All 14 tullab were aware of a power struggle going on between the two leading ayatollahs of Shiraz during the summer of 1979. Each of the ayatollahs controlled large organizations of which the madrasehs constituted only one institution. The tullab themselves were not attached to a particular madraseh or ayatollah, but studied in the madrasehs of both. The tullab did have personal loyalties to one or the other ayatollahs, and there was an even split. Subsequently, the majority of tullab would transfer their loyalties to the ayatollah who became identified as Khomeini's representative.

Summary: The above data reveal some interesting patterns about an important section of the clergy in the city of Shiraz. Among these youthful mollas (born between 1955 and 1960), about 80 percent came from small towns or rural areas. All were from families of modest means— lower middle class, working class, or peasant. All had some secular education before entering the madraseh system. In terms of social attitudes, especially as pertain to the status of women, they were very conservative. They were enthusiastic supporters of Khomeini and had become very politicized. Additional data obtained since 1979 indicate that their politicization has intensified, and their loyalty to Khomeini has remained firm.

To what degree the patterns observable in Shiraz are applicable generally is unclear. Obviously serious errors of judgment can result from trying to draw nationwide conclusions based upon such a narrow sample. Nevertheless, one can compare these data with limited data available in other sources in order to find what similarities or differences may exist. If similar patterns are found, then it is possible to make some tentative generalizations about the social origins of Iran's politically active clergy. My own research into the origins of clerical political activists in Tehran presents some interesting parallels to data gathered in Shiraz. For Tehran I have been collecting information from Persian newspapers. Again my focus has been upon the preachers, in this case those who had completed their studies prior to the revolution. In a sample of 40 mollas who have been politically active after the revolution the following results have emerged.

1. All forty belong to the generation born between 1930 and 1954.

2. 50 percent come from small towns; 24 percent from rural areas; and only 26 percent from one of the twelve largest cities.

3. At least 50 percent have had a secular education through primary school; 40 percent have attended at least one year of secular high

school (data on educational background is incomplete).

4. All had studied at least one year at Qom (data are incomplete). 60 percent of those who studied in Qom prior to 1964 when Khomeini was exiled to Turkey studied under him (I assume that the other 40 percent who studied in Qom prior to 1964 also were Khomeini's students since it is common for tullab to attend the classes of several different mujtahids; this information is unavailable, however). In addition, at least 10 percent of the mollas studied under Khomeini at his madraseh in Iraq between 1965–78, although data on the length of study there is lacking.

5. All forty are loyal, even militant, supporters of Khomeini.

The data for Tehran mollas are for an older generation of mollas. Nevertheless some similarities in the data are observable. For both the clergy in Tehran and Shiraz one can notice that the preachers who are most supportive of the present political system come from small town or rural backgrounds. They tend to have had a mix of secular and religious education. And they are devoted to Khomeini and his interpretations of Islam which sanction an active role for the clergy in politics.

The preliminary nature of these data cannot be over-emphasized. Nevertheless, they do provide a basis for some tentative observations about the social origins of the politically active clergy and suggest some possible motivations for clerical involvement in politics. For example, the prevalence of small-town and lower-class backgrounds among both the Tehran and Shiraz clergy makes it reasonable to conclude that clerical occupations may have been viewed, at least unconsciously, as a means of upward mobility. This would explain the initial attraction for entering the madraseh system during the 25 years preceding the revolution.

If becoming a molla seemed to be a way of acquiring status for young men contemplating a religious vocation, certainly at some point during their studies awareness of "reality" must have developed. "Reality" in this case would have been the generally ambivalent status which mollas actually occupied in Iranian society doing the 1960's and 1970's. There was a strong current of anti-clericalism in Iran at this time. I encountered it in all areas and among all social groups while doing research in Iran between 1966 and 1979. Its most typical expression took the form of satirical, even derogatory, jokes about mollas. The clergy were often described in unflattering terms as venal, greedy, and hypocritical. At the same time that Iranians were critical of mollas, they were respectful of mujtahids, who were generally described as pious and learned. In fact, the majority of Iranians whom I have known do consider themselves to be religious, even though they are negative in their opinions of mollas. Of course, there is also a strong secular current in Iran which has been associated with the political elites under both Pahlavi shahs. Prior to 1979 the central government adopted various secularizing policies which had the effect of undermining the role of the clergy and reinforcing the negative attitudes toward them.

Becoming a molla, then, was not as prestigious an accomplishment at the end of studies as it may have appeared at the beginning. A preacher, at least during the 1970s, could not expect to enjoy widespread respect. Indeed, in one study of seminary students in Qom during 1975, it was found that many tullab actually were trying to complete secular secondary school simultaneously with their madraseh program in order to have more options for employment opportunities.[9] The ambivalent nature of their social status prior to the revolution is significant because it has had an influence on how they have perceived the revolution and their role in it.

The revolution and subsequent political developments since 1979 have had the effect of reversing the role of mollas in society. Whereas in the past preachers did not have extensive influence, now they are the political elite. They are in effective control of the principal executive, legislative, and judicial offices of government. One can reasonably assume that a majority of mollas are satisfied with their new status. And, likewise, now that they have consolidated their position, it is unreasonable to assume that they would accept a return to their status quo ante with ease.

Clerical involvement in politics has been controversial. The clergy itself has been divided. In the first years after the revolution, several senior mujtahids warned against the corrupting effect of political power.[10] The politically active clergy were impatient with scholastic arguments. With the support of Khomeini they successfully imposed their views upon the dissenting clerics by using such tactics as public rebuke and ridicule, intimidation, censorship and house arrest.[11]

Even though the views of Khomeini and his supporters among the clergy presently dominate politics, it still is not possible to predict whether clerical political activism will remain a permanent feature in Iran. For some prominent mutjahids and many lay persons, Khomeini's conception of rule by the clergy is considered to represent an innovation which is incompatible with traditionally accepted interpretations of Shi'i Islam. Obviously, they would prefer considerably less clerical involvement in government. Nevertheless, there are a number of factors which may aid the continuation of the current trends. First, those mollas who have gained political power can be expected to be reluctant to return to the mosques to become once again simply preachers. Second, the fact that so many politically active mollas come from lower-class backgrounds, and also that so many of the tullab have similar origins, means that their support of the concept of clerical political activism is tantamount to having an assured means of upward social mobility. Third, clerical control of the government has meant clerical control of government revenues, and thus financial independence from the traditional support of private, lay persons. Fourth is the fact that mollas have been successful to date in mobilizing support among a significant portion of the population for their vision of an Islamic Republic in which they are the chief decision makers. And finally, the mollas have established a mass party base which is used to recruit lay political activists who—at least to date—have been willing to serve both as allies and agents of the clergy.

CONCLUSIONS

This preliminary study can be summarized briefly. The clerical political elite of post-revolutionary Iran is largely composed of men of lower-class origins whose accession to political power has meant an elevation in social status. They have striven to create a political system in which ultimate authority is vested in a religious scholar, or faqih, and subordinate authority is exercised by men trained in religious law which they believe should be the basis for governing society. As the interpreters of religious laws, mollas have thus acquired a direct role in national and local government. This represents a dramatic role reversal for the preachers, especially since prior to the revolution their prestige generally was low. This development has precipitated a controversy within the hierarchy of the Shi'i clerical establishment regarding the proper role of the clergy in politics. Whether or not clerical rule will prevail in the long term is unclear, but it is reasonable to assume that the politically active mollas will not surrender their newly acquired status and power voluntarily.

Continuing observation of the political role of the clergy during the four years since the above chapter was written tends to confirm the trends noted. The new political elite consists primarily of younger clerics (and their numerous lay allies) who come from predominantly middle and lower class backgrounds. They base their status upon the exercise of authority, rather than upon the attainment of scholarly erudition. An excellent example is Ayatollah Hosein Ali Montazeri who was chosen in November 1985 to be Khomeini's successor as faqih. Montazeri is the son of a peasant and a former student of Khomeini. His reputation does not derive from traditional scholarship and theological rhetorics, but from his political activities. By the time of the revolution, he already was a veteran of the former shah's political prisons; since the revolution, he has participated in several of the new political organizations. He is visible as a political molla who is loyal to Khomeini and his vision of a theocratic society.

In contrast to Montazeri, many of the more senior clerics have refrained from political activity since the revolution. These are men who were born prior to 1920 and proudly trace their family origins to prestigious ulama or influential politicians and merchants of the Qajar period. As the institutions of the Islamic Republic continue to consolidate, many of these senior theologians have remained in the seminary centers of Mashhad and Qom apprehensively observing a process about which they remain ambivalent. In particular, they have still not provided unambiguous support for the concept of *velayat-e faqih*. However, as time passes these clergymen will probably have less and less influence in defining what is appropriate behavior—political or otherwise—for Shi'is in Iran.

Notes

1. I wish to acknowledge the helpful suggestions of Nikki Keddie and Jahangir Salehi who have read earlier drafts of this paper.

2. There are two pioneering studies of the Iranian clergy during the Pahlavi dynasty. See Shahrough Akhavi, *Religion and Politics in Contemporary Iran* (Albany: SUNY Press, 1980): and Michael Fischer, *Iran: From Religious Dispute to Revolution* (Cambridge: Harvard University Press, 1980).

3. These colleagues must remain anonymous at their own request.

4. For more detail see Nikki R. Keddie, *Roots of Revolution* (New Haven: Yale University Press, 1981), p. 21.

5. Census data is from Akhavi, p. 200.

6. For more detail on courses of study in the madrasehs see Fischer, *Iran*, pp. 61–86.

7. Based upon writer's field research, 1979.

8. Actually both of the tullab said they had taken the college entrance exam *(konkur)* before coming to the madraseh. The other student said he "passed," but wanted to come to the seminary.

9. Fischer, *Iran*, p. 59.

10. See, for example, the brief discussion in Michael Fisher, "Becoming Mollah: Reflections on Iranian Clerics in a Revolutionary Age," *Iranian Studies*, 13(1980): 87; some of Ayatollah Shariatmadari's views about the role of the clergy in politics are presented in *Ettelaat*, 20 Khordad 1358/10 June 1979.

11. The most dramatic incident was the convening of a special theological "court" in Qom in the spring of 1982 to investigate Shariatmadari's alleged involvement in an abortive coup d'etat plot. The ulama participating in this assembly took the unprecedented step of declaring Shariatmadari, widely regarded as Iran's most erudite Shi'i scholar and theologian, unfit to serve as a spiritual guide for Muslims.

DISCUSSANT'S REMARKS
Ervand Abrahamian

I am going to comment on the question of stability and instability in present-day Iran. On this question, most Western commentators have drastically changed their views in the last several years: right after the revolution, they prophesized the imminent doom of the new regime; now they predict the full consolidation of a clerical one-party totalitarian state. My own assessment is that the regime will neither fall—since there is no political organization capable of destroying it—nor will it fully consolidate itself, since the ruling clergy—particularly the Islamic Republican Party—are sharply divided by intense cultural, social, and political issues.

In predicting the future, the role of the Islamic Republican Party is highly relevant. When Ayatollah Beheshti first established the IRP, it appeared as if Iran was obtaining its own clerical version of a highly structured and disciplined communist party with its "politburo," "central committee," "chairman," "first secretary," and so on. In actual fact, the IRP was a very loosely organized party containing not only many independent local notables, especially provincial ayatollahs and hojjat al-Islams, but also diverse religious organizations, particularly the Hojjatiyeh that had started in the early 1960s as a fanatically anti-Baha'i group as well as the Mojahedin-e Islami that had been created in 1979 by religious-minded radical laymen eager to carry through a social revolution but also anxious not to alienate the clerics surrounding Ayatollah Khomeini. Although both the Hojjatiyeh and the Mojahedin-e Islami continue to support Khomeini and both are usually described as radical, they are radical in very different ways. The former's radicalism focuses on destroying root-and-branch the judicial system set up by the Pahlavi dynasty and replacing it with independent clerics rigidly applying Quranic laws. This group opposes land reform and nationalization of foreign trade on the grounds that Islam protects the rights of private property. The latter's radicalism focuses on land reform, nationalization of foreign trade, redistribution of wealth, and stringent controls on the bazaars. Thus the Hojjatiyeh can be described as radical on cultural-legal issues, but conservative on social-economic issues. And the Mojahedin-e Islami can be described as radical in social-economic issues but relatively unconcerned with legal-cultural problems. Although the Mojahedin-e Islami is led predominantly by laymen, it carries considerable weight within the ruling circles partly because it is well organized, partly because its technocrats control many of the important ministries, and partly because its leader,

Behzad Nabavi, has established himself as the regime's main trouble-shooter.

The IRP is divided not only along these organization lines, but also along major issues. One such issue is land reform, which is supported not only by the Mojahedin-e Islami but also by some radical clerics such as Ayatollah Montazeri. Many of the radical clerics, it should be noted, come from rural lower-class backgrounds. Meanwhile, land reform is opposed not only by the Hojjatiyeh but also by many senior clerics such as Ayatollah Golpayegani and Ayatollah Marashi. It should also be noted that many of these conservative clerics tend to come from better-off families. Although land reform has received the support of Ayatollahs Khomeini and Montazeri, as well as the endorsement of some 124 parliamentary deputies, the opposition to it is widespread enough to prevent its passage through the Majlis. The issue of land reform is likely to remain a thorn in the flesh of the new regime.

Another issue that divides the ruling circles is the problem of Khomeini's succession. This is directly tied to the social issue, particularly the land issue, since social radicals such as the Mojahedin-e Islami, want Montazeri to be declared the heir apparent, while the social conservatives, notably the Hojjatiyeh, want a committee of clerical leaders to replace Khomeini as the leading faqih. This issue of succession will probably turn into a theological conflict with one side arguing that Shi'i Islam favors the concept of one spiritual leader and the other side counter-arguing that the position of leadership is too scared to give to one living person. It should be noted that the Hojjatiyeh were very reluctant to give the label of imam to Khomeini, arguing that such a title would be incompatable with the traditions of Shi'ism.

Yet another issue that will divide the leadership is the Iraqi war. While many of the government leaders openly insisted that Iran would not carry the war into Iraqi territory and would cease hostilities once the invading armies were forced out of Iranian territory, other government leaders have brazenly stated that Islam knows no national boundaries, that Iran will continue the war until Iraq is liberated from Saddam Hussein's "fascist dictatorship," and that Ayatollah Khomeini should be the Imam of Iraq as well as that of Iran. On this question of whether the revolution is for export or not, one may well find that social conservatives, such as the Hojjatiyeh, may advocate a more adventurist foreign policy in order to divert attention from internal social problems, especially the problem of land reform.

The cultural-legal issue will also keep on dividing the regime. Whereas the true fundamentalists, such as the Hojjatiyeh, will continue to argue that local shari'a judges should have full and final authority in enforcing the laws, especially the laws against moral offenders, the more pragmatic clerics will argue that the country needs a central judicial system to curb the extremist behavior of some of the local clerics. It should be noted that clerics (such as the late Ayatollah Beheshti) who are often described by the Western press as "fundamentalist" are highly innovative and unorthodox in the Islamic tradition in that they reject the idea that local judges should have full authority and instead favor the creation of a highly centralized, albeit Islamic, judicial system.

These cultural, foreign policy, and social issues will probably keep the new regime divided for years to come and will continue to undermine the organizational unity of the IRP—something that is clearly noticeable since the time of Beheshti's assassination. Inevitably, the differences will develop into political conflicts, with each side trying to gain and retain as many governmental, judicial, and military positions as possible. In the struggle for power, it is possible that the competing elements *within* the ruling circles will seek support from groups *outside* their own circles—even among groups that neither supported the revolution nor are even religious-oriented. For example, social conservatives, such as the Hojjatiyeh, may well form an alliance with high-ranking ayatollahs who joined the revolution only in its final stages. They might also seek support among conservative elements in the military. Meanwhile, social radicals, notably the Mojahedin-e Islami, may well further cement their alliance with the Tudeh Party and the Majority Wing of the Fedayan-e Khalq. They may also seek help among radical elements in the military and the revolutionary guards. Thus political conflicts within the ruling elite could easily spill over into society and bring in their wake years of instability with no one group capable of monopolizing power and exercising full authority.

GENERAL DISCUSSION

Rose: I was wondering, Prof. Hooglund, if in your data you ran into any sense of animosity, or lesser repect, for Ayatollah Dastghaib as opposed to Ayatollah Mahallati because of the lateness of his age when Dastghaib became a mujtahid? He didn't begin studying to be a mujtahid until he was 57. Also, was there any animosity in the Shiraz area toward the introduction of tullab from Qom into the post-revolutionary governmental structure, particularly the komitehs?

Hooglund: I would say it was just the reverse. The Dastghaib organization was clearly beginning to overwhelm the Mahallati organization as early as the summer of 1979. By the end of the year the Dastghaib people won, mainly because of their close identification with Khomeini, even though Mahallati had been associated with Khomeini since the early 1960s. But Mahallati also was identified with the Shiraz branch of the Freedom Movement. Nationally the Freedom Movement regarded Ayatollah Taleqani as one of its leaders. Mahallati respected Taleqani, eventually becoming a close friend and ally. Thus, he supported Taleqani's reservations about the participation of the clergy in politics. Dastghaib and his followers, in contrast, welcomed an active political role for the clergy, an enthusiasm obviously shared by the tullab from Qom. The local tullab, I would argue, saw the participation of the clergy in politics as a means of upward social mobility, perceived that it would be more advantageous to be associated with Dastghaib and some actually joined the campaign of personal vilification directed against Mahallati.

Abrahamian: Just to add to that, the Dastghaib family was not only non-political before, but actually cooperated with the shah's regime. There are plenty of documents indicating their request to SAVAK to come rid Shiraz of religious radicals. It must have been very late, probably in 1978, that Dastghaib decided to join the bandwagon.

Najmabadi: Is there any information on how the factions of the IRP sorted out their differences on certain political issues? For example, when the IRP decided to give support to Bani Sadr for the presidential election, how did the factions reach a consensus on this issue?

Akhavi: It's unclear why the IRP supported Bani Sadr at that time. Some people have speculated that it was because their own candidate had been found unacceptable and the IRP needed a last-minute candidate. Bani Sadr had been close to Khomeini, and it was largely upon a reputational basis that he was isolated out as the individual to aggregate interests nationwide. And he was familiar to the secular groups, as well as to the religious. But are you asking how the IRP rationalized their earlier backing of Bani Sadr after he began to be anti-IRP?

Najmabadi: The IRP probably knew they had deep differences with Bani Sadr, and recognized that these would eventually come out. So the question is, how and why did the IRP decide to back Bani Sadr for president?

Akhavi: Presumably it was a tactical move, to have Bani Sadr as the front runner, then deal with him later as an exposed and relatively powerless person within the bureaucracy. But I don't have any more specific information.

Abrahamian: I think this case shows that the IRP was not really a tightly organized party. The IRP as a whole never really supported Bani Sadr. That is, Beheshti and much of the leadership supported Habibi. Habibi actually was more secular than Bani Sadr. He would have caused the IRP more trouble in the long-run than Bani Sadr did.

Najmabadi: But wasn't the IRP support for Habibi just a face-saving maneuver? In the end Bani Sadr could not have been elected without the votes of IRP members.

Abrahamiam: I doubt that the IRP actually got out the votes for Bani Sadr. The party organization didn't endorse him completely.

Akhavi: Of course, the other candidate was Admiral Madani, the second runner up. He was even less appealing to the IRP.

Najmabadi: One more question. On Abrahamian's point about "permanent instability." Could you please clarify what that means? Instability can't last forever. There has to be resolution at some point: a consolidation of power by one group; or another revolution; or a complete social disintegration. Could you indicate what direction you think the current instability will lead to in the long run?

Abrahamian: I use "permanent" to mean the long term, a good ten or fifteen years. Beyond that I don't think we can speculate.

Sick: Back in February Khomeini made a speech which is very interesting in view of what has recently happened to Shariatmadari. Let me quote from the speech. "An important unaddressed issue is that of order and discipline in the Qom seminaries. We need to prevent admission of deviant elements. Otherwise corrupt elements will make the nation lose faith in the clergy and purges are necessary in the seminaries and universities." What corrupt elements is he talking about? Is this simply a matter of clerical politics, or is he referring to a deeper problem related to the whole course of the revolutionary movement in Iran?

Hooglund: Clerical politics and the future of the revolution, at least to Khomeini, are intimately related. The seminaries in Qom are important because it is in these colleges the future political cadres are being trained.

Presently, there are at least sixteen thousand students in Qom. The most influential teachers there are the mujtahids, in particular the three grand ayatollahs: Shariatmadari, Golpayegani, and Marashi. None of the three has yet made a clear statement of support for the concept of velayat-e faqih. Indeed, Shariatmadari is known to debate the religious justifications for this concept with his students, strongly suggesting that the whole notion is an "innovation"—perhaps even a heresy—and therfore is religiously suspect. Khomeini certainly must be uncomfortable with the principal scholars and teachers in Qom. In fact, it is widely believed that the primary reason Ayatollah Montazeri was sent to Qom was to teach Khomeini's ideas and thus counter the influence of senior clerics like Shariatmadari.

Khomeini, looking to the future, has cause for concern about the influence of the traditional teachers. He sees the seminary students and young preachers as the standard bearers of the revolution and it is important that their commitment not be diluted by mujtahids using their religious authority to challenge the new order. He and his followers must be especially worried about what will happen upon Khomeini's death. Traditionally in Imami Shi'ism the view of a *living* mujtahid must take precedence over one who has died. In theory, then, if Khomeini passed away suddenly, the five remaining grand ayatollahs could issue an opinion saying that the principle of velayat-e faqih is unsound and participation by the clergy in government is wrong; all practicing Shi'ites would be obliged to respect such a ruling. The prevention of just such an eventuality is one of the factors behind the Shariatmadari incident. That is, he needs to be discredited so that his influence will be permanently eroded, if not destroyed. If such a respected scholar as Shariatmadari can be successfully humiliated, then Khomeini and his followers can more easily purge other "corrupt" majtahids. "Corrupt" is thus a euphemism applied to clerics who disagree with Khomeini's and the IRP's policies. They feel threatened by the potential ability of the religious scholars to undo the revolution and want to pre-empt that possibility.

Akhavi: Khomeini's speech reminds me of the speeches made by non-IRP–related clerics in 1980. Men like Ayatollahs Tehrani, Tabataba'i, and Shirazi. In particular I recall the speech of Ayatollah Tehrani—I'll call him ayatollah even though he rejects that title, saying he is only a Hojjat al-Islam—in which he said: "There are an estimated three hundred teachers in Qom. Only fourteen of them belong to the IRP, and only three of those are worth anything." Thus, Qom is by no means filled with teachers and instructors who are Khomeini-oriented. And as Hooglund suggested, that is a cause for concern.

Sick: Is the concept of velayat-e faqih sufficiently institutionalized to survive after Khomeini? Or can it be changed or even abolished?

Abrahamian: I think the concept of velayat-e faqih is loose enough to continue. In Khomeini's original concept of velayat-e faqih the clergy would not rule directly, but only supervise the government. The force of circumstances brought them into the executive. Ideally, velayat-e faqih means that the clergy control the judiciary while the executive is in the hands of non-clerical politicians. The legislative is open, depending upon the electoral results. There can be many different interpretations of the concept, but I can't see how the Khomeinists would lose. Senior clerics like Shariatmadari oppose, and will continue to oppose, the velayat-e faqih, but for the lower ranks of the clergy the concept makes rational sense. In essence, velayat-e faqih means clericalism, and the clergy as a group will gravitate toward it. Already the clergy have been in power for three years. It is not usual for a group in power to say it made a mistake by entering government and then hand over power to someone else. Especially after all the bloodshed, to resign now would be like signing their own death warrants. So, I don't see the clergy withdrawing willingly from the scene.

III

Change in a Rural Area

AN EYEWITNESS VIEW

ECONOMIC CHANGES in a RURAL AREA SINCE 1979

Reinhold Loeffler

THIS IS A DESCRIPTION, in broad outlines, of the economic conditions prevailing in 1980–81 in the southern province of Kuhgiluye and Boir Ahmad, in Southwest Iran. The material on which it is based was collected in the area between September 1980 and July 1981.[1] A final section deals with changes as of 1983. Much of this description can be phrased in terms of continuities and change.

1. The View from Above

As Table 1 shows, the government allocation for development in the province was in 1980–81 almost five times as high as in the last year of the shah's regime.

Government officials present this fact as evidence that the present regime, unlike the previous, does indeed devote the country's resources to the people's welfare. The figures do not, however, reflect real increases, as they are not corrected for inflation. To do so is rather difficult. The official inflation figures of 10 to 20 percent are probably unrealistically low. According to my own estimates in 1980–81 inflation in common consumer goods was running at least at 100 percent per year. But factors entering development expenses may be less affected by inflation. Certainly, the prices of construction materials have soared since the revolution, but unskilled-labor wages rose only 50 percent, and the losses to corruption are now presumably much smaller than in the past. Overall, it appears safe to say that since the revolution real allocation—and probably actual spending—for development has indeed increased, although this increase may not be as dramatic as government officials like to present it.

TABLE 1

DEVELOPMENT BUDGETS of KUHGILUYE and BOIR AHMAD, 1976–1981[2]

Year	US $ million (70 *rials* = $1.00)
1976–77	8.57
1977–78	11.14
1978–79	15.00
1979–80	31.43
1980–81	71.17

The importance of development in the province is also revealed by the fact that the development budget was, as shown in Table 2, almost as high as the current budget (while on the national level, its size was only about a third of the latter). This unusual proportion reflects the fact that this is an essentially rural region (with only one major town of 26,000 inhabitants) where effective government administration was not established until some 20 years ago. Therefore, government liabilities are as yet relatively low (60 percent of the current budget goes to education—mainly in the form of teachers' salaries—and another 22 percent to the operation of government health clinics) while on the other side the need for development expenses is relatively high. This budgetary importance of development mirrors the pervasive fervor and dedication to development which is currently perceptible among top provincial administrators.

Local planners profess it is their central goal to develop agriculture so as to assist in the national effort to achieve economic self-sufficiency. However, they argue that without adequate motor roads no development program can be effectively delivered. It is for this reason that they have allocated a staggering proportion of the development budget— nearly 50 percent—to this purpose. The effects of this policy are impressive. Construction teams are everywhere in evidence and areas which two years ago had been cut off from the world were in the summer of 1981 accessible by automobile. Officials assert—and they appear to be quite right—that the same speedy development would not have taken place under the previous regime.

But as under the previous regime planning and management

mistakes are frequent. An unnecessarily wide road is being built in very difficult terrain with plans calling even for asphalt surfacing—120 km from the nearest similar road. Other roads were so badly engineered that they did not survive the first winter. And contracts are given to private, unqualified self-styled entrepreneurs who themselves admit that this is a great way to make money.

As a consequence of this emphasis on roads, the funds allocated to agricultural development remain necessarily small—in fact too small in the view of the planners themselves. In the following year's budget, they say, they intend to go for a figure three times as high. Even so, in 1981 they could already show an impressive list of ongoing projects, among others

TABLE 2

EXPENDITURE BUDGET OF THE OSTAN [district of] BOIR AHMAD AND KUHGILUYE, 1980–81[2]

U.S. $ million (70 rials = $1.00)

Current	77.49			
Development	71.17			
		Basic	47.21	
			School and education	5.31
			Public Health	6.36
			Roads	23.32
			Urban Development	1.27
			Housing	1.37
			Water Pipelines	3.33
			Agricultural, Animal Husbandry, and tribal development	4.57
			Handicraft	1.31
			Other	0.37
		One-day oil income[3]	19.14[4]	
		Jehad-e sazandegi	4.65[4]	
		Other	0.17[4]	

the construction of twenty-two new major irrigation canals, designed to turn, according to varying claims, some thirty thousand to one hundred fifty thousand acres of dry cultivation or wasteland into irrigated fields. Even entrenched royalists among the people admit that in this area the regime is accomplishing things which the shah should have done a long time ago.

Many of the currently visible, smaller-scale development projects are conducted by a special, Khomeini-instituted agency called *Jehad-e sazandegi* (Reconstruction Crusade). The core of its personnel is formed by idealistic, educated youths who volunteer for the work with little or no pay. They consider themselves the young elite of the present state, devoutly religious and selflessly dedicated to the welfare of the common people. They say that in the two years since creation of the agency they have accomplished more than the shah in ten years. This is of course a gross exaggeration, but in relation to their very limited budget (Table 2) their activities are indeed impressive. These range from the construction of bathhouses, mosques, and tributary roads to the provision to farmers of tractors at half the going fee. The Jehad's accomplishments are so obvious that even opponents of the regime fully acknowledge them. Jehad members attribute their success to their religiously motivated, total commitment to the cause, and they make no bones about their disregard for the bureaucrats and technocrats whom they consider self-interested and grossly inefficient.

In another approach to rural development, the government is giving loans to groups of people, usually young but not as highly educated for setting up small enterprises (Islamic Cooperatives) such as the establishment of a sheep and goat farm for meat production. The success of such investments is highly questionable. Although they are examined by experts before approval, the projects are usually ill-conceived, and the would-be entrepreneurs are in most cases totally inexperienced for the task. If their enterprise should fail, they can simply declare it unfeasible and return to the government what is left of it. Meanwhile, they will have had their salary, which is built into the loan, and as locals point out, they will have stashed away some of the investment money as well.

Thus this regime makes more definite and visible efforts in the direction of rural development. Until now, however, these efforts appear to be a patchwork, lacking an overall coherent scheme. The emphasis seems to be almost exclusively on agricultural rather than industrial projects. A number of such industrial projects, initiated by the shah, have even been discarded because of economic, political, and ideological considerations.

One such project is the development of oil production in this province. The Italian national oil company, AGIP, had in the 70s drilled over a dozen oil wells which were intended to be connected to the southern oil industry. This would have provided a great number of job and training opportunities for the local population. The present regime ordered a complete breakoff of the operation on the grounds that the wells were not productive enough; in the summer of 1981 all installations were dismantled and transported to the Gulf coast. Another discontinued project is the construction of the second gas pipeline to the Soviet Union which should have, like the first, traversed the whole length of the province. Work was in full progress in the area when the revolution started, but then abruptly cut off. Miles of pipe segments strung out along the bald swath bulldozed straight across the mountainside to be welded and ditched have become a permanent feature of the landscape. More sections of the 52-inch pipes are rusting away in huge stockpiles, and the special caterpillar construction vehicles seem to be gradually decaying in guarded parks. Finally, the development of all tourism in this climatically and scenically attractive region was suspended—not becasue there was no tourism, but as a matter of principle; it is seen as compromising national independence.

2. The View from Below

The economic conditions of this area under the shah did not conform to the rather dismal stereotype about rural Iran which has emerged during and after the revolution. For one thing, in this area land reform had indeed been carried through; the peasants did become the owners of the fields they worked. Only in a few cases could former landlords hold on to larger landholdings through mechanization; and there was no stratum of laborers who remained landless after land reform. But even more important for the peasants than actual ownership of the land was the fact—almost always ignored in discussions of land reform—that the former landlords were totally divested of all coercive, armed power. In the past they had wielded power over the peasants by means of their own riflemen or bribing gendarmerie officials. The peasants were now completely safe from the wanton extortions which had been imposed over and beyond the regular land rents and had left them with the means for bare survival. More than the rents themselves, these extortions formed the root of their lack of enterprise. As soon as security was established, they began vigorously to expand cultivation and herd sizes.

Under the shah, the people of this area did not become poorer, as revolutionary rhetoric had it, and as economists,[5] relying on inadequate data,[6] claim has happened to 40 percent of the rural households in Iran. On the contrary, especially since the mid-70s, this area saw a dramatic improvement of living standards and expansion of salaried positions, wage labor, private small enterprise, and educational opportunities. As a consequence of these developments people began—probably for the first time in their history—to see the light at the end of a long tunnel, an end to age-old poverty and a brighter future for their children. There prevailed a certain confidence in the way things were going. This has changed now.

In contrast to the enthusiasm and optimism which pervades in government planning circles, the attitude of a great many people is one of discontent, frustration, or plain indifference. In evaluating their economic condition, the people do not look so much at government road building and other activities but at their own immediate livelihood. And there they see a marked deterioration.

On the one hand, there has been no improvement in the conditions of agricultural production programs initiated under the shah, like the provision of veterinary antibiotics, synthetic fertilizers, and fruit-tree seedlings, at subsidized prices. These are being nominally continued, but obtaining the now scarce fertilizer has become difficult and the planting of orchards (which would provide better incomes to the peasants) is not encouraged. The government's effort is directed toward achieving self-sufficiency in wheat supplies. As under the shah, the real issues of agricultural development have not as yet been faced, much less tackled. There are no effectual programs afoot for a comprehensive land consolidation; for the introduction of high-yield crops like fruits, which grow excellently in the area; for the protection and regeneration of pasture land; for a modernization of animal husbandry; for an organized marketing system; or for a reliable price structure of agricultural produce. All of these would be essential reforms to make agriculture a reasonably profitable undertaking, but their realization lies far beyond the capacities of individual peasants.

On the other hand, since the revolution—starting well before the Iraq-Iran war and in intensified measure since then—the living standard of the people has been seriously impaired by a combination of soaring inflation rates (100 to 300 percent), chronic shortages, and above all, drastically reduced opportunities for wage labor.

To understand the critical importance of wage labor one must realize that in most of this mountainous region the incomes from agriculture and animal husbandry alone do not allow the peasant to raise his living standard in any significant way. Agriculture is too underdeveloped, the operation of herds has become too expensive,[7] the population is increasing too fast (3.8 percent in my estimate). The landholdings are too small (mostly around 5 acres per family) although the land reform was carried through with minor exceptions which now have been corrected and although there was no *khoshneshin* (landless laborer) population in the area. Consequently, in the attempt to gain additional incomes peasants have always experimented with migrant labor in the cities. But it was not until the sharp increase of labor wages in the mid-70's allowed the peasants to make worthwhile savings that they turned to this new source of income in large numbers.

Characteristically, they did not settle in the cities. The external circumstances of city life as well as the separation from their kin and the forsaking of their landed properties effectively precluded such a move. Rather, they took up work in a city for three to six months during the agricultural slack season, trying to maximize their savings by living under extremely austere conditions, and then returned home. The resulting flow of cash to the villages, together with the salaries of the growing number of educated young people—all of whom desired and found local employment—profoundly transformed the livelihood of these people. Of the many variants of this pattern I will give two examples.

A. THE VILLAGE OF SISAKHT

At the beginning of the 60's this was a tight cluster of sun-dried brick houses exhibiting the usual desolate character of Iranian villages at the time. Its inhabitants lived on a subsistence economy of agriculture and herding; clothing was threadbare; food was inadequate and seriously deficient in protein and vitamins during the winter months; acorn bread was still a common staple. A family of seven or eight lived in a single eleven- by eighteen-foot room plus a veranda of the same floor space. There was no motor road, no hygienic drinking water, no doctor, no electricity, not even toilets. There were four teachers, whose classes in part were crowded in deserted stables.

By the time of the revolution, most of the families had built or were in the process of building spacious, modern houses furnished with plumbing, electricity, and bathroom facilities. In many houses there was a refrigerator, a sewing machine, and a television set, and in some also a washing machine. Eighteen families owned a private car. The quality of food was adequate; meat and fruits were consumed year round. A local partnership had established a plaster factory which provided local employment as well as much needed building material. Young men, making use of skills acquired in the cities, had set up shops offering such new services as auto repair, welding, plumbing, painting, even photography. There were ten dump trucks, three minibuses, seven pickup trucks, and a tractor, all owned and operated by villagers as business enterprises. Still other villagers had opened new grocery and dry-good stores.

All this had been generated neither by government development programs, nor from agricultural surplus production, but from wage and salary incomes. About a quarter of the married men earned a salary or a regular income from an enterprise, craft, or trade. The remainder of the men still carried out their peasant activities, but in addition, most earned wages from part-year seasonal labor—more than half of them in an Iranian city, another ten percent in Kuwait, and many more in the village. An unmarried youth might also add wages to a household income. In all, there was hardly a single household which did not benefit from at least one salary or one seasonal wage. Looking at the village as a whole, the total agricultural production—with incomes from surpluses in some areas compensating for shortfalls in others—covered just about the very basic food needs; all the remaining expenses were met by outside incomes.

Under the circumstances of such an economic upsurge it is understandable that from the outset the peasants of this village were very skeptical about the revolution. As they saw it, a change of things could only be a change for the worse. Presently, they felt their fears had come true. At first the large government and foreign construction sites had been shut down. Then, with the war and shortages of all kinds, the small-scale private housing industry also declined sharply. As a consequence, for the Sisakhtis, wage labor opportunities in the cities have all but dried up. The remaining possibilities (work in Kuwait, at local government projects, or on houses being built by salaried persons) could not compensate for this loss; if anything, their profitableness and availability has diminished rather than risen.

Nor are the peasants willing to go back to intensive animal husbandry. Eighty percent of these farmers had given it up, or cut down, during the 70s when other sources of income had become more profitable. The troubles, risks, and relatively low returns (in spite of the fact that the price paid for butterfat has increased 500 percent since the revolution) make the local transhumant herding no longer an attractive enterprise.

This drastic decline in cash earning potential, compounded by skyrocketing inflation, shortages, unemployment of high school-graduate sons, and close-down of universities, signified for the Sisakhtis an abrupt halt to their prosperity. Hardly surprisingly, they feel frustration and anger toward the clerical regime which they hold responsible for the situation. They are deeply committed Muslims, but they do not approve of the regime simply because it calls itself Islamic. In their view, a regime which cannot provide for all its people is not truly Islamic at all.

B. THE KE ALI KHAN SECTION OF THE OULAD MIRZA ALI

This is a tent-dwelling tribal unit having winter quarters in the vicinity of the city of Behbahan. In the 1960s and early 70s they lived in conditions of exigency even more severe than those of the southern tribes. This was partly due to the loss of access to their summer quarters in the course of a tribal feud in 1963. As a result they suffered a depletion of their herds. Also, as a consequence of chronic malnutrition they had become hopelessly dependent on tea and sugar as stimulants, a habit which put inordinate strain on their economy. As was usual in Iran under such conditions of indigence, they had become trapped in relations of debt and dependency to urban moneylenders, in their case the traders of Behbahan. This deepened their poverty. Possessing no ready cash, they were charged up to double the ordinary price on everything they bought, but they were credited with only half the retail price for the goods they delivered, like yogurt. When such products proved insufficient to pay for their debts, the tribesmen were forced either to sell off some of their animals for cash, or to transfer ownership of animals in their flocks to the Behbahani creditors who were then entitled to a major share (normally 50 percent) of the products from those animals. In either case, the tribesmen's earning capacity was even further diminished. Government loans provided from around 1970 onwards were not big enough to free the tribesmen from this dependency.

Then in the mid-70s, opportunities for wage labor with companies operating in the area became available and were readily utilized. Typically, one or more members of an extended-family household would take up such work while the others looked after the traditional economy. In adaptation to this pattern, the tribesmen would pitch their tents close to a highway, allowing a company truck to pick up the workers of a camp in the morning and return them at sunset. Also, some individuals earned cash as sheep buyers responding to the growing demand of urban wholesalers. The income from these outside sources became the major mechanism through which the tribesmen could free themselves from their bondage to the Behbahani traders, and raise their standard of living.

When I visited the section again in 1981, a new feeling of prosperity and control had replaced the former despondent mood. The tribesmen had become the full owners of their herds. No longer forced to decimate the herds in order to meet debt payments, and being free to manage them according to maximizing principles, they had been even able to increase their sizes significantly. No longer obligated to produce yogurt for Behbahani creditors, they now allowed the lambs and kids to have all the milk, thereby almost doubling the value of these animals by the time they were sold, and generating a much higher profit than marketing of the milk in the form of yogurt would have yielded. Herding was also profitable because they still used their children as shepherds—something that had been taboo in Sisakht for at least fifteen years—and so saved on the cripplingly high shepherd wages. They even had now the means, unthinkable ten years ago, to buy large amounts of barley to compensate for poor pasture conditions in winter, and to improve the sale value of their livestock.

Using incomes from wage labor as well as from the now profitable herding, many families had bought land outside Behbahan, and after the revolution when the Shah's land-use regulations were temporarily revoked, they had built houses there. Those who settled in the new village year-round were mainly the younger generation who had been taking up work in Behbahan or were operating the family pickup truck as a business operation. But for some tribesmen the houses became their new summer quarters. In late spring, when tribes who had access to summer quarters in the mountains started their migration, these tribesmen rolled up their tents and moved into the relative comfort of their new homes furnished with fans and refrigerators and offering a plentiful water supply from a nearby irrigation canal.

The decrease of wage-earning opportunities has hit this group much less hard than the Sisakhtis. The reasons are evident. Most of the Sisakhti migrant workers, conforming to new standards of life style and status representation, had sunk their savings into new houses, furniture, and consumer goods. The tent group, however, had created through the regeneration of their flocks a viable productive base which now—especially with meat prices up 300 percent since the revolution—continues to yield good returns. Also, as very few new cars are getting into circulation, their pickup trucks, like those of the Sisakhti entrepreneurs, are carting in very good profits.

To summarize: following its professed aim to achieve national self-sufficiency, the government is making noticeable efforts to develop the province of Kuhgiluye and Boir Ahmad. The yearly budgets allocated to the purpose since the revolution are probably higher, in real value, than any time under the shah, and vigorous activity is visible everywhere. However, these efforts have yet to make their impact on the immediate economic conditions of the people. In the meantime, trends in the national economy (radical decline of wage labor opportunities, high inflation, shortages of all kinds) have led to an abrupt halt of the unprecedented economic upsurge people in wide parts of the area had experienced since the mid-70s. This has converted their former economic confidence into frustration and anger. Only those groups and individuals who had before the revolution invested their cash incomes into productive enterprises (for example, trucking service or herding under favorable conditions) fare better, and can even profit from the inflation.

In 1983 I was able to visit the province again. The preceding two years had been characterized by war and terror, the effects of which were clearly discernible in economic and social life.

1. THE VIEW FROM ABOVE

The former optimism and enthusiasm in regard to development among technocrat officials had subsided considerably. They appeared to be frustrated with policy making, quite as it was under the shah. The development budget, which showed yearly increases of over 100 percent for the first two years after the revolution (see above), had grown only by 36 percent per year, far below the inflation rate. Officials admitted that development goals were not being realized and attributed this failure to four principal reasons: lack of heavy machinery; shortage of construction materials; shortages of skilled manpower, that is, technicians and engineers; and periodic requisition of material and machinery for the war front.

But engineers saw the reasons much more in misplanning and mismanagement, both of which they said resulted in tremendous waste of time and funds. Also, they argued that a much greater engineering staff would be needed to run operations efficiently. Not that engineers were not available, they said, but the administration shirks from hiring them because of political risks; engineers tend to be liberals. Thus, although many different projects were under way, engineers were not very confident about them. They felt that projects were executed sloppily and cheaply, and therefore if completed at all were bound to decay rapidly.

Many of these conditions could be clearly observed. One major irrigation canal, which in 1981 was one of the showpieces of the Jehad's activity in the northern part of the province, stood half-finished and abandoned. When its course had hit a rock wall, it had been decided that completion would be too expensive. The planned asphalt road mentioned above never got beyond primary earth-moving—wiping out a whole stretch of agricultural land in the process—because the construction company allegedly declared insolvency. New roads had been partly washed away because proper drainage and pipes for irrigation canals had not been provided.

Nevertheless, given the high costs of the war, one was amazed at the number of construction sites—roads, bridges, school buildings and clinics—and at the scale of the plans—among others, two major factories—for the future. Of course, it should be kept in mind that the summer of 1983 saw the beginning of a concerted effort on part of the regime to meet the demands of businessmen and technocrats by launching an ambitious five-year plan and allowing a 40 percent increase in imports. As it turned out, oil earnings then fell far short of expectations, which necessitated drastic cutbacks and restrictions in 1984. This process will undoubtedly have had a dampening effect on the development plans in this province.

Especially impressive in 1983 was the growth of small enterprises like plumbing, welding, carpentry, metal lathing, transport operations, and cottage-style rug weaving. In the northern part of the province alone, over one hundred so-called Islamic cooperatives had emerged. These enterprises are started by government loans. Once the operation produces a net profit, the loan is to be paid back and the group of entrepreneurs are to become the owners. In this way, everything from chicken farms to tile factories and minibus operations were established. Many of the projects were obviously productive and flourishing, others were barely keeping afloat, and still others were generally acknowledged failures. One of these was a major livestock farm which, after one million dollars invested in two unfinished buildings, was already in the hands of the third set of would-be entrepreneurs. It was generally doubted that the project would ever become operational because of the lack of adequate water supply in the area. Although it was said that controls over these projects are now stricter, insiders claimed that there is still much unrealistic planning and incompetent personnel. In addition, operations were generally impaired by the unavailability or poor quality of necessary production supplies.

2. THE VIEW FROM BELOW

In 1983, some eight staple items were provided by the government in rationed quantities (that is, 1.2 kg sugar per person, per month), and at subsidized prices ranging between one-half and one-eighth of the free-market price. These rations seemed to meet a good portion of actual requirements. Besides, there were also special distribution systems which made industrial goods like refrigerators and automobiles available at subsidized prices. Although these items were made available in only very limited quantities (that is, four television sets in a village of three thousand people in the summer of 1983) people sensed an attempt on part of the regime to normalize situations and to meet their demands. Thus, when a teacher who had been fired in the 1980 purge because of too-liberal views was allotted a dump truck which guaranteed him incomes far superior to his former salary, he took this as an effort by the regime to co-opt him.

But inflation has risen unabatedly and by 1983 had reached a level where consumer items ranging from meat and clothes to cars and houses were four to seven times more expensive than at the time of the revolution. As a consequence, teachers and government employees, whose salaries were frozen at 1979 levels, had lost much of their former prosperity. While formerly they were able to build a new house within a year, it now took them three to five years. This class considered themselves the real losers of the revolution. Also, for small-scale mixed farmers, agricultural incomes had generally not kept up with the inflation. Farmers with larger landholdings encountered different problems: broken-down combines that could not be repaired in time, pesticides unavailable when needed, wage-labor costs that jeopardized agricultural profits. The wheat price—already depressed before the revolution because of subsidized imports—had increased only 200 percent since the revolution, so that it was, in some areas at least, far below total production costs.

In contrast, the price of herding products tended to keep up with inflation. The resulting good incomes seemed to have stimulated the growth of herds in certain areas, so that officials estimate there were overall three to four times as many animals as pastures could support in 1983. Consequently, with the help of government loans, pastoralists were buying large amounts of animal feed, mainly barley, imported from abroad.

Wage labor, both locally and in the cities, had become available to a greater extent. This allowed peasants again to supplement their agricultural incomes and promoted the growth of a local working class. Also, migrant work in Kuwait had again become possible, though reportedly only for the old-timers, as the Kuwaiti government refuses to issue new work permits. Although the Iranian government was imposing hefty fees on Kuwait-migrants, proceeds from such work had become very remunerative due to the steep increase of wages for laborers in Kuwait (from five to fifteen Kuwaiti dinars per day), and the dramatic devaluation of the Iranian rial in Kuwaiti banks from two hundred sixty to fourteen hundred rials per dinar since the revolution.

Finally, the trend towards wider use of birth control under the shah had become visibly reversed, due ultimately to the regime's attitude on this matter. The population now seems to be soaring at unprecedented rates. My own data for the village of Sisakht suggests a natural-increase rate of almost 3.9 percent.

The political attitudes of the population had generally changed little. Resentment among those who disapprove of the regime seemed to have become even more intense, but—hardly amazing after the terror this province also had witnessed—expression of such attitudes had become very cautious and guarded. On the other hand, especially among the salaried classes, there was a noticeable tendency towards going along to get along, an increase in at least outward conformity accompanied by an effort to express more positive attitudes towards the regime.

As of 1985, when I visited the area again, the trends observed in 1983 continued in more or less the same form. Development activity was in evidence over the whole area, notably the construction of residential, school, and office buildings, new roads, clinics, water pipelines, and small-scale industry like tile factories; the development of projects to improve agricultural and pastoral productivity; and the completion of asphalting of all major roads which connect the centers of the region to the general Iranian road network. The number and scale of the projects completed or in progress were truly amazing in view of the fact that Iran at the time spent reportedly some 25 to 33 percent of its budget on the war with Iraq. I observed no significant changes in regard to popular attitudes.

In conclusion, we must address the unavoidable question of how far the described conditions may be considered typical of rural Iran in general. The question can be answered only in cautious and tentative terms because only very few other persons here had the opportunity to study post-revolutionary rural conditions. The eliciting of actual political attitudes is under the present circumstances not only extremely difficult, but fraught with real danger for researcher and informant alike.

But making do with what we have, I think we can assume that conditions more or less like the ones described here prevail all along the Zagros range. This suggestion is based, for one thing, on the basic uniformity of rural conditions in this culture area, and, more specifically, on empirical evidence from the provinces of Luristan and Hamadan, some 700 kilometers to the north of the province here considered. Research in Luristan villages indicates that during the shah's reign peasants "had experienced rapid economic change: increased credit, more tractors, and new opportunities for cash crops." Also parallel to the Boir Ahmad case, they reportedly "were lacking in 'Islamic and revolutionary spirit.' "[8] As to Hamadan province, a 1975 study of a small village suggests that the cash flow from migrant urban labor, carried out on a massive scale (48 percent of the male population over fifteen in that village), was affecting the economic and social conditions even in villages so remote that the men had to travel five hundred kilometers to their city.[9]

Turning to regions outside the Zagros range, we find that in rural Laristan in the 1970's living standards had significantly risen as a consequence of high cash incomes earned by large numbers of migrant men in the oil states.[10] One can speculate that with the outbreak of the war, when travel to the Gulf states was first altogether suspended and then became encumbered with extra expenses and red-tape, migrants may have seen their new prosperity jeopardized and consequently developed unfavorable sentiments toward the new regime. Also, I observed, such migrants tend to be critical of the regime anyway. Unimpressed by its ideological claims, they frequently come to adopt the conditions in their host countries as exemplars of how a government should provide for workers. Finally, as to the north of Iran, I am informed that recent research has found conditions which are also quite similar to the ones described above.[11]

Although these data are clearly not conclusive, they seem nevertheless to indicate that the situation reported here is not unique, and that in broad outlines it can be probably generalized to a great part of Iran, especially to areas of genuinely rural, peasant cultures.[12] In villages surrounding the large urban centers, however, evidence suggests the existence of different types of development, and the prevalence of attitudes akin to those of the lower bazaar classes whose milieu exerts, through a multitude of channels, an intense acculturative effect on these communities.[13]

NOTES

1. Support for this research by grants from the Social Science Research Council and Western Michigan University is gratefully acknowledged.

2. Based on material provided by the Planning and Budget Organization. Compare also: *Yek sal kushesh va sazandegi.* An activity report of the *Ostandari Kughiluye va Boir Ahmad,* for the year 1359 (1980–81).

3. By decree of Imam Khomeini every ostan is to be allocated for development projects the proceeds from one day of oil income, to be administered by the Development Office of the Imam.

4. A more detailed breakdown of these figures was not available; it was said to follow the general pattern.

5. Manoucher Parvin and Amir N. Zamani, "Political Economy of Growth and Destruction: A Statistical Interpretation of the Iranian Case," *Iranian Studies,* 12, 1–2 (1979), 50.

6. Anonymous, "Reply to Manoucher Parvin," *Iranian Studies* 1 (1984), 135–137.

7. See Reinhold Loeffler, "Recent Economic Changes in Boir Ahmad: Regional Growth without Development," *Iranian Studies,* 9, 4 (1976), 266–87.

8. Emad Ferdows, "The Reconstruction Crusade and Class Conflict in Iran," *MERIP Reports* 13, 3 (1983), 14.

9. Carol Kramer, *Village Ethnoarchaeology,* (New York: Academic Press, 1982).

10. Emily Wells McIntire, personal communication.

11. Ahmad Ashraf, personal communication.

12. See also: Eric Hooglund, "Rural Iran and the Clerics," *MERIP Reports* 12, 3 (1982), 25.

13. Mary Hooglund, "The Village Women of Aliabad and the Iranian Revolution, " *RIPEH* 4, 2 (1980) and 5, 1 (1981). Mary Hooglund, "Religious Ritual and Political Struggle in an Iranian Village," *MERIP Reports,* 12, 1 (1982).

GENERAL DISCUSSION

Question: Considering the widespread perception that the clergy traditionally have been against land reform, do the peasants regard Khomeini as supportive of or opposed to their interests?

Loeffler: For the peasants in the area which I have studied it makes absolutely no difference what Khomeini says. What he did, in their view, was to oppose the land reform of the shah in 1963. In their eyes this act alone discredited him way before the revolution. The people believe land reform is completely legitimate. For them it is not a matter of dispute in the Islamic or any other sense.

Keddie: Scholars have spent a great deal of time trying to find any statement by Khomeini in the early 1960s opposing land reform. If what you say is true, it implies the peasants were extrapolating from Khomeini's opposition to the shah in general that he was also opposed to land reform.

Salehi: I am confused about how someone like Khomeini or the clergy came to be associated with opposition to land reform in terms of their own statements. It is common to read in the history of this period that Khomeini was against land reform—Prof. Loeffler has suggested that just now. But other scholars such as Professors Keddie and Hooglund say that there is no evidence in terms of his statements that Khomeini was opposed to land reform. Can Prof. Loeffler clarify this issue?

Loeffler: It is not my view that Khomeini actually opposed land reform. I don't know. But the perception of the peasants is that Khomeini opposed land reform. I can tell you how they acquired this view. In 1963 there were plans for an uprising which was put down by the shah in June. The Boir Ahmadi tribal chiefs were participating in that plot. They did strike out, raiding gendarmerie stations and similar actions. This was a major uprising in the Boir Ahmadi area. The Boir Ahmadi paramount chief had the support of Khomeini. Last year when I was with one son of the tribal chief he even showed me documents in writing in which Khomeini gave his support for the tribal leaders. It is because of his support to the tribal chiefs that the peasants concluded that Khomeini was simply against land reform. That has been their perception since 1963.

Abrahamian: The issue of land reform is very important in terms of what it shows of the working of Khomeini's mind. Even in the early 1960s he was a maverick among ayatollahs, a man who was consciously creating a new populist Islam. While other ayatollahs explicitly denounced land reform, Khomeini was careful not to get the label of black reaction. In fact, in specific regard to a question on land reform he said "I'm not opposed." Then he used to give a listing of all the reasons why he opposed the regime. In these listings one never finds land reform. He used to attack the regime on a host of issues, but not land reform. This is significant because at that time (1963) the ayatollahs who were attacking the regime focused on land reform. Khomeini saw his constituency as being different.

On the other hand, Khomeini didn't come out clearly in favor of land reform because again he didn't want to erode the support he had among the bazaar middle class. So he developed a radical popular ideology which appeals both to the propertied class and the propertyless. He has been consistent in this right up to the present time and even now has not taken a clear position. He doesn't want to lose support from either group.

IV

Ideology

IS SHI'ISM REVOLUTIONARY?

Nikki R. Keddie

TODAY, SHI'ISM SEEMS A SCHOOL that encourages political dissidence, as in Lebanon, Iraq, Arabia, Pakistan, and elsewhere, or even revolution, as in Iran. At various times, however, Shi'is have supported the status quo. Like nearly every religion, sect, or even political doctrine, Shi'ism is seen as essentially unchanging by its adherents. When revolution is in the air among many Shi'is they will tend to stress revolutionary antecedents, and when quietism and support for the ruling powers is considered doctrinal, as it often was, these will be considered the doctrines of Shi'ism's founders. Given the fact that Shi'ism comprises a whole series of religious schools over more than a thousand-year period, it is not surprising that the widest variety of political and religious doctrines should have been followed under the Shi'i rubric. With the growth of populist Islamic politics (a more accurate phrase than "Islamic revival") in recent years, there has been a trend among different groups of Shi'is to include everything from socialism through totalitarianism under the heading of Shi'ism, just as there has been a trend in both Shi'i and Sunni countries to call Islamic whatever one wishes to advocate. One outstanding Islamicist has said orally that "any religion can be made to mean anything," and while this may seem a cynical comment, the varied history of religious ideas and practices makes it seem at least partially true.

The potential for such variability in Shi'ism, which could be matched in other religions, may be illustrated by the varying use of two central Shi'i concepts. One is the messianic *mahdi*, of whom it is said that he will return "to fill the earth with justice and equity as it is now filled with injustice and oppression." Although mahdist ideas came into Sunnism as well as Shi'ism, they apparently originated among early Shi'is. The first Shi'is were those who felt that leadership of the Muslim community should pass in the house of Prophet via his son-in-law and cousin Ali. Messianic and other so-called extremist ideas entered Shi'ism in Iraq from non-Arab converts to Islam from religions with messianic ideas. Early messianic revolts were carried out not only in the name of Ali's sons and descendants, but even of more distant relatives of Muhammad, in the seventh and eighth centuries A.D. Some were carried out only in the name of an absent member of the family, but most revolts shared a conviction that their named leader was the mahdi who would overturn the disliked social system and bring justice to earth.[1] These revolts clearly represented social tensions, which are sometimes explicitly quoted in the sources—indeed the tagline of the mahdi cited above already shows great alienation from the existing system. Among the causes of rebellion in the first Muslim centuries (which centered in the popular classes) were the rapid movement of Arab tribes into Iraqi and other towns, the overthrow of the old rulers among non-Arabs, the imposition of new taxes, and the rapid urbanization of non-Arabs as second-class citizens in Arab camp cities. In this period, as in various later periods of Shi'i messianic revolt, the mahdi was considered to be already alive, or to be coming in the lifetime of believers, and hence the mahdist concept had a rebellious or even revolutionary significance.

Very different was the development of the mahdist concept for most of the life of that line of Shi'is known as Twelvers or imamis, who now make up the majority of Shi'is both within and outside Iran. After the period when Shi'is were small fractionalized sects following different imams, the main body of Shi'is came to follow the line of Ali's second son, Hosein, who was killed in a hopeless battle against the Umayyads for leadership of the Muslim community. After the militance of Hosein, many Shi'is became more quietist, and this was one reason for the split in the community. One line followed the descendants of Ismail, eldest son of the great sixth Imam Ja'far as-Sadeq, and become known later as the Ismailis or Seveners (although Ismail is not their last imam). Another line followed a different son and his descendants. The first line in the early centuries generally kept the revolutionary and rebellious traditions of Shi'ism and mahdism, naturally with variations over time. The second became increasingly quietistic, in line with Ja'far's separation of imamate from caliphate; it was represented by high officials of the court of the Abbasid caliphate at Baghdad, and increasingly put messianism off into a distant future. Although a number of different sects and beliefs were found in both lines, the second, quietist, one finally coalesced in a doctrine saying that the eleventh imam had an infant son who disappeared, but remains alive on earth and will return as mahdi. At first many expected his imminent return, but not those high ranking Abbasid Shi'i officials who promoted the doctrine of disappearance, apparently largely to remove any potential conflict between theoretically infallible imams and temporal rulers. In time, Twelver Shi'is became accustomed to an indefinite wait for the mahdi (similar events occurred in Christianity), and so the distant mahdi became more a source of vague comfort about an indefinite future than an incitement to revolt—indeed he was made to discourage revolt or efforts to bring him back before his time. Hence, the idea of the mahdi has been both rebellious and anti-rebellious, depending on circumstances and doctrines to which they give rise.[2]

A similar use of a central Shi'i concept first quietist, then rebellious, was observed in Iran over a two-year period, before and during the 1978–79 revolution. In this case the concept involves the meaning of the martyrdom of Ali's son Hosein, a central event in Shi'i thought and ritual, commemorated in Iran by special readings, passion plays that may last ten days, and processions which often include self-flagellation. The anthropologist Mary Hegland was concerned to find out what Hosein's death meant to villagers, which in large part reflected both their experiences and what they were being told by the clergy. Before the revolution, emphasis was placed on Hosein as an interceder for people with God, an idea widespread among Shi'is. (Several studies have also shown that the death of Hosein's party, including women and children, enables people to bear their own incomprehensible family losses). During the revolution, however, the meaning of Hosein's struggle and death changed to an activist and revolutionary one; Hosein was now an active and courageous hero leading a battle against odds in order to establish justice, and it was his role as a fighter, not an interceder, which called forth emulation. As had happened in the 1906 revolution and other struggles, the shah and his men were compared to evil Umayyad caliphs who killed Hosein and fought Ali and his descendants, while the fighting opposition represented the party of Hosein and of righteousness. As revolutionary fervor cooled, Mary Hegland found a synthesis of the two views emerging. A wide range of uses of the Hosein story covers a variety of political groups and circumstances, as well as personal problems.[3]

Doctrine can thus change from revolutionary to quietist, quickly or slowly, and when we know enough of the circumstances we can usually explain the nonideological reasons for this change. There are three clear historical cases where revolutionary Shi'is wanted a fundamental change in society, and with their messianic ideas helped install a dynasty. Once installed, these dynasties returned to doing things largely in the prerevolutionary way, and put down their former "extremist" supporters. These were the Fatimids, who began in A.D. 909 in North Africa and took their capital of Cairo in 969; the Abbasid caliphate, which ruled, in theory,

750–1258 from Baghdad; and the Iranian Safavids, 1501–1722. Naturally their stories are far from identical, but the circumstances of their rise to power and what they did thereafter have major parallels.

The Fatimids arose out of a branch of the Ismailis or Qarmatians. These were at first essentially the same group, but the Qarmatians succeeded almost uniquely in setting up small states that did carry out some radical measures, while the Fatimids in power behaved differently. The ninth-century leaders of the Fatimid movement, which existed before it had a state, claimed descent from the imams. They claimed to be imams, and looked upon the taking of territory as part of their messianic mission. The first Fatimid territorial rulers made messianic claims, but perfection failed to appear, and so there developed a "routinization of charisma," with a stress on observance of the old law and a suppression of religious "extremists." It is true that the Fatimids may be regarded as historically "progressive" for their encouragement of science, literature, and economic measures, but they remained within the framework of an ordinary Islamic state, not a messianic or radical one.[4]

More dramatic is the case of the Abbasids, whose forcible taking of power in most of the Islamic world is often called the "Abbasid Revolution."[5] Although several forces with underground propaganda and preparations participated in this revolution, there is no doubt that Shi'i participation was both extensive and crucial. The Shi'is hated the Umayyads as their long-time persecutors, and propagandists for the Abbasid cause assured the Shi'is that they were working to bring back the caliphate to the rightful control of the family of Ali. (More broadly they might speak of "people of the Prophet's house"—Ahl al-bayt, whom the Alids thought meant them, but others meant rather descendants of Muhammad's paternal uncle, the Abbasids.) Hence Shi'i participation in the anti-Umayyad movements and battles was high. Once the Abbasid movement took power, they were clearly not Alids (descendants of Ali) or Shi'is, and they moved against their "left," both Shi'i and non-Shi'i. A group of Rafidis (Shi'is) who regarded the first Abbasid caliph as divine were forcibly suppressed, as were Alids who claimed the right to rule. While their practical policies were strikingly new only in their incorporation of broader non-Arab groups into full rights in the polity, the Abbasids nonetheless retained remnants of their Shi'i past. Among these were their messianic reign-names, including, al-Mahdi, and the abortive naming by the Caliph al-Ma'mun of the Imam Ali ar-Rida to be his successor caliph. As noted, the late Twelver imams and the subsequent Twelver movement also got along with the Abbasids, but this was more because the Twelvers had become tamed and non-revolutionary, especially from the time of the sixth imam, Ja'far as-Sadeq, than because of any radicalizing of the

Abbasids. From the point of view of political position and alliances, Imami Shi'is and Abbasids often worked together as a moderate to conservative force opposing the Fatimids and other Ismailis on the other side, in this period.

Learned Twelver Shi'is and their followers centered in Iraq, Syria, and Bahrain, remained quietist and conservative for many centuries. The next major radical Twelver Shi'i movements arose not from them but from popular sects in Turkey, Iran, and Syria (centering first among Turkic tribes), which revered the twelve imams but in their messianism and radicalism remind us more of some of the Ismailis than they do of official Twelver Shi'ism. The originally Sunni Sufi order called the Safavids took on these radical Shi'i ideas in the fifteenth century when two of its leaders lived and fought among Turkic tribes in Anatolia who resented centralizing efforts of the Ottoman leaders. Sources tell us that these leaders, and then Shah Ismail Safavi who took the Iranian capital, Tabriz, in 1501, held a series of "extremist" ideas, including divine incarnations in leaders and messianism, and that among their Turkmen followers, "there is neither mine nor thine." Again, however, once Ismail began to conquer Iran he incorporated conservative Persian bureaucrats in his state, and he and his followers imported learned Shi'is from Arab lands. One element retained by early Safavid leaders was belief in their own divinity.

The pattern of rulers suppressing the left of a movement that brought them to power is not exclusive to Islam. What is special in Islam is that this "left" was almost always sectarian and religious, and often wholly or partly Shi'i.

An exception to the conservative pattern of Shi'i states is found in the small Qarmatian state of Bahrain, and the nearby Qarmatian community in the Sawad. They were contemporaries of the Fatimids and Abbasids who followed strikingly egalitarian socioeconomic policies even after taking power. Although the Qarmatians and Ismailis seem to have had common origins they increasingly diverged, especially with the setting up of competing states with contrasting policies. Both Qarmatian states aided the poor and avoided extremes of poverty and wealth. The Bahrain state intervened in the economy to encourage production and owned or controlled some key parts of the economy, while the Sawad community for a time abolished private property and at all times was able to get popular support via donations to its treasury.[7] The early centuries of Islam also saw egalitarian movements and revolts in Iran, some with a Shi'i tinge, but unsurprisingly for a pre-modern period, these movements could control only rather small territories, for a short time.[8] Even when the will to be revolutionary and egalitarian continued beyond the initial revolt, socioeconomic circumstances were not ripe to uphold these small states against the major ones that surrounded them. These movements show a recurring revolutionary or rebellious spirit chiefly among the popular classes, especially in the early centuries of Islam when socioeconomic change was rapid, but they also show that it was impossible to sustain this spirit over a large territory and a long period of time, given the objective impossibility of transforming the Muslim world at that time. When such movements were on the upswing their ideologies were usually revolutionary or rebellious; when things began to look hopeless the same doctrinal elements would be interpreted in a quietist fashion.

A partial, but not complete, exception to this pattern of suppression is found in the Nizari Ismailis, known by their enemies as Assassins, and centering in Iran. An indirect offshoot of the Fatimids, they set up a new state consisting of noncontiguous territories, mostly outside major cities. While the centuries up to AD 1055 had seen a gradual rise in Shi'i influence in the Middle East, with Buyid Shi'is ruling in Iran from 945 to 1055, overlapping the Fatimid Ismaili Shi'is in Egypt, the invasion of the militantly Sunni Seljuq Turks in Iran and Turkey signalled a strong orthodox and anti-Shi'i trend. The Nizaris were no match for the Seljuqs, but they could keep them on the defensive by new tactics. The most famous of these, which today has a modern ring, was assassination of leading men, notably the most important Seljuq Vizir, Nizam al-Molk. Many stories have come down about the Assassins, such as the story of the paradise-garden into which young men were drugged and told they had to kill to return, or the myth of the oath of the three supposed schoolfellows, Omar Khayyam, Nizam al-Molk, and the Assassin chief Hasan-e Sabbah. Their real story, as unravelled by Marshall Hodgson, Bernard Lewis, and others, is almost as strange, involving one leader who said the messianic revolution had arrived, and another who returned his followers to Sunnism. From the point of view of the dynastic paradigm above, however, the most interesting point is that the Assassins, for most of their history, did not become just another status quo state, but rather retained or revived revolutionary fervor and close messianic expectations over a long period. Whether they would have done so had they succeeded in building a large state with contiguous territory is, however, uncertain. The kind of incomplete state they had was likely to keep an ideology of constant warfare against the Sunnis, carried out by devoted *feda'is*—self-sacrificers—again a concept that reappears in modern times.

Also distinct from the Abbasid-Fatimid-Safavid pattern is the story of the growing power of the Iranian ulama (religious leaders) since early Safavid times. This is not intrinsically either a revolutionary or a conservative development; the ulama were more often conservative than revolutionary, although their rebellious or revolutionary role in 1891,

1905–11, 1963, and the 1970s has naturally attracted more attention. The crucial fact was a dramatic growth in ulama power over time; this power was used in a variety of ways, often in the same period by ulama with different ideas and interests. Indeed many of the disagreements now appearing among scholars in the West about the role of the ulama at various times have roots in the fact that there was no single line followed by the ulama at any time, and so it is often possible to quote ulama on a number of sides of any issue.[9]

Despite this, one may point to general trends that have helped bring Iran and its ulama to where they are today. As noted, from about the time of the sixth imam, Twelver Shi'i leaders were predominantly quietist and cooperative with the powers that be—they supported both the Abbasid caliphs and the Buyid rulers, and did nothing that we know of against the more militantly Sunni Seljuqs and Ottomans. Shi'i movements against such Sunnis were either Assassin or popular-twelver, unconnected with the learned ulama. These ulama centered in Syria, Iraq, and Bahrain, and were largely Traditionists who worked on the reported sayings of the Prophet and Imams, and legal scholars (Twelver Shi'ism had a different school of law than the four Sunni schools). We do not know exactly when the important institution of the mujtahid arose, but the relative silence of the sources suggests it had modest beginnings and for long made no claims against temporal rulers.

As noted, the Safavids early began to import orthodox Shi'i scholars from Arabic-speaking lands, partly as a counterweight to their radical Turkmen followers. At first these imported scholars were dependent on Safavid pay and good will, and appear to have been docile. As their *vaqf* and other income and following grew, however, some became increasingly independent, and native ulama were always more independent. In the late seventeenth century, the well-informed Chardin tells us that one group of mujtahids claimed that they were more qualified to rule than were the wine-bibbing impious shahs—the first we hear of this later-repeated claim. While kings were needed to protect Iran's borders and for other such matters, other questions could and should, this group said, be decided by mujtahids and carried out by temporal rulers.[10]

The eighteenth century saw a decisive struggle between two groups of religious thinkers. The Akhbaris said that believers themselves were able to make decisions based on interpreting the Traditions *(akhbar)* of the prophet and the Imams. The Usulis or Mujtahidis denied this and said that every believer must choose a learned mujtahid whose opinions he would follow in matters of law and practice. By the late eighteenth century the Mujtahidis won out.[11] In the nineteenth century a new institution developed of a top mujtahid to whom all must defer unless he chose not to rule on a given subject, in which case people could defer to the mujtahid they found most learned. Although it was not necessary to have a head mujtahid, and there has not always been one (it is moot whether there is one today), this was the ideal.[12]

The distinctive role of the mujtahid is to exercise *ijtihad,* "learned judgement," about matters referred to him and to issue decrees ruling on them. Mujtahids, and particularly those at the top, gained their position by learning and a consensus that they are the most learned. Unlike the imams, their judgements are fallible, and the mujtahids lack divine qualities. Hence, argued the Mujtahidis, it is forbidden to follow the rulings of a dead mujtahid, which can be wrong, but one must always refer to the writings and judgements of a living mujtahid. (In practice much continuity was maintained, as mujtahids often incorporated much or all of the work of earlier ones in their own treatises.) This system gave great power to living mujtahids, particularly the one or group at the top. Older mujtahids are now often called ayatollahs ("ayatollah" was formerly reserved for a few top mujtahids but is now widely used for many respected older mujtahids).

Besides this doctrinal development, Iran's top mujtahids retained more wealth than their Sunni counterparts, and lived away from the control of the Iranian government, in Iraq, from the early eighteenth century until after World War I. Both these factors added to their power, as did the relative weakness of the Iranian state before 1925. All of this gave the ulama considerable power to influence or even oppose the government. The ulama's power was shown in their role in promoting war with Russia in 1826; in the killing of the Russian envoy Griboyedov and his party in 1829; in anti-Babi and anti-Baha'i movements from the 1840s on; in the dismissal of Prime Minister Mirza Hosein Khan and the cancelling of the Reuter concession in the 1870s; and most dramatically in the successful movement against a British tobacco concession in 1891–92. The last movement saw an alliance between a variety of bazaar merchants, liberals, and radicals with the ulama, whose influence over the population was increasingly recognized even by liberals and radicals who were often anti-clerical. As in more recent times, their hostility to governmental policies outweighed their anti-clericalism, and so they hid their views and encouraged ulama leadership.[13]

This same policy was followed in the Constitutional Revolution of 1905–11, which represented much the same alliance of forces. In that revolution, however, the constitution and laws achieved were, perhaps ironically, far more "modern" and secular than were those that followed the revolution in the "modernized" Iran of 1979. How can this paradox be explained? Chiefly, it seems it is explicable on the basis of the main enemy who was being fought in each case. Although foreigners were a target both times, many in the first stages of the constitutional revolution were friendly towards England and also towards Western countries that had not interfered in Iran. The chief enemy was a dynasty that had largely rejected modernization and self-strengthening and it was the unchecked actions of that dynasty that were blamed for Iran's backwardness and dependence. Japan's victory over Russia in 1904–1905 was taken as evidence that a Western-style constitution was a secret of strength for Asian countries, as the only Asian constitutional power had defeated the only major European nonconstitutional power. Although the early ulama participation in protests against the government involved no demand for a constitution, several key ulama let themselves be convinced of the virtues of a Western-type constitution in limiting the power of shahs. As time went on and many ulama saw that the constitution and the laws passed under it would limit their powers in such spheres as law and education, many turned against the Western-style constitution, but other key ulama remained its partisans until the end of the revolution and beyond.[14]

In the 1979 revolution the key enemy was again the dynasty, but this time it was a shah associated with total Westernization at the expense of both Islam and local custom which might be identified as Islam, and also with subservience to Western governments. By 1979 many people had had time to become disillusioned with what they saw as the West—its mass culture, its changes in male-female relations perceived as breaking Islamic norms, and its massive presence in Iran, which involved cultural clashes and pushed up the prices of housing and other necessities. By the 1970s there were two cultures in Iran: that of the new, Westernized middle and upper classes, and the more traditional and Islamic culture of the bazaar classes, the mass of urban migrants from the countryside, and the ulama. In 1979, despite their increase in size from 1905, the Westernized classes were no longer able to manipulate the ulama opposition; in fact, the opposite happened. By the 1970s secular opposition groups had been decimated or forced into exile. The religious opposition was far harder for the shah to control. While a few obvious leaders were jailed or exiled, it was impossible to jail every preacher who spoke eloquently in a recognized code about, say, Umayyad oppression, and the martyrdom of Hosein. Finally, secular opponents lacked (and often still lack) contact with the Iranian masses and understanding of how they think and act, while many religious opponents have direct contact with them.[15]

Also, the themes of liberal democracy voiced by the secularists, while not opposed by the masses, were less inspiring than the increasingly totalistic and in some ways messianic themes voiced by Ayatollah Khomeini.[16] Khomeini's bold attacks on the shah and his program, and on subservience to the U.S. and ties to Israel, struck a more responsive chord than the compromise positions of the liberals; this was already true in 1963, and even more so during Khomeini's exile. Khomeini's belief that a return to true Islam would solve Iran's problems had the virtue of simplicity and of appealing to nostalgia at a time of rapid and often discriminatory socioeconomic changes. Although Khomeini did not claim to be the mahdi, his appeal had messianic elements; like Ali, Hosein, and other Shi'i heroes he was oppressed by an unjust temporal ruler, forced to withdraw from the center of power and gather his forces, and then do battle against the tyrant—but in his case the battle was successful. The messianic title of Imam accorded to him, for whatever reason, added to this quality. The title in Iran normally means the Twelfth Imam, who will return as mahdi. Khomeini sees himself as the possessor of the truth, and probably expected his various allies to come around to his viewpoint; they in turn expected him to move into the background, which he might have done only were he convinced that all those running the country were following the upright path.

Looking at the previous paradigms, the only one that shows significant resemblance to events and personalities in Iran from 1978 through 1981 is that of the Nizari Ismailis, who similarly had violence-prone leaders convinced they possessed the absolute truth.

Like the revolutionary movements discussed above, the 1979 revolution has seen a breakup of the coalition that brought it to power and persecution of the losers in that coalition by the winners. In this case the breakup is more extreme than in the past, partly because there are more politically aware groups than ever before. It should also be noted that while Fatimid, Abbasid, and Nizari leaders had titles that gave them a traditional hold on the loyalty of their subjects, this is less true of Khomeini. He had been declared faqih under the new constitution, but the concept of rule by a faqih is new with Khomeini and is not accepted even by many of his ulama colleagues, some of whom also have other objections to him. Most of the other "great ayatollahs" opposed Khomeini in the first few years after the Revolution, whether on conservative or liberal grounds or both, and several spoke out. Even among the ulama there is no unity about him, beyond what is forced by repressive policies, or about current policies. Struggles within the Islamic Republican Party over issues including the premiership, Khomeini's successor, and land reform, indicate, splits among the ulama along with other social tensions.

A non-ulama trend towards a radical or socialist interpretation of Shi'ism dates from the late 1960s, with the formation of the Mojahedin-e Khalq and the lectures of Ali Shariati (d. 1977).[17] The former has been an underground organization for most of its existence. It felt it could bring down the shah by beginning with urban guerrilla warfare directed largely against Iranian opponents and American military advisors. The Mojahedin's radical interpretation of Islam paralleled and took some inspiration from that of Ali Shariati, whose political activity was confined to teaching. Like many past ideologists, the Mojahedin and Shariati often give what appear to non-followers to be forced interpretations of Islam and Shi'ism; but this is also true in somewhat different fashion for Khomeini. Islam and Shi'ism have changed through the centuries, despite their unchanging sacred texts, largely through new interpretations of those texts. A more serious criticism of the Mojahedin and Shariati (as of their counterparts in Egypt and elsewhere), is that the time some of them spend showing their programs to be in accord with the Quran and the Traditions might better be spent in working out a socioeconomic program with the aid of sympathetic experts that would really take into account Iran's economic and human problems. Most of these groups are rather vague and apologetic in their social and economic programs, and they tend to rely on a few simple programs and slogans that tie their simplified ideals to Islam and to independence.

Also, many Islamic leftists and liberals in Iran contributed to Khomeini's victory and access to great power. In several cases of men who actively backed Khomeini's accession this is clearly true—ranging from the liberals Bazargan and Ayatollah Taleqani within Iran, through the younger ex-student leaders Yazdi, Bani Sadr, and Qotbzadeh, who were with Khomeini in France. They helped him come to power, and participated in high governmental positions. For the Mojahedin it is less clear. Khomeini broke with them soon after their armed struggle, along with the leftist Fedayan who also helped him take power. On the other hand, the vagueness of the Mojahedin's social and economic programs compares with that of Bani Sadr. Although the Mojahedin are probably the most effectively organized oppositional group in Iran, they share with exile groups an over-optimism that helped precipitate their open armed opposition to the government in the summer of 1981 which brought them tremendous losses. Perhaps having learned something from experience, the Mojahedin and Bani Sadr now talk and write less about details of the consistency of their program with the Quran—a ground on which trained theologians like Khomeini can outdo them—and more about Iran's current problems, although some of their tactics remain open to criticism.

Throughout history, Shi'i themes have at appropriate times taken on rebellious and revolutionary meaning, and have given an ideological basis to revolts and rebellions that have usually deviated quite soon from the hopes for a better life that moved their followers. The co-opting of Shi'ism in the interest of one powerful group in the revolutionary coalition is not unique to Khomeini, though his regime controls new means of terror, nor is such co-option of revolutions peculiar to Shi'i ones. Shi'ism, owing to its rebellious origins, provided special elements for revolutionary syntheses, but like many religions can as well be adapted to conservative causes.[18]

NOTES

1. On early Shi'ism see especially several articles by W. M. Watt, including one in *Religion and Politics in Iran,* ed., N. R. Keddie, (New Haven, Yale University Press, 1983); and W. M. Watt, *Islam and the Integration of Society* (London, Routledge and Kegan Paul, 1961); and M. Hodgson, "How Did the Early Shi'a Become Sectarian?," *Journal of the American Oriental Society,* 75 (1955), 1–13. See also the articles of E. Kohlberg and of W. F. Tucker, and his unpublished dissertation, "Chiliasm: A Study of the Bayaniyyah, Mughiriyya, Mansurriyah and Janahiyya Sects of the Extreme Shi'a," (Bloomington, Indiana University, 1971).

2. See the cited works by Watt; A. Sachedina, *Islamic Messianism* (Albany, SUNY Press, 1981); C. Cahen, "La changeante portée sociale de quelques doctrines religieuses," *L'Elaboration de l'Islam,* (Paris, Presses Universitaires de France, 1961).

3. Mary Hegland has discussed her findings in N. R. Keddie, ed., *Religion and Politics in Iran.* See also the varying meanings and uses of the Hosein story discussed in the articles by G. Thaiss, E. W. and R. Fernea, and H. Algar in N. R. Keddie, ed., *Scholars, Saints, and Sufis* (Berkeley and Los Angeles, University of California Press, 1972), and in M. Fischer, *Iran: From Religious Dispute to Revolution* (Cambridge, Harvard University Press, 1980).

4. On the Ismailis and Fatimids see the introductory chapter of M. Hodgson, *The Order of the Assassins* (The Hague, Mouton, 1955); B. Lewis, *The Origins of Ismailism* (Cambridge, Cambridge University Press, 1940); and articles by S. M. Stern, including "Ismailis and Qarmatians" in *L'Elaboration de l'Islam.*

5. Claude Cahen and M. A. Sha'ban have written about this concept. Prof. M. Perlmann noted orally that the term *daula* in Arabic was first applied in a political sense to the Abbasid movement by its followers, with the "Abbasid daula" meaning literally "the Abbasid revolution," in the sense of a complete turning. (The closest English meaning for this daula is "turn" in the sense of "his turn"—personal communication by Bernard Lewis.) As the Abbasids became conservative, the same "Abbasid daula" came to mean "Abbasid government," with daula becoming a standard term for government, not revolution. This linguistic change epitomizes the change from revolution to regime of the Abbasids and other religious rebels discussed herein. See also B. Lewis, "Islamic Concepts of Revolution," in his *Islam in History* (New York, The Library Press, 1973).

6. See the discussion and references in N. Keddie, "The Roots of the Ulama's Power in Modern Iran," *Scholars, Saints, and Sufis.* Further study of the period 1501–1800 is being carried out by Said Arjomand, Andrew Newman, Roger Savory, A. Sachedina, J. Cole, and others.

7. Thanks to a detailed unpublished study of the Qarmatians by O. Hamed, UCLA.

8. See A. Bausani, *Persia Religiosa* (Milan, Saggiatore, 1959), and G. H. Sadiqi, *Les mouvements religieux iraniens au IIᵉ et au IIIᵉ siecle de l'hegire* (Paris, Les Presses Modernes, 1938).

9. Different views on the majority ulama position have been expressed in articles and book chapters by S. Arjomand, N. Keddie, H. Enayat, and others, and in the book by H. Algar, *Religion and State in Iran, 1785–1906* (Berkeley and Los Angeles: University of California Press, 1969). On ulama power see N. Keddie, "The Roots of the Ulama's Power in Modern Iran." On the Nizari Ismailis see M. Hodgson, *The Order of Assassins* (London, 1967).

10. *Voyages de Monsieur le Chevalier Chardin en Perse,* II (Amsterdam, 1711), pp. 206–208. More complete coverage of the Safavid ulama is found in a U.C.L.A. dissertation in progress by Andrew Newman.

11. G. Scarcia, "Intorno alle controversie tra ahbari e usuli presso gli imamiti di Persia," *Rivista degli studi orientali,* 33 (December, 1958), 211–250; J. Cole's article in N. R. Keddie, ed., *Religion and Politics in Iran;* and H. Algar, *Religion and State in Iran 1785–1906.*

12. Cole, *op. cit.*

13. N. R. Keddie, *Religion and Rebellion in Iran* (London, Cass, 1966); "Religion and Irreligion in Early Iranian Nationalism," in N. Keddie, *Iran: Religion, Politics and Society* (London, Cass, 1980); and *Sayyid Jamal ad- Din "al-Afghani": A Political Biography* (Berkeley and Los Angeles, University of California Press, 1972). There is not space here to discuss dissident movements within nineteenth century Shi'ism, well analyzed in M. Bayat, *Mysticism and Dissent: Socioreligious Thought in Qajar Iran* (Syracuse, Syracuse University Press, 1982). The above works give references to the main Iranian sources of the period.

14. E. G. Browne, *The Persian Revolution of 1905–1909* (Cambridge, Cambridge University Press, 1910); S. A. Arjomand, "Religion and Ideology in the Constitutional Revolution," *Iranian Studies,* 12, 3–4 (1979), 283–291, and "The Ulama's Traditional Opposition to Parliamentarianism, *Middle Eastern Studies,* 17, 2 (April, 1981); and A. K. S. Lambton, "The Persian Ulama and Constitutional Reform," *Le Shi'isme Imamite* (Paris, PUF, 1970). Important Iranian works include those by Kasravi, Taqizadeh, Adamiyyat, Malekzadeh, Rezvani, and Naini.

15. N. R. Keddie, *Roots of Revolution: An Interpretative History of Modern Iran* (New Haven, Yale University Press, 1981); "Iran: Comparing Revolutions," *AHR,* 88 (June, 1983), 579–598; and "Iran: Change in Islam; Islam and Change," *International Journal of Middle East Studies,* 11 (1980), 527–42.

16. See Keddie, *Roots;* F. Kazemi, ed., *The Iranian Revolution in Perspective, Iranian Studies,* 13, 1–4 (1980); H. Algar, trans. and ed., *Islam and Revolution: Writings and Declarations of Imam Khomeini* (Berkeley, Mizan Press, 1981), and Gregory Rose, "Vilayat-i Faqih and the Recovery of Islamic Identity in the Thought of Ayatollah Khomeini," in N. Keddie, ed., *Religion and Politics in Iran.*

17. Analyses of Shariati are found in the section by Yann Richard in Keddie, *Roots of Revolution;* in S. Akhavi, *Religion and Politics in Contemporary Iran* (Albany, SUNY Press, 1980), and in his article in Keddie, ed., *Religion and Politics in Iran.* Selections from Shariati have been translated by the Hosainiyeh Ershad and elsewhere; the most

accessible are A. Shariati, *Marxism and Other Western Fallacies: An Islamic Critique,* trans. R. Campbell (Berkeley, Mizan Press, 1980), and his *On the Sociology of Iran,* trans. H. Algar (Berkeley, Mizan Press, 1979). On the Mojahedin see especially E. Abrahamian, "The Guerilla Movement in Iran, 1963–1977," *MERIP Reports,* 86 (March–April, 1980), 3–21. Many Mojahedin pamphlets, newspapers, and interviews exist in English.

18. Further analyses of Shi'i politics are in J. R. I. Cole and N. R. Keddie, eds., *Shi'ism and Social Protest* (New Haven, Yale University Press, 1986).

SHARIATI and KHOMEINI on WOMEN

Adele Ferdows

THE ISLAMIC RADICAL, Ali Shariati (d. 1977), approaches the understanding of women's roles from two angles. From one, he advocates the study of the Quran along with Islamic history, while from the other, he examines and vehemently rejects Western theories and practices concerning the role of women in society. He regards the Quran as a compendium of all human knowledge and as such it must be read and comprehended by all generations in accordance with changing times. Because its language is a symbolic and religious one, he considers it open to appropriate new interpretations by each generation.[1] To illustrate this, Shariati uses polygyny as an example of a state both degrading and morally decadent to contemporary women, but one which was considered logical and acceptable in the time of the Prophet. Before Islam, he states, women were bought and sold as slaves; men could marry an unlimited number of wives while women were denied all economic and social rights as individuals.[2] Hence, Shariati finds the Quranic permission to marry up to four wives a limitation and not an encouragement of polygyny.

He also finds the use of the veil acceptable in the past, given environmental circumstances, but as degrading and unbecoming to women's status in the modern world. He acknowledges the inevitability of change in Muslim societies such as Iran and the effect that currents of change will have on the status of women, and he advocates adjusting to those currents.

Shariati espouses the belief that the challenge of change in the role of women is the responsibility of the intellectuals. They are the ones who must educate and inform women on how to become "new women." But women themselves must also be prepared to adjust to the changing conditions and grasp the forces of change. "We must break down the age-old barriers imposed on women in the name of religion."[3] Shariati distinguishes between Islam as a true religion and the Islam practiced by Iranians and advocated by their religious authorities. He claims that the Islam practiced in Iran has very little similarity to the Quran's intention and the Prophet's and Imams' legacy. Although evidence to the contrary is available,[4] Shariati finds the distorted religious teachings in Iran as dangerous as the threat of infiltration of Western immorality and materialistic values concerning the role of women. He considers the body of Islamic teachings and practices to be fanatical and decadent as well as non-intellectual and misleading. He regards the ulama as the group responsible for propagating these values through their own backward fanaticism and considers them as strong a barrier to the development of true Islam as are the corrupt forces of Western moral and social imperialism. He also blames Iranian Muslim men for pushing women to Western lifestyles by their enslavement of women, having kept them backward and ignorant.

To challenge the threat of the demoralizing foreign influences, Shariati suggests that the only avenue open is to grant basic human and Islamic rights to women. With these rights, he argues, Muslim women will become the best tools for defending the Muslim system.

Shariati rejects the claim that Iranian society is a Muslim society. Instead, he regards it as a pseudo-Islamic one, where many of the basic human rights granted women by the Quran are denied them. Woman's personality has been lowered to such a level that she is not even called by her name but referred to as "the mother of the kids."[5]

Shariati blames the media for presenting a distorted view of Western women, accusing them of using movie stars and sex symbols as models for Iranian women. Through the media's publication of articles on vulgar, immoral lifestyles which inspire adultery, corruption, and promiscuity, they promote the misconception that to be a "modern" or "Westernized" woman is to imitate these idols. Shariati criticizes the media for ignoring the life stories of "such heroic women as Angela Davis, freedom fighters, prominent political figures, or scientific and intellectual leaders," thus misrepresenting Western women.[6]

Shariati is concerned that the image created by the Iranian media is, in fact, a far cry from the true European woman. In an apparent contradiction, Shariati on the one hand seems obsessed with the position of Western woman as the slave of commercialism and consumerism, sexually exploited for capitalistic purposes by the large corporations; while on the other hand, he decries the misrepresentation of the true European woman by the Iranian media and the distortion of her true role in the family and society. In Europe, he states, the woman is a partner with her husband, a coproducer; educated and free, she is raised equally with men and thus is experienced in meeting the challenges of life. Being a responsible member of society, she participates fully in the decision-making process at all levels. At home she is "a spouse, a partner, and equal to her husband," because she is educated, aware, and responsible. He says that Western women are deprived of many rights that Islam has given women. But, he further cautions that freedom and rights, "are not meant to be sexual freedom but human freedom and societal rights." Unfortunately, he rarely, if ever, defines or explains what he means by these social rights or human freedoms.

Shariati's dilemma becomes more clearly evident when he describes the nature of the changes in the role of women of the West which took place as a result of their economic independence. He states that once women worked outside the home and became economically self-supporting and independent of their husbands, economic calculations and logical reasoning replaced love in their relationships with men. He claims that they shirked their "family obligations and standards of behavior," by which one can assume he probably refers to the traditional role of housekeeper and mother, subservient and secluded by her male family members, a role which he condemns in another place. At the same time, however, he abhors the new woman, independent and free, who "becomes a realist instead of an idealist, using logic instead of emotion and romanticism, calculating economic benefits instead of love, aspiring toward the fulfillment of herself instead of her family."[7] He concludes that women, by becoming free and independent, also become alone. Shariati further blames the failure of Western family structure on the sexual freedom of women. Through early sexual contacts with men, women's sexual desires diminish until they are left tired and bored. They seek men with wealth and position and settle into marriages which are unexciting, devoid of love, and concerned with the pursuit of fulfillment of their own selfish ambitions. Hating each other and creating a miserable family environment, they produce children whose only escape is through alcohol and drugs.

Shariati then suggests that the answer will not be found in the prevention of change and the imposition of traditional standards of morality; nor will it be found in the Western model of immorality and decadence. The answer will be found in Islamic history, in the form of Fatima, daughter of Prophet Mohammad. This is his "third alternative" offered as the only reasonable choice for Iranian women: the legacy of Fatima. He challenges Iranian women to learn about Fatima's life, personality, and contributions, and he exhorts them to strive to emulate her.

Viewing Fatima as the symbol of freedom, equality, and integrity most compatible with Islam, he wishes to present her legacy and traditions to Iranian women so that they may identify with her.

Fatima's role as a devoted, hardworking wife to Ali and mother to their children (Hasan, Hosein, and Zainab) is regarded by Shariati as the exemplification of the ideal Muslim woman. In short, the two roles of Fatima, a devoted self-sacrificing wife and mother attending to her family's needs, and courageous untiring fighter for social justice, are the roles Shariati presents to Iranian women for imitation and emulation. The greatest emphasis, however, is put on her role as the perpetuator of the Prophet's line and the special role she acquires through her position as the mother of Hasan and Hosein, the two Imams who later epitomize martyr-dom and heroism in the struggle against evil and tyranny. Fatima is credited with raising sons who gave their lives for the fulfillment of the Prophet's work as well as defense of social justice and who became leaders of the Muslim community.

AYATOLLAH KHOMEINI'S POSITION ON WOMEN

The examination of Khomeini's writings, statements and speeches yields a complex image of his stand on women's issues. On the one hand there were his writings prior to the revolution which were foursquare in the major tradition. On the other hand, his messages and speeches while in exile in Paris present a very different image of that role. This image shows Iranian women as equal partners in all of the economic, social, and political arenas, with complete freedom of choice. His and his government's rulings since his return to Iran, however, correspond much more closely to the former than to the latter position. Among the most revealing pieces of Khomeini's writing on women's role are a few pages of his critique on the shah's well-known Family Protection Act of 1967. Kho-meini condemns the Act as being contrary to Islam, not only because of its content but because it was passed by an illegitimate, anti-Islamic legis-lative body. He declares the Act null and void and calls for its violation by the people. More interesting, he warns the enforcers of the Act that they are sinners and will be punished according to the *shari'a*. His most fascinating proclamation, however, is that all women who had been granted divorce under the Act are still legally married to their former husbands (under the shari'a). If they have knowingly remarried, they have, in fact, committed adultery and if any children have been born from these marriages, those children are illegitimate and as such have no inheritance rights.[8] His proclamation was carried out on February 26, 1979, when Khomeini instructed the Ministry of Justice to strike all those provisions of the Act which he believed contravened Islam. This ruling was put into effect by that Ministry on August 9, 1979. Khomeini asks that women recognize and accept the necessity that there be limitations on women's individual freedoms; that although women may vote, be elected, and choose professions, those things must be done within the framework of Islam.

Khomeini, like Shariati, refers with pride to the provision of women's rights to property ownership as an indication of their economic independence while at the same time, in his criticism of the Western women's lifestyles, he pinpoints their economic independence as the major cause for the downfall and deterioration of the family institution, absence of love, and prevalence of immorality in the society. Shariati, like Khomeini, upholds the man's position as the primary provider for the family, thus indirectly minimizing or dismissing womens' need or desire to hold jobs and be financially independent. Thus the fear of an independent woman as the disrupter of the normal family is shared by the two men.

Khomeini and Shariati both express their fear of women's sexuality, although in different ways. Shariati is very careful about the sense of the term "freedom" that he advocates for women. He promotes freedom for women but is very adamant in saying that it does not include sexual freedom. To him, sexual freedom for women is tantamount to immorality, promiscuity, and the collapse of the family. His basic belief, one may deduce, is that, since women are naturally sexual animals, they will tempt and corrupt men and lead them to passion and lust, which will in turn lead to adultery, promiscuity, and moral corruption. This line of thinking is identical to those of the traditional religious leaders like Khomeini, Motahhari, and others. The solution seems to be the control and regulation of women's behavior; the same old story of blaming Eve for the Fall of Adam. They both agree that women must understand that these limitations on them are in their own interest.

Ayatollah Khomeini demonstrated a disdain for those women who participated in demonstrations on March 8, 1979, against his directives to various government agencies on the adoption of the *hejab,* an "Islamic dress code" for women. He discredited them, stating that they were not "proper young women" and that they opposed the hejab because they had been educated and brainwashed under the shah's system of education. He blamed their moral corruption on their ignorance and deprivation of an Islamic education, which would be corrected under the Islamic government.

On the question of education for women, although Khomeini

supports it, he clearly defines the content of that education in limited terms as that which would prepare women to be mothers, housekeepers, and devout Muslims, while Shariati apparently aspires to the goal of women's education in all areas of the arts and the sciences that are open to men. Shariati opposes Khomeini's dictum of the segregation of the sexes in schools, professions, and in society in general.

After the revolution, a series of articles appeared in Tehran newspapers and various religious personalities were interviewed on television regarding the issue of the veil and the Quran's directives on it. There is a striking uniformity of approach present in these comments that is compatible with Khomeini's own statements to the protesters on veiling. "Those women are the remnants of the Pahlavi regime. To wear the hejab does not imply suppression or seclusion."[9] Here Shariati differs. With some historical justification, he regards it as an Iranian (presumably pre-Islamic) custom which the Muslim religious leaders have adopted and imposed on women through their misrepresentation of religion in order to subjugate them to men. This is perhaps the only truly opposite view that Shariati holds from that of Khomeini and his cohorts. Although condemning the extravagance in Western dress styles as immoral and vulgar, he in no uncertain terms opposes any form of forced veiling for women and accuses the clergy of the promotion of this non-Islamic practice.

Interestingly, for all those opposed to the veil, there were many more women who marched in support of it, shouting: "Death to foreign dolls!" It was not surprising that thousands of chador-clad women poured into the streets of Tehran against their uncovered sisters because these women represented the vast majority of Iranian women who, by their sheer numbers, could drown the voices of their "modern" sisters. Since 1979, on the whole, women have not demonstrated an overwhelming opposition to the Islamic Republic's rulings on women. One explanation may be the division and polarization among Iranian women on the proper role and position of women. It can perhaps be estimated that the majority of women support Khomeini's stand and interpretation of what their rights and role should be.

Immediately after the revolution a series of articles written by women appeared which on first glimpse had a refreshingly new approach to the role of women in Iran and Islam. They dealt with the concept of equality of rights with the claim that by returning to the Quran one finds harmony between Islam and nature. Women are created equal and are equal before God. However, men and women are created biologically, physically, and emotionally different so that they complete and complement each other. They stated that while Muslim women and men have equal rights, they do not necessarily have the same rights. It was further explained that since men and women are created with different natural and biological characteristics they therefore have different roles and responsibilities to their families and society. It was particularly emphasized that equality of rights did not mean sameness of rights as is believed in the West and that differences did not mean inferiority.[10] This view of biological difference was presented as an alternative basis for identity and self-esteem for women. By emphasizing the biological differences they concentrated on the privileges of femininity, thus giving women a status men can never attain and indicating that any suggestion of making her equal to men would be demeaning. This approach created an elusive world of femininity that made women appear crazy to choose anything but be a "true Muslim woman." They thus transformed the biological difference and child-bearing capacity of women into a blessing which in turn created the impression among many women of a desirable and positive choice.

The impact of the basic philosophical and logical method used by Shariati is very clear in these writings, in which the authors have elaborated on and supported his analyses through direct application of the Quran. In addition, Shariati's line of argument is followed in offering the true alternative as the model for the new revolutionary Iranian woman to identify with and find fulfillment in Islam. The new woman is characterized as free, independent, and aware of her rights through her knowledge of the Quran and all those rights that the Quran has bestowed upon her. Realizing that the social, religious, and intellectual revolution is only just beginning for Iranian women, they forsee the road to achievement as a long and arduous one, filled with many obstacles and struggles. Among the major obstacles, and one which will admittedly require a very long time to change, is women's own perception of themselves as inferior, second-class citizens. The above-presented line of argument, however, does not seem to promote a change. Those women who have become Shariati's disciples have themselves accomodated themselves to the traditionalist values and have become the defenders and advocates of those practices.

CONCLUSION

The analysis of Shariati's writing on the position and role of women in society shows the reader a dual image of his thoughts. On the one hand he opposes the traditionalist clerical interpretations of the Quran, presenting a logical approach to his seemingly enlightened conclusion that the only way the true meaning of the Quran and the intention of Islam will be understood is by educating men and women to the Quran as well as to the history of Islam. On the other hand, he presents a superficial understanding of the position of women in the West. He paints a confused picture of Western women, rejecting them as models for Muslim women in Iran to follow, choosing instead Fatima as the only suitable model. But his characterization of Fatima is not very different in substance from that of the traditional ulama whom he attacks. In addition, he emerges as a utopian who has closed his eyes to the actual discriminatory provisions of the Quran which make change and reinterpretation very difficult if not impossible. Shariati raises the issue of women's role but does not address it.

Khomeini's position on women's rights is much clearer. He represents the conservative traditionalist school of Shi'i *fiqh* and *hadith* transmitted by the clerics before him for centuries; clerics such as Allamah Mohammad Baqir Majlisi and his very well-known and widely relied-on collections of Shi'i hadith. one does not find much variation from these hadith in the rulings of the Islamic Republic and Khomeini himself on issues relating to women. One most recent ruling concerning women perhaps represents the general tone of that position: all unmarried women employees of the government must present a physician's certificate indicating their virginity status. Any woman who is not found to be a virgin will be immediately dismissed from her job.

The most significant fact perhaps is that no clear view of women's role exists among Iranian women. No doubt the revolution has affected the man-woman relationship in many families. Yet a majority of illiterate men and women continue to think women are inferior. Thus the circulation of the post-revolutionary writings on the subject is limited to a small number of Iranians—primarily Western-educated, middle or upper-middle class women. Furthermore, any clarification of the position of women in Islamic thinking would need much more substantiation of women's individual freedoms than is offered by Shariati and others.

Since 1979, the Quran and the shari'a have been used by the Islamic Republic as guidelines for the establishment and preservation of a virtuous and moral society where provisions dealing with the role of women and the family are emphasized as core factors. The constitution of the Islamic Republic in its Preamble devotes one section to the "Women in the Constitution" and states: "The family unit is the foundation of society and the main institution for the growth and advancement of mankind. . . . It is the principal duty of the Islamic government to regard women as the unifying factor of the family unit and its position. They are a factor in . . . renewing the vital and valuable duty of motherhood in raising educated human beings. . . . As a result, motherhood is accepted as a most profound responsibility in the Muslim viewpoint and will, therefore, be accorded the highest value and generosity."[11] In Principle 10 of Chapter 1, it reads: "The family being the fundamental unit of the Islamic society, . . . should be based on Islamic standards and moral concepts." In Principle 21: "The government is responsible for guaranteeing the rights of women in all areas according to Islamic standards. . . ." These standards were later explained and clarified by the passage of the Qisas (Retribution, Revenge) law passed by the parliament in August 1982.[12] The provisions of this law are carried out in Iran daily and its rules are implemented in the form of the public flogging and execution of men and women for adultery, prostitution, and fornication, and compulsory veiling and en-masse dismissals of women from government positions. Polygyny, temporary marriage, male unilateral rights of divorce and its denial to women, are examples of the enforcement of these sets of laws. Although these laws also have great consequences for the population as a whole, their impact on the lives of women is enormous. Women are held responsible for shortcomings of the society without being given authority to control the direction in which the society is moving. Ayatollah Khomeini's declaration on the occasion of Woman's Day in 1982 is a good reflection of this situation: "The role of women in the world has special peculiarities. The virtues and vices of society originate from the virtues and vices of women."[13]

The *Law of Qisas* is perhaps the most definitive document of the regime's interpretation of the Islamic moral codes and social standards within which the constitution is to operate. Here we will refer only to a few provisions affecting women. Two areas that occupy most attention deal with punishments for murder and sexual offenses.

Rules governing the practice of blood revenge of a murdered person are detailed in Chapter 1. If a murdered man's family decide to kill the murderer, they may do so in order that justice is carried out. If the murdered person is a woman, however, her relatives are obligated to pay one-half of the murderer's life-value *(dieh)* to him before killing him.[14] The logic of this rule may be viewed from two perspectives. One may be that the life value of a woman is worth only one-half that of a man, hence her relatives' obligation to make a payment to the killer to compensate him for the remaining half of the life-value that is the difference between the victim's and the killer's life. Or, that since the murderer (man) is responsible for the support of his family, after his killing, his family will be at least partially supported by the receipt of the dieh money. The woman who is murdered, however, did not have financial obligation to her family according to the Quran, thus no payment for blood-value is necessary. Either way, it is the discrepancy in the evaluation of one's contribution while living and life-value while dead, solely based on the sex of the person.

In cases of non-premeditated murder, in order to carry out the punishment, two male witnesses are required. One man and two women or only one man would be sufficient if he would take an oath to be truthful. The end result probably is that women are rarely asked to testify.

A long section of the law deals with the illicit sexual relations between married, homosexual, and unmarried men and women. The most revealing provisions are perhaps those cases when a woman has either been raped violently or simply claims to have had intercourse with a man against her consent.[15] In the latter case, "if it is seen as true," her claim is accepted. There are no explanations, however, of how a claim is seen as true or by which authority, and whether, upon the acceptance of her claim, she is absolved of all punishment. Meanwhile, one can assume that the man who had intercourse with her by force is subject to punishment and if so how? In the case of rape the maximum punishment, stoning to death, is prescribed for the rapist "if the victim dies" as a result of the act.[16] One is left wondering if any provision for justice is made if she does not die although it may perhaps be assumed that a punishment of less than execution may be in order.

Here, another article must be reported which explicitly deals only with the case of pregnancy of an unmarried woman but which I think deals with rape. It is stated that if the pregnant woman's adultery is not proven, she will not be stoned to death (but one may expect that she will be whipped one hundred lashes), which implies that in cases of pregnancy as a result of rape, the woman is punished for being a victim of sexual abuse. Perhaps it is assumed that she had consented to the intercourse which resulted in pregnancy, which could not be proven.

It seems appropriate to mention that the form of execution used for adultery is stoning to death (which is detailed in procedure) and the less severe punishment is the Quranic ruling of one hundred lashes.[17] The overview of the law of Qisas seems sufficient to give us insight into the values, standards, and social codes that the rulers of Iran believe in and enforce in relation to rights and position of women. In addition to these laws, there have been numerous orders and rulings regarding women, generally limiting their options and opportunities for development and participation as full citizens. Among them is the restriction on married young women's attending public schools which, given the customary early age of marriage for girls, encouraged by the regime, reduces their chances of getting an education. Throughout history, men have learned the value of knowledge and discerned it as a means of progress. Thus, by limiting this source of power to men, they have prevented women from acquiring knowledge in order to continue men's control of women. Official legalization of polygyny and *mut'a* (temporary marriage), as well as the tremendous emphasis on motherhood and revocation of women's right to divorce, discouragement of women's working outside the home, etc., can be seen as the factors limiting their participation in the social and political life of the country.

As mentioned before, the general government policy in Iran has been aimed at limitation of women's active participation in those areas secondary to the Islamic preference of motherhood and household management. Within the context of the "proper" role of women, the government has launched extensive and long-term socialization and education programs through a complete overhaul of the content of all elementary and secondary textbooks; sexual segregation of teachers and students; establishment of Islamic dress codes for both female students and teachers; and encouragement of peer pressure for absolute compliance with those codes of behavior and belief systems. Hence the earlier views of Khomeini, and not those he expressed during the revolution or those of Shariati, have essentially triumphed for the present.

NOTES

1. Ali Shariati, *Islam Shenasi* (Knowing Islam), V. 7, p. 87.

2. Idem, *Zan dar Cheshm va Del-e Mohammad* (Woman in Mohammad's Eye and Heart), pp. 23–24.

3. *Idem, Fatemeh Fatemeh Ast* (Fatima Is Fatima), p. 90.

4. Adele and Amir Ferdows, "Women in Shi'i Fiqh: Images Through the Hadith," in *Women and Revolution in Iran*, ed. Guity Nashat (Boulder: Westview Press, 1982).

5. Shariati, *Fatemeh*, p. 77.

6. Ibid., pp. 57–58.

7. Ibid., p. 67.

8. Ruhallah Khomeini, *Tauzih al-Masa'el* (Explanation of Problems), pp. 463–64.

9. Mujtahid Shabastari, "Islamic hejab is not equal to oppression," Interview on Tehran television as reported in *Keyhan*, March 11, 1979.

10. Shahin Tabatabai, "Women in Islam," *Islamic Revolution*, No. 1 (1979), pp. 14–17.

11. *The Constitution of the Islamic Republic of Iran* (in Persian).

12. *The Law of Qisas* (in Persian).

13. Interview with Ayatollah Khomeini in *Mahjoobeh Weekly*, Tehran, V. 2, No. 2 (1982), p. 9.

14. *The Law of Qisas*, Art. 6.
15. Ibid., Art. 84.
16. Ibid., Art. 99.
17. Ibid., Art. 100, 115, 117.

DISCUSSANT'S REMARKS

Nikki R. Keddie

I FOUND FERDOWS' PAPER VERY INTERESTING, but I feel that, probably because of the limits of time, the interconnections between society, politics, and ideology got a little lost. Perhaps they can come out more in the discussion.

Why is it, exactly, not only in intellectual terms but in other terms, that you have people like Shariati and Khomeini appearing just when they do? I think this is a very important question.

Another extremely important question which is raised by implication in Dr. Ferdows' paper is: why is it that in Islamic society the retention of women in what we might loosely call a traditional status (although I am one of those who believes that is not a very accurate term) is so much more pervasive and sticky an issue than it is in many non-Islamic societies? That is, there are also traditional customs in non-Islamic societies: Christian, Jewish, Hindu. Indian women were made or volunteered to throw themselves on their husbands' funeral pyres until not too long ago. I happened to hear from one of my colleagues that there are still a very few who do it. Among Chinese women foot-binding disappeared very quickly, and I don't know of anybody even before the communists calling for its revival. And yet, in the Muslim world you still have customs that are somehow parallel which keep recurring, and you find many arguments even from people who consider themselves modernists. Shariati is not alone in this. I've been reading in some people from the Arab world many arguments about the natural inferiority of women. It is a very common argument.

This is a question which deserves much more serious consideration than most scholars have been able to give to it, perhaps because scholars are a little bit hesitant to make an unfavorable comparison of one group to another group, which late 20th century scholars don't like to.

Part of it does go back to the notion that the Quran must be taken literally, but there must be more to it than that.

GENERAL DISCUSSION

Rose: Running the risk of doing what western scholars are supposed to be loath to do, let me address a couple of issues to Dr. Ferdows. It seems to me that by dismissing Shariati's writings on Fatima as confused or somehow question-begging, that you have missed in part what Shariati is getting at in the study.

It seems to me that in talking of Fatima as the mother of Imams Hosein and Hasan, he's talking about the role of women as the molders of Islamic consciousness. And since Shariati believes that Islamic identity has been fundamentally lost in the Muslim world, he is in fact assigning to woman an incredibly important role in terms of regenerating this Islamic identity within the context of his world view. It is secondarily the perspective characterized from his description of Fatima as the wife of Ali. In that book he characterizes her as the fundamental contributor to Ali's struggle against *zulm* and the suppression of the rights of his followers. That also, within Shariati's system, is an extremely important role. When you see Shariati's writings as approaching the question of how to reconstruct Islamic identity in a time when virtually the Period of Ignorance had returned to Islam, then what he says in his book on Fatima becomes a much more significant comment than you suggest.

Also, it seems to me that you can regard Shariati as question-begging only if you assume that his project is supposed to end up looking like Western liberalism. That may be a fine argument and a polemic to hold, but is not at all what I think Ali Shariati was about. Looked at as primarily a reformer, there is no question-begging, no inconsistency. There is a fairly clear position. You may disagree with that position, but it is not question-begging.

As for Khomeini, it seems to me that you characterize him as being more conservative than he is. For instance, Ayatollah Kho'i is much more conservative than Khomeini on the question of women. When Kho'i and Khomeini were in Najaf, both were asked whether women could meet with men to discuss political questions. Kho'i issued a *fatva* saying that under no circumstances, except for Friday prayer, could men and women who were not married gather together. Khomeini, on the other hand, licensed it in his fatva. So, there are extremely more conservative mujtahids than Khomeini.

Ferdows: In response to your first comment about Shariati. Number one, I don't dismiss Shariati's work, because it has had a tremendous effect on the youth in Iran. Many people are still his followers and disciples. I'm not dismissing him; I'm stating that he does picture Fatima as struggling all her life for Ali's cause, for social justice, for fighting against tyranny. The injustice was the fact that Ali was not selected as the first Imam, which Shariati felt should have been done legitimately, as the Imamis would. Now, whether that struggle is a fight against tyranny or simply a political struggle depends on one's Islamic beliefs. I'm not trying to look at it as a believer or a non-believer, but simply trying to understand the cause Ali was fighting for and which Fatima supported. Shariati's claim is that this is a fight against tyranny and injustice.

Rose: The content of that struggle of Ali's was not simply for the right of succession to the caliphate but a fight for an entire philosophy of social justice. Shariati repeatedly cites Imam Ali's works as exemplifying this holistic social philosophy. That is what Fatima in *Fatima Fatima ast* is fighting for, the entire complex of social justice issues.

Ferdows: Within the Ithna Ashari Shi'i Islam complex.

Salehi: To follow up on Rose's comment. As I understood the substance of Ferdows' paper, Shariati, much like Rose's comments about him, failed to realize that Fatima's legitimization is constantly through her function for males, either as the mother of Hosein, or the wife of Ali, not for what she does as a woman in terms of her own attitudes, beliefs, expressions, or contributions. Constantly she receives her value in relationship to males. This is the same attitude that Khomeini exhibits, in different particulars, but the same attitude. I think the typical attitude is expressed by saying that one thinks: of course women are equal, one couldn't live without them, *men* need them. The barrier that neither Shariati nor Khomeini breaks through is the one that gives women value outside of males altogether, in and of themselves. That is the way I understood Ferdows' argument.

Ferdows: Yes, that is right. At one point Khomeini makes the point that Fatima was such a great woman that if she had been a man she would have been the Prophet himself.

Question: During the revolution we saw that Iranian women were very active. I am wondering what is the significance of this politicization for today's Iranian woman?

Bayat: I think that it is important to recall that women's consciousness was not new with the revolution but has a long tradition in Iran. For example, many years ago I prepared an article about women in Iran at the suggestion of Nikki Keddie. It was about the role of Iranian women in the Constitutional Revolution of 1905–1906. Women were politically active even then. Even earlier in the 19th century there were instances of women going into the streets in their *chadors* and instigating bread riots. It is from this tradition of women playing a very effective role as street agitators that you find women playing a political role in the Constitutional Revolution.

My own research on the Shaykhis, a 19th century Shi'i sect based in Kerman, covered letters their leaders had sent to the shah requesting him to send royal troops to save them from religious rioters. In these letters the Shaykhis said that the worst agitators against them were women. Thus, women participated in religious and political disturbances as well as bread riots.

I don't want to be an advocate of women's role in 19th-century Iran, but let me cite just one more example. I have studied many unpublished letters written by women. These were obviously elite women because not many women had even an elementary education in the 19th century. Nevertheless, women wrote polemics in response to male charges that women were inferior and unequal. These women rejected such views and insisted they were equal to men. If men said "I challenge any woman to write a poem as good as a man," women would write poems and gather a following of female friends and admirers who praised their work.

Thus, female consciousness did exist long before the present revolution. Of course, that consciousness has been considerably heightened as a consequence of all the secularization of the past fifty years. And women who wear chadors are affected as much as "westernized" Iranian women. It is important to recognize that women who wear chadors are conscious about women's rights. Take Taleqani's daughter for example. I really admire her as a courageous woman. She always wears a chador, but she is very active on behalf of women. When some judges ordered that women found guilty of adultery be stoned, Taleqani's daughter stood up in the Majlis and attacked this policy as un-Islamic. In fact she has said she considers herself a representative of women's rights in the Majlis. Of course, her conception of women's rights may be different from mine. Still, I can respect her—although that doesn't mean she would grant me the same honor.

Thus, it is not necessary to be "westernized" to fight for women. But for the "westernized" women in Iran life is difficult. Women who haven't worn the chador are being forced to wear it. Such women are suffering a great deal. These are also educated women, and they are being dismissed from their jobs. They are not being offered job opportunities. They are being harrassed because of their education. For these women the problem is very acute.

Regarding the broader question of Khomeini's thought, I have begun a study of Khomeini's *Hokumat-e Islami* and have some preliminary points to suggest.

> (A) His analysis of the development of Islamic government in the seventh century A.D. is distorted history. This distortion reflects Khomeini's own political need to justify his claim for an Islamic government.
>
> (b) Khomeini projects a slightly Sunni version of the position of laws in Islamic society and Islamic government.

The reason for both tendencies is that Khomeini wants to establish an Islamic government. However, no imam except Ali established an Islamic government, and Ali was head as a caliph, not as an imam. The other imams did not establish an Islamic government, and by the time of the imamate of Ja'far as-Sadeq in the second half of the 8th century there was a postponement of the claim to political rule. Thus, Khomeini is forced to accept as a historical reference the Sunni Umayyad and Abbasid caliphates in preference to the Shi'i Safavid or Qajar states in Iran. It is also important that he does undermine the most important qualification of the imam, and that is direct descent from the Prophet. He does say in several places that the dispute over leadership of the community and the succession to the Prophet was not over qualifications, but the identity of the leader. And he says that Ali was the legitimate successor because he knew Islamic law. That is a radical transformation of the imamate doctrine which believes that the imam is imam by hereditary right.

One can understand why he wants to undermine this whole issue of the right to succession by hereditary right. It is because by 1970–71 he had reached the stage of declaring the monarchy un-Islamic because it was hereditary. It is interesting that when he does use the Umayyads and Abbasids as references for an Islamic government, he notes that they were perverted. But they were perverted not because they were non-Shi'is, but because they were monarchical. This is a very significant view for a modern Shi'i religious leader.

Another point. In Sunni Islam it is the law which is central in the establishment of the government. In Imami Shi'ism it is the imam who is central. The imam is not only the executor, but he is also the interpreter of the law. This is the traditional doctrinal exposition of the imamate. Khomeini undermines this position by speaking of the imam as the executor of the law revealed by the Prophet Mohammad, and he makes no other claims for the imam.

When Khomeini comes to his own claim for establishing Islamic government, he also goes far beyond Shi'i doctrinal consideration by saying in a very revolutionary way that the faqih is the successor of the Prophet after the imams. He states many times in his book that the authority of the faqih is equal to that of the imams and the Prophet, and people should obey the faqih just as they would the Prophet and the imams. This view is very different from the doctrinal exposition of the position of the imam as far as authority in the Shi'i community is concerned.

From where does Khomeini get his conception of faqih? Partly it seems to be derived from 19th-century mystics and radical religious philosophers who tried to advance the claims of an authoritative jurisprudent during the occultation of the imam. But it is also true that his conception of faqih goes far beyond these philosophers. An important basis for the faqih, then, is neither traditional nor radical Shi'i religious thought, but really the tradition of 20th-century popular revolutionaries.

V

The Opposition

MYSTIFICATIONS of the PAST and ILLUSIONS of the FUTURE

Afsaneh Najmabadi

EW MODERN REVOLUTIONS have given rise, in so short a period, to such gaping disparities between the expectations of its supporters and the emergent reality as did the Iranian revolution of 1979.

For certain strata of the population—national and ethnic minorities (Kurds, Turkmen, secular women, and intellectuals)—the disillusionment came in the first few weeks and months, as they found themselves under attack with their rights curtailed, and all hopes for a blossoming of national and democratic liberties crushed. With the exception of the Kurds, the subsequent resistance of these social layers faded into demoralization or depoliticization as the repression rapidly achieved its purpose of atomizing and breaking up their political identity, established in the course of the turbulent months before the overthrow of the Pahlavi regime.

Even before the first anniversary of the fall of the Pahlavis, political forces such as the National Front and the Freedom Movement *(Nehzat-e Azadi),* headed by Bazargan, had already been forced out of governmental positions, into opposition, to be joined a short while later by Bani Sadr and his supporters. The Mojahedin, after suffering continuous attacks over a period of two years, were finally forced into frontal opposition in July 1981 and have lost thousands of militants since. The secular left enjoyed barely six months of open activity before the first organized wave of repression in August 1979.

For the organized political groupings in Iranian society such events have forced a re-evaluation of the recent past. Both for active participants in the struggle against the shah's regime and for sections of the leadership alliance that had essentially controlled or directly administered state power in post-1979 Iran, it has become an existential problem to situate their political role in the evolution of events, as the outcome was clearly not foreseen, even as a theoretical possibility, by any Iranian political current.

This paper will present a critical review of these re-evaluations of the 1979 revolution. It will attempt to sketch from this standpoint the views and practices of political currents across the whole spectrum, from the National Front and the Freedom Movement, to Bani Sadr, the Mojahedin and the secular left.

I. THE NATIONAL FRONT, FREEDOM MOVEMENT, AND BANI SADR

Those currents and individual politicians who originally considered themselves part of the post-revolutionary alliance, and were subsequently driven out, have presented remarkably similar reasons for the way events have turned out.

According to the National Front (NF), in the name of Islam the population was deceived by those who had designs to monopolize power—that is, the Islamic Republican Party (IRP), which in fact controls all institutions of state power in Iran today. The IRP is accused of opportunistically using the religious sentiment of the masses to brand all its opponents as "enemies of Islam"; to cover up their own faults and inadequacies; and for the purpose of imposing their sole authority over society.[1]

Bazargan, on the other hand, does not attribute any insidious intention to the IRP. He attributes the IRP's takeover of all state institutions to a certain type of ideological elitism: sectors of the clergy, the IRP, and the revolutionary youth genuinely believe that only they know what is best for the people and the revolution. They are, therefore, impatient with and intolerant of all other views, and out of this conviction have hegemonized all positions of responsibility and power in the country.[2]

In more recent, and more exhaustive writings, Bazargan has introduced new arguments. He claims that many of the ideas and actions of the IRP, "the youth," and the clergy in the post-1979 period were shaped under the influence of—if not actual infiltration by—communists. Once the monarchy was overthrown, numerous leftist groups raised "extreme demands," according to Bazargan. They penetrated the factories, set up armed headquarters, and in some regions took up arms against the new government. The IRP and the radical Muslim youth did not want to be outflanked by these groups.

The Muslim groups, therefore, took up many of the leftists' demands, such as nationalization of banks and industries, radical land

and wealth confiscations, and redistribution, putting workers' committees in charge of enterprises. They insisted on ideological loyalty rather than professionalism in the workforce, introducing anti-imperialism and the idea of expanding the revolution beyond the Iranian borders, talking of the oppressed and the toilers, championing a cultural revolution, and so on. According to Bazargan such issues were not part of the original aims of the movement, and took the movement towards internationalist communist goals, regardless of whether anyone was explicitly conscious that this was going on. He further states that the Tudeh Party's support for the government and their infiltration of various government bodies and "revolutionary institutions" also contributed to this process.[3]

These "new" arguments fit neatly into a longstanding implicit theme of both the National Front and Bazargan's Freedom Movement, to the effect that "we" started the movement, while "they"—the clergy—jumped on its bandwagon and "hijacked" the revolution.[4] Bani Sadr, since moving into exile, has become much more categorical: he accuses Khomeini in person of betraying his own promises and of having turned into a dictator.[5] Indeed, Bani Sadr's book-length "testimony to the young generation" is in part devoted to arguing that Khomeini in Paris, under his influence and a number of his close associates, accepted a completely different notion of an Islamic government than the one he had formulated in his series of lectures entitled *Velayet-e faqih* (government of the jurisprudent), first published in the early 1970s.[6] According to Bani Sadr, in Paris, in the last few months before the revolution, Khomeini abandoned an idea—velayet-e faqih—he had developed over the last thirty years and accepted that government was accountable to the governed and not God. Once in power in Tehran, however, he reverted back to his old ideas and Bani Sadr found out that a leopard does not change his spots. Although he attributes Khomeini's change of mind in Paris to his own influence, he explains the second transformation by Khomeini's psychological traits, such as weakness of character, incapacity to take bold and decisive initiatives, and his readiness to be easily influenced by whoever surrounds him. His own mission, Bani Sadr explains, over the period that he remained loyal to, if at times critical of, Khomeini, was to try to turn Khomeini back again into his Paris self.

The problems with these explanations lie at several levels. First, instead of providing us with any answers, they remove the question from one level ("what went wrong?") to another ("why did it happen that way?"). The NF's "monopolization" theory has to explain why it was so easy for Khomeini and the IRP to "take over" the movement against the shah and then later to push out NF ministers from Bazargan's cabinet without any popular dissent. Similar questions arise with Bazargan's more guarded approach. The Islamic militants, for example, who by taking over the U.S. Embassy brought about Bazargan's resignation, did not simply decide for the populace what was good for them and the revolution. Clearly, they had the support of a very large majority of the population who agreed with them that this action was in the interests of the revolution.

In addition, the influence of communism in Iran is exaggerated beyond all recognition. Given the hegemonic hold of Khomeini and the clergy on the mass movement against the shah, it was the communists who were adopting the slogans of the Islamic movement, reading into them their own notions, rather than the other way around.

In both cases, however, to admit to the obvious fact that it was Khomeini who had the support of the masses and whose program for a radical Islamic government had gained genuine political hegemony would amount to a recognition of one's own political irrelevancy. Despite the NF's repeated references to "the religious sentiment of the people" (to which it has tried to make its own accommodations), it could hardly be expected openly to recognize that the political actions of the masses were (and for those still politically active still *are* to a large extent) formed not by nationalism—as once was the case in the days of Mosaddeq—*but by their newly-found allegiance to Islam as the political alternative that they began to feel has the potential to address itself to their needs.*

Similarly, although Bazargan frequently brags about the historic role of the Freedom Movement (FM) in bringing the clergy into national politics,[7] he cannot bring himself to admit that *the very success of this project* has ironically eliminated much of a role for the FM itself. Once the clergy—that section under Khomeini's leadership—became convinced of its role in politics, they no longer needed lay politicians and spokesmen, except at the beginning as "front men," in order to smooth out the transition from the then relatively secular order to the building of a theocratic Islamic alternative.

The second—more serious—problem with these arguments is that, whether implied or explicit, the charge that Khomeini betrayed his promises does not stand the scrutiny of recorded history. Indeed, in the modern history of Iran few political leaders have been so faithful to their ideas and formulated program as Khomeini.

We are of course not privy to the personal discussions that went on in Paris among Bazargan, Bani Sadr, and others with Khomeini. We do, however, have access to all his written works, essays, published interviews and many of his daily lectures while in exile in Paris.[8] It seems highly improbable, given the state of the movement at the time, the critical international focus on Khomeini's views, and the concern with democratic rights amongst sections of the anti-shah opposition, that a politician as shrewd as Khomeini would have made promises *in private* that were more in tune with a democratic government than his internationally reported interviews or semi-public audiences. Whatever one may think of Khomeini's views, it cannot be denied that as a politician he has a certain integrity and single-mindedness of purpose which is part of what made him so popular. Bazargan's claim, for example, that Khomeini had agreed to the formulation of "Democratic Islamic Republic" as the title of the new state and only changed his mind when back in Iran calling it an "Islamic Republic," seems very dubious.[9] A close scrutiny of Khomeini's interviews and speeches for the period before the overthrow of the shah shows that he consistently spoke of the establishment of an "Islamic Republican Government." More often he simply referred to an Islamic government. The label "Republic" came later into Khomeini's discourse and as a counter-position to some of the earlier positions of the NF and the FM that considered the possibility of preserving a limited monarchy without the shah—"like those in Britain and Belgium," as they would say. Naturally, Khomeini, in response to questions from interviewers in particular, would say that an Islamic government would be democratic. He would say so today. But his definition of democracy and liberty should be scrutinized carefully. The charges of Bani Sadr and others that Khomeini had promised democratic rights, women's rights, and so on while in opposition, but reneged on them once in power ignores the fact that practically all of Khomeini's statements on such issues were qualified with phrases like: "provided such liberties are not harmful to the people"; "if they do not damage Islam"; "provided they do not cause corruption"; and "if Islamic norms are taken into account"; etc. In his daily speeches in Paris, Khomeini repeatedly emphasizes that Islam is the only criterion for working out the new governmental and social system, and that all Islamic rules (including the Islamic punishments) would be carried out *once conditions were suitable* and the necessary preparatory work had been done. Bani Sadr's recent discovery that velayat-e faqih is tantamount to a clerical dictatorship is somewhat behind the time, if not outright hypocritical. Khomeini's views on this topic were formulated, in writings and speeches, and never once retracted in over a decade. They were inserted explicitly into the new constitution (in the summer of 1979) and Bani Sadr himself voted for them in the December 1979 referendum on the constitution. As long as the Imam held him in favor, Bani Sadr used the authority of the supreme *faqih* to his own advantage (for example, in the presidential elections), only to discover the dictatorial nature of velayat-e faqih after he became the subject of its wrath.

Clearly, Khomeini, like any intelligent political leader, would attempt to implement his program only to the extent that political conditions were suited, and "the necessary preparatory work" had been done. Nevertheless, he was remarkably consistent in trying to implement his ideas.

For example, on the issue of women's rights Khomeini had said women were free to participate in all activities, as long as they did not cause corruption. But as Bazargan and Bani Sadr know full well—particularly Bani Sadr with his personal contribution on the subject of women's hair and its effect on men's sexual response—a woman's unveiled body is considered a cause of corruption in Islam. Therefore, Khomeini's early attempt in March 1979 to impose the veil was no breach of his previous statements. That he retreated temporarily on this front at that time because of the unexpectedly forceful and spontaneous demonstrations of women, only to come back to it more forcefully in the early summer of 1980, shows how attuned his political instincts and sense of timing were. In March 1979, he was in need of more "preparatory work."

Another issue for which Khomeini has been repeatedly accused of betrayal of promises is the role of the clergy in the new state. It is said that he had declared on many occasions that the clergy would not take charge of the day-to-day functioning of the state. On this issue, Khomeini has admitted his change of mind openly. For instance, when addressing the Council of the Guardians on December 11, 1983, he said, "Before the revolution, I used to think that once the revolution would be victorious, there would be virtuous individuals who would run our affairs according to Islam. Therefore, I repeatedly said that the clergy would attend to their own affairs. But later I realized that in their majority they [the available people] were not virtuous. I saw that I had been wrong. So I declared openly that I had made a mistake."

Similarly, Khomeini's statements on democratic rights (freedom of the press, of association, and self-determination) were always qualified. As early as August 1979 censorship and repression of the press began on the grounds that what was being printed was not in the interests of the people or Islam. Papers were banned, meetings attacked, parties declared illegal because the Imam considered them damaging to the Islamic revolution and the people, and causing corruption and incitement of the populace against Islam. Again, the extent to which such repression was actually carried out and against whom depended on the relationship of political forces that prevailed at the time. But at no time can this selectivity and testing of the political ground be considered in contradiction with Khomeini's previously expressed views regarding the nature of an Islamic government.

The fact that these ideas of Khomeini and in particular his

qualifications on democracy *were largely ignored by many political forces* at the time stems from two considerations.

First, there was a powerful element of self-delusion. Given the overwhelming ideological, political, and organizational hegemony of Khomeini over the mass movement against the shah, many political currents tended to read their own political beliefs—which they could not see supported by the masses—into Khomeini's views. Forces on the socialist left searched for social justice, egalitarianism, and even some sort of socialist society. Betrayed by their own illusions, they now accuse Khomeini of betrayals.

To his credit, Bani Sadr admits that in Paris he and his colleagues tried to give "an expression to the revolution" through Khomeini, since "without using Khomeini as a cover, it was impossible." He admits that they tried to make Khomeini say that in its first phase, the Islamic government would be a national government committed to independence and freedom. According to Bani Sadr, on the third day of Khomeini's arrival in Paris, he had a meeting with him, during which Bani Sadr brought to his attention a list of criticisms raised by "the international press and Iranian intellectuals" about the ideas formulated on Islamic Government. He pointed out to Khomeini that there were anxieties that velayat-e faqih would be a more severe and reactionary dictatorship than that of the shah. Bani Sadr argued that world public opinion had turned against the shah because of his suppression of liberties and that this same public opinion had contributed greatly in isolating the shah internationally, depriving him of the support of Western governments. He, therefore, pointed out to Khomeini that if it were not emphasized that an Islamic government would be based on the popular will, there would be much propaganda that Khomeini intended to replace the shah's dictatorship with his own and that this would be used against them.

After much discussion, Bani Sadr states, Khomeini agreed with him and Bani Sadr was assigned the task of formulating these various objections against the Islamic government and appropriate responses to them. He summarized these into nineteen points, with corresponding clarifications and Khomeini agreed to study them and answer the press interviews accordingly. Furthermore, according to Bani Sadr, they made arrangements so that reporters had to hand in their questions ahead of time and a team composed of Bani Sadr, Yazdi, Qotbzadeh, Ahmad Khomeini, and later Kho'iniha—the cleric who led the students in the occupation of the U.S. Embassy in November 1979—would prepare the answers and give them to Khomeini prior to the actual interview. If the description is accurate, it amounts to a very big "public relations" exercise that was so successful it deceived Bani Sadr himself! To be fair to Bani

Sadr, he admits that this may be construed as being a cover-up of Khomeini's true face—that of a dictator worse than the shah. He dismisses this
charge, however, on the grounds that he had believed, at the time, that
Khomeini had genuinely changed his views. Conveniently, he ignores the
fact that over the same period, in his lectures and audiences to his Iranian
followers in Paris, Khomeini had reiterated his own views on the nature of
the Islamic government, as discussed above. What is totally unreasonable
is Bani Sadr's insistence on using Khomeini's interviews with the international press—namely, the very formulations that he and his colleagues had
put into Khomeini's mouth—as a proof of Khomeini's betrayal of his
illusions.[10] The second consideration is that many of Khomeini's ideas,
particularly the notion of qualified and conditional democracy were, and
still are, shared by many of the political currents and organizations that
took part in the revolution. They simply have *different* qualifications and
limitations on democratic rights. For example, "the Transitional Government of the Democratic Islamic Republic of Iran," of which Bani Sadr,
until his recent (spring 1984) split, was president, promises to exclude
pro-Khomeini and pro-shah candidates from its "free elections." Its freedom of the press, political parties, and gatherings, like Khomeini's, do not
include "counter-revolutionary parties and groupings." It promises to
"replace the use of violence with democratic loyalty."[11] Khomeini prefers
the concept of "Islamic loyalty," but in essence both would agree that
"loyalty" is the operative concept. After all, if currents with far smaller
mass bases can give themselves the right to decide for people whom they
can or cannot elect and who constitutes a counter-revolutionary, why
shouldn't Khomeini make the same claims, with his vastly greater popular
authority, particularly at the height of the movement against the shah and
the immediate post-revolutionary period?

What appears to be shared is the same deepseated contempt for
an individual's right to political democracy as is the case with so many
Third Worldist and nationalist currents all over the world. When they are
in opposition the rallying call of political democracy is a most expedient
banner to wave about; however, once they are in power it is treated as an
unpleasant nuisance to be curtailed or done away with at the earliest
convenience.

II. THE MOJAHEDIN

Ever since the Mojahedin were forced into opposition, they have taken the
implicit logic of the above positions to their very end. They now assert that

Khomeini "usurped" the leadership of the movement and "snatched" the revolution, using the open status and relative security of the mosques during the shah's reign combined with the authority of Islam, to organize, and to fill the political vaccum left as a result of the repression of all other political forces. Today, they claim that as early as 1970 they were aware of the reactionary nature of Khomeini. However, because of his mass popularity, they could not say so. They had to wait for the right moment (June 1981) to denounce him openly.[12]

To begin with, this is a contradictory position: if Khomeini was popular to the extent that the Mojahedin could not criticize him then, he neither could nor did he need to "usurp" or "snatch" the leadership of the revolution. His very popularity *guaranteed* him uncontested leadership. Furthermore, to keep silent on the reactionary character of Khomeini when he was popular and to attack him when that popularity is declining is opportunist and politically vacuous. After all, what is the role of the Mojahedin in bringing about a decline in that popularity?

More importantly, however, it is factually false that the Mojahedin kept silent about Khomeini. A reading of their organ, *Mojahed*, over the past years shows that prior to late spring 1980 they actually *praised* Khomeini and gave him explicit political support. It was between the spring of 1980 and 1981 that they kept silent with respect to Khomeini while attacking the IRP, only to move finally into open opposition in late June 1981, calling for Khomeini's overthrow.

The early issues of *Mojahed* are full of praise for Khomeini as the leader of the revolution, the father of the people, the expression of the depth and the authenticity of the popular movement, etc. Although the Mojahedin were critical of the constitution and the formalization of the position of velayat-e faqih within it, they nevertheless declared their acceptance of Khomeini as the supreme leader of the people in his lifetime. In December 1979, they proposed that Khomeini personally should stand as the presidential candidate. Only after it was clear that Khomeini had no such intentions, did the Mojahedin leader Rajavi stand as a candidate, only to be disqualified by Khomeini himself for his opposition to the new constitution.

As late as February 1981, Rajavi described Khomeini's role in the revolution in the following words, "The overall historical and social situation necessitated that Ayatollah Khomeini . . . all by himself should take the responsiblity and role of a united front and then as the leader, the Imam, of the revolutionary masses, take charge of all affairs and responsibilities."[13]

In another interview in March 1981 (only three months before the Mojahedin's call for the overthrow of Khomeini) Rajavi states that the

Mojahedin accept "the anti-imperialist positions of the Imam" and expresses concern that the excessive adulation of Khomeini by certain people "reduces the status of his leadership in the revolution against the monarchy."[14]

Clearly, the written record does not bear out the Mojahedin's current claims, unless one assumes that they had been playing a very cynical game over the first two years, in which case there is even less reason to take their positions seriously.

III. THE SECULAR LEFT AND THE ISLAMIC REPUBLIC

The problem facing the secular left has been different in character from that of the Islamic dissidents.[15] Whereas the main problem for the Islamic dissidents as well as for the NF has been their characterization of Khomeini—because they had seen themselves as part of a leadership bloc—for the secular left, the issue has been their relationship with the masses.[16] As the masses are presumed to be revolutionary in their actions, almost by definition, the major problem has become to explain how they supported and followed a reactionary leader. The resolution of this dilemma clearly has enormous repercussions for the projected trajectory of mass action and the role of the left.

Khomeini's popularity and the political and organizational hegemony of the clergy are explained by emphasizing one combination or another of the following considerations:

1. The repression of all political forces under the shah, with the exception of the clergy, who enjoyed relative freedom of political agitation and organization through the mosques;

2. Socio-economic changes since the 1960s that brought millions of rural laborers and peasants into the cities, but failed to provide them with adequate jobs, housing etc., thereby creating an urban mass susceptible to populist ideas and with no previous history of political struggle;

3. Khomeini's intransigence against the shah in contrast to other forces (for example, the NF or the FM) who were open to various compromises;

4. The political discrediting of other major parties, like the NF and the Tudeh Party, who had been tested historically (1941–53) and failed.

Linked with these explanations, there are various notions about the aspirations of the masses. It is often stated that the masses knew what they were struggling against (the shah and all the problems associated with his regime), but they did not have a clear idea of what type of regime would take its place. Alternatively, the explanation is along the lines that the masses did not have any formulated notion about what an Islamic republic meant. They were primarily concerned with their material needs (jobs, better living conditions, etc.) and with political liberties. The clergy, it is frequently said, used their traditional prestige as part of the opposition and their organizational apparatus, to deceive the masses, and possibly the left, to dull their political sensibilities, and to come to power on the back of their struggles. The implications of this line of argument, often drawn by the left, particularly in the early days, are that through a comparatively speedy process the masses will come to realize that the regime is incapable of fulfilling their demands. They will therefore cease to support it, and move to the left towards socialist solutions in a continuously deepening revolutionary process.

The main problem with the above scenario is not that it does not contain important elements of reality, such as the factors contributing to Khomeini's powerful hold over the mass movement. The problem lies in refusing to see one very important consequence of (and contributor to) this hold: namely the genuine political identification of the masses with Islam. This refusal leads to completely voluntaristic conclusions, such as the incessant, totally unrealistic, expectations of the left for a break of the masses from Khomeini and a turn to socialism in a new revolutionary upsurge.

The struggle for higher wages, welfare, housing, etc., in and of themselves are not political struggles challenging state power. At no time in human history have masses of people made a revolution in the sense of a fundamental change in the structure of political and social power for this or that specific demand. Repression may lead to widespread protest movements; bad working conditions and low wages may lead to strikes; high prices may lead to riots, but in and of themselves such explosions in isolation will not lead to revolution, unless through a much more complicated socio-political process the masses come to the political conclusion that there is no alternative. In other words, they come to identify their struggle for this or that demand with the necessity of implementing a radically different political-economic-social system, and a positive desire to change the structure of power itself.

This means that in the struggle against the shah, by the time the multi-million street demonstrations were calling into question the legitimacy of the regime and calling for the downfall of the shah and for an Islamic government, they were no longer simply fighting for this or that demand. They had already reached a level of *political* consciousness that

identified the satisfaction of their various demands and aspirations with
the coming to power of an Islamic government and the implementation of
its Islamic program.

Once this is recognized, it becomes clear that the process of mass
differentiation from the new regime, their change of consciousness and
willingness to go out on the street for a totally different political program,
is an immensely more complicated process than mere disillusionment with
their clerical leaders. For one thing, some of the demands can be partially
satisfied, at least for certain sectors of the population. This would intensify
their allegiance and support for the regime, particularly since it arose as a
result of a prolonged and bloody struggle.

Secondly, even if masses of people experience a worsening of life
compared to that under the old regime (unemployment and inflation have
risen drastically, common consumer goods are scarce, and now with the
war tremendous hardship and rationing are added), this does not necessarily and immediately lead to a political break from the regime or from
an Islamic program. Broad historical conclusions (the undesirability of
theocratic rule, for example) are not reached from short partial experiences. Instead, the popular masses may attribute these failures to a whole
series of other factors and react accordingly.

For example, they may believe the problems are due to sabotage
by an internal "fifth column" (royalist opposition, "the liberals," the
communists, the atheists, etc.). They may attribute the failures to powerful
external factors (imperialist conspiracies, the present Iraqi-Iranian war).
Even if, after a few years of experience, they come to see something wrong
with the government itself, the most obvious reaction is to assume that
their ideals are not being implemented properly, and therefore to try
reforming what they have got, rather than moving towards its replacement
with another. For example, initially the Bazargan government enjoyed
tremendous popular support. This support was gradually lost over the
following nine months, not to socialists or even to the Mojahedin, but to
the clerical Islamic Republican Party. The masses associated the failures
with Bazargan's *insufficiently* Islamic government. The U.S. Embassy
seige marked a high point in this process. A year later, the IRP, with its
clearly catastrophic policies in all areas, began to lose support to Bani
Sadr and to a general awareness that maybe the clergy did not know how
to run a country. This important partial shift in mass consciousness, away
from direct involvement of the clergy in daily management of national
politics, still remained within an Islamic framework. Sectors of the masses
simply concluded that the clergy may be good for implementing religious
and social aspects of Islam, but they may not know enough about an
Islamic economy, army, etc. This shift in consciousness although positive

in itself is far from class consciousness, or from any *political* break from Islam.

Third, the simplistic notions of a mass break away from Khomeini totally ignore the severely *negative* effects of the past three years on mass consciousness and activity. The clergy have done everything to curb any development of independent mass activity. Working class militants opposing the prevailing policies on even the most elementary trade union or economic issues have been jailed or sacked. Corporative consultative committees have been set up to replace any remnants of the independent workers' committees formed during the struggle against the shah. Strikes are declared acts of treachery. Austerity measures, justified by reference to the fight against the U.S. and now Iraq have reduced even further the level of employment. Under these conditions, workers themselves avoid head-on clashes, strikes, etc., and are suspicious of militants who propose such actions. Particularly since the outbreak of the war, the drive for longer working hours and higher productivity has further narrowed the possibilities of independent trade-union type work.

Moreover, politically and ideologically, the clergy have consistently campaigned for (and implemented) a system of government beyond accountability: *they* are the ones who know what is best for the Moslem community. Their success in this is a factor in reducing the self-confidence and willingness of the masses to undertake independent activity.

Fourth, those sectors of the mass opposition against the shah who indeed had followed the clergy-dominated movement out of sheer illusion (for example, wide sectors of state employees, intellectuals, and professional women) and within a few months after the change-over realized what they had helped to effect, were ill-prepared to do anything about their disillusionment. For one thing, prior to the fall of the shah they had seen their struggles as part of the general movement, while objectively their demands (freedom of press and association, equal rights for women, etc.) were at odds with the requirements of an Islamic regime. This made it difficult to make a sudden organized turn-about. Instead, opposition to the Islamic regime on these issues was partial, disorganized, atomized; and easily defused and defeated. Moreover, faced with a regime that enjoyed militant mass support, it seemed impossible and futile to put up any resistance or open struggle: all were branded acts of counter-revolution, isolated from the workers and urban poor.

Once these factors are taken into account, then it becomes clear why none of the simplistic projections of the left have borne much resemblance to reality. Political differentiations and changes of allegiance have occurred and will continue to occur for some time to come within an Islamic framework. These are the new politics into which the masses have put their hopes and are prepared to experiment with. In this context the popularity of the Mojahedin is notable. Despite the tremendous losses and repression that they have suffered, they will remain one of the main currents to whom fresh layers of Islamic militants will turn. Political developments towards secular political programs will be much slower, given the deep disillusionment with nationalism and the undemocratic nature of those countries which call themselves socialist. Poland has become yet another proof, from this point of view, of the undesirability of "socialism."

It is this basic problem with which the current evaluations of nationalist and left groups fail to come to terms. It is of course for different reasons that both currents fail to appreciate the significance of the mass turn to Islam as the central feature of the political development in Iran in the recent past. I have argued that for nationalist currents the reason is an existential one: the turn to Islam has occurred partially as a result of their failures as well as their partial cooptation by the shah's regime. The turn to Islam is at the same time a *rejection* of nationalism in the historical sense.

Yet, the actual experience of an Islamic government may be, in fact, preparing the ground for genuine secularization. Ever since the Constitutional Revolution (1905–11), an underlying tension has existed in the relation between the ideas of modern political systems and Islam. Secular constitutionalism formed under the influence of European political thought and experience. As such it had strong tendencies towards the elevation of the sciences and of European critical thought, and away from religion. It was skeptical of the traditional clergy, but the break with religion was very limited. Shi'ism in Iran, having been the ideology of a strong Iranian dynasty (the Safavids in the seventeenth century), had historical as well as mythical roots. Therefore, while Iranian nationalists could fall back on pre-Islamic Iran as a source of national identity, Shi'ism also lent itself to becoming integrated into Iranian nationalism. The tensions posed by these tendencies towards secularization, pre-Islamic identification, and pro-Shi'ite allegiances were all reflected in the 1906–07 constitution. This constitution, on the one hand, attempted to draw on the European experience and set up a government based on the idea of separation of powers and the secularization of the judiciary and legislature. On the other hand, it conceded that no laws contrary to the Islamic shari'a could be legitimate. Similarly, during the reign of Reza Shah, although much secular legislation was drafted, the civil code remained based on shari'a.

The Pahlavis emphasized pre-Islamic nationalism and partial secularization, without actually attacking the prerogatives of the clerical establishment and the requirements of Islamic jurisprudence. They failed.

The Islamic Republic, on the other hand, by basing itself solely on religion, has dissolved this historic tension by abrogating the nationalist idea along with secularization and by committing itself to building a theocratic state and reconstructing some kind of Islamic religious community. When it is challenged, secularism will of necessity be a central political issue. This is already indicated by the heated debates amongst oppositionists of various shades on the issue of separation of religion and state. Old debates and old political lineups have collapsed in the face of an unforeseen and unpredicted revolution; new lineups are shaping up around issues posed by this new development.

NOTES

1. See, for example, "The Statement of the National Front on the Occasion of the Second Anniversary of the Glorious Revolution of 22nd of Bahman," in its organ, *Payam-e Jebhe-ye Melli* (The Message of National Front), No. 52, February 10, 1981. The same theme is repeated in many articles and editorials of this paper.

2. See Bazargan's speech on the occasion of the second anniversary of the revolution, printed in *Mizan*, February 23, 1981.

3. See Bazargan, *Enqelab-e Iran dar do harekat* (The Iranian Revolution in Two Motions), in Persian (Naraqi: Tehran, 1984). It must be mentioned that this "new" explanation conveniently followed the farcical prosecution (and execution) of many Tudeh members and leaders.

4. The reference is to the open letters of protest to the shah in the spring of 1977 by NF leaders and the declaration of the Iranian Committee for Human Rights formulated by many leaders and members of the two organizations.

5. See, for example, "Payam-e Riyasat-e Jomhuri be mellat-e Iran" (the message of the presidency to the Iranian nation) in the newspaper *Enqelab-e Islami dar Hejrat* (Islamic Revolution in Emigration), No. 6 (December 10, 1981); also an August 1981 interview with Bani Sadr, by Fred Halliday, in *MERIP Reports* (March–April 1982).

6. See Bani Sadr, *Khianat be omid* (Hope Betrayed) (Paris, 1982). The very title of the book indicates the delusionary character of its thesis: How could Khomeini be accused of betraying what were the subjective aspirations and hopes of another person?

7. This theme is present in many of Bazargan's speeches. See for example, the reference in Note 2.

8. See *Neda-ye Haqq (The Call of Truth—A Collection of Messages, Interviews, and Speeches by Imam Khomeini in Paris)*, Volume I covers from October 9, 1978 through

November 21, 1978. No further volumes seem to have come out. Other interviews have appeared in the Iranian daily press of this period.

9. See Bazargan's interview with *Nouvel Observateur* reported in the Iranian daily press of April 14, 1979.

10. To his credit, Bani Sadr, later in the book, admits that he censored himself on the character of Khomeini's views on government. As he puts it, "we did not want to know anything bad about him . . . we thought that since Khomeini had said certain things, in Paris, in front of the world press, he would not back off from them. . . . We were very proud of our achievement in Paris. . . . Like little children, we were happy to hear good stories."

11. See *The Program of the Transitional Government of the Democratic Islamic Republic of Iran,* particularly pages 7–8, and 26–27.

12. See Mas'ud Rajavi's message on the occasion of the third anniversary of the revolution, "Victory is Imminent." Excerpts appear in the English *Weekly Publication of the Moslem Student Society—Britain,* No. 7, 19 February 1982. Also Rajavi's interview with *Iranshahr,* an English translation of which appears in the above publication, Nos. 4–5. See also Fred Halliday's interview with Rajavi (August 1981) in *MERIP Reports* (March–April 1982).

13. See *Mojahed,* No. 108, February 5, 1981.

14. See *Mojahed,* No. 113, March 12, 1981.

15. In speaking of "the secular left" I exclude those groups who for the first crucial years supported Khomeini's regime (the Tudeh Party, and Majority Faction of the Fedayan). The exclusion is not for political reasons, but because a position of support for the regime had a different internal logical consistency. Nor do I take up the position of every group separately. The multiplicity of the leftist groups in post-revolutionary Iran is so large that such a review would require a book. The arguments presented here, however, do appear in varying combinations and with different emphases in all major left groups' positions.

16. I do not mean that characterization of Khomeini and his regime is unimportant, nor that it was not problematic for the left. On the contrary, the literature of the left in the first year of the new regime was primarily concerned with such questions as: Is Khomeini progressive? Anti-imperialist? Should he be supported? Critically? Unconditionally? Which class does he represent? etc. However, as the policies of the new regime began to speak louder than the often scholastic debates, these questions receded to the background, with everyone (excluding Tudeh, et al.) agreeing that the new regime was reactionary and conveniently forgetting about the left's initial support for Khomeini. The concern then shifted to the problems I am discussing here.

DISCUSSANT'S REMARKS

Patrick Clawson

BEFORE OPENING THE FLOOR TO QUESTIONS and comments I would like to monopolize my position as chair to make a few remarks on the paper.

First, I was struck that Afsaneh Najmahbadi did not talk about the social bases of the opposition. I think that all the organized opposition comes from much the same social background. All of the groups, which I would divide into three—the Monarchists, Islamic liberals such as the Mojahedin, and the secular liberals, come from the top ten percent of the income scale. And they are in one degree or another Western educated. This is obviously less true for the Mojahedin. For example, the neighborhoods where all their street actions took place were not the poor neighborhoods in south Tehran, but the wealthier sections in north Tehran. That's where the Mojahedin support seemed to be centered.

In any case, I think that if we are going to examine the opposition we have to look at their social base carefully. I think that one of the reasons for the increasing cooperation between all these movements lies in their similar social backgrounds. And there is increasing cooperation among them. When I was in France recently I was certainly struck by the kind of literature coming from the Mojahedin these days. They were trying to explain why support for the Mojahedin would be logical for the United States, and especially for France. I was in Paris for the May Day celebrations organized by the socialists, the ruling party in France. The Mojahedin were there handing out their leaflets which were so sycophantic about the French Government and explained how they represent the interests of the West. But there were no Mojahedin at the larger communist May Day demonstration. The Khatt-e Imam, the followers of the Imam, and the Tudeh were there but not the Mojahedin supporters.

Another question that I think is very important in examining the opposition is their attitude toward foreigners. I think that this is one of the major reasons for the Islamic character of the current opposition. Let's take the radical left as a whole, for instance. For years their major argument was that the shah was a U.S. puppet, and that U.S. imperialism is the main enemy of the people of Iran. Now correspondingly there was little analysis of the internal problems of Iranian politics from this touchstone. What was their approach? Now the question of Khomeini. There is no question that he is very virulently opposed to the current U.S. government. As a result the left-wing opposition movements thought that this would mean that Khomeini was basically on their side; all his other statements were ignored. This was told to me time and again by leftist Iranian students: "on the key question Khomeini is on our side." This continues to be the position of the Tudeh, the Fedayan (Majority), the Trotskyites, etc., that Khomeini has two aspects, his anti-imperialist aspect and his reactionary internal aspect. The main question facing Iran is its approach to international issues and dependence on the West. There Khomeini has the right position and therefore we should support him, even though we support him critically.

Furthermore, by making what could best be called xenophobia the touchstone of political debate and discussion, the way was opened for Islam. For if we were going to reject the West and Western ideology, then clearly we have to turn towards something which isn't Western, and there the obvious response was to turn to Islam. Thus there was no way for liberals to defend the good aspects of the Western cultural heritage such as political democracy or civil liberties and civil rights.

Another justification the left used for failing to criticize Khomeini is that "we know he's wrong, but we are going to ally with him now and later on we are going to explain to people how he is wrong." That fits in with a long heritage in Iranian culture of contempt for mass knowledge. It is felt that the masses don't know very much; those who understand things are a small elite really capable of comprehending the issues that most people can't. That also demonstrates the social basis of the opposition. The opposition didn't feel any identification, at a gut level, with the masses of Iranian people but still felt a distance from them. They were the political elite that could understand the political issues.

On this question of approach towards foreigners, let's look at the Monarchists. The Monarchists in general are looking to the United States and other foreign powers to restore them to power in Iran. I think that Leslie Gelb's piece in the *New York Times* about eight thousand exile-led troops in Turkey is a good example of how Aryana and the others are trying to inflate their power and strength by saying they have U.S. support. The implication is that they would come to power if only the United States would back them. And they have some amazing conspiracy theories about why the revolution succeeded and why the United States wanted to throw the shah out. But on the whole, the underlying theme throughout all these Monarchists' discussions is that foreigners caused the revolution for one reason or another, and that only foreigners will overthrow the Khomeini regime.

GENERAL DISCUSSION

Hooglund: I'd like to comment on what Clawson said about the social origins of the Mojahedin. My own research contradicts some of the things he is saying. First, in terms of where the Mojahedin's activities take place. The single most important area in Tehran, in terms of numbers of incidents, has been in Yakshirabad, not Shemiran. Yakshirabad, as anyone who has lived in Tehran knows, is a very crude slum with hardly any running water nor any sewage system. It is one of the worst slums in Tehran. Another important area is the section formerly called Bist-o-panjom-e Sharivar. It is a low-income housing development in south Tehran near Shahr-e Rayy. The third most important area for Mojahedin activities has been east Tehran, beyond Meydan-e Jaleh. And there have been a number of incidents in the downtown university and bazaar areas. But contrary to what he says, there is no evidence of significant Mojahedin activities in Shemiran or other wealthy sections of Tehran, although incidents have occurred there. The same pattern is true of other cities. In Shiraz, for example, nearly 70 percent of incidents between June, 1981 and January, 1982, took place in low-income neighborhoods, especially in the area called Dalilabad which is an atrocious slum made out of oil cans. So to say that these activities are taking place mostly in the wealthy area is inaccurate. The government of Iran announces the locations of all incidents, and the evidence is clear that Shemiran and similar areas have not been the locus of many activities at all.

Second, there are about three of us in this room who have actually interviewed Mojahedin in Iran, and I think that they would agree with me on this: most of the Mojahedin in Iran, as opposed to those you might find in the U.S., do not come from the top percent income brackets of the population. They come from the same classes which support the clergy, the working and lower-middle classes, especially bazaar families. I interviewed many Mojahedin in 1979 and the overwhelming majority were of lower-class origin. It is a very different origin than many Mojahedin whom you find in this country. I think it is very significant that there are these class differences in the composition of the domestic and expatriate Mojahedin, but it is important to point out here that the support for the Mojahedin in Iran is not the wealthy upper 10 percent of the population, but rather the lower middle class.

Salehi: I agree that it is vital to understand the class identification of the opposition. But I also disagree with your representation of the opposition as being confined to the top 10 percent income of the population. Perhaps the top 30 percent. The Mojahedin are described, even by their opponents such as the Fedayan, as petit bourgeois, and not as part of the elite classes, the court or Shemiran. If it is important to identify class affiliation, it is also a danger to mistakenly typify any opposition.

I think Afsaneh Najmabadi's paper is important because she accurately points out the dual attraction of the Mojahedin: they do not represent the ruling class, the top 10%, and despite the Fedayan contention that their Islamic identity is a liability, they are an Islamic alternative.

I think that is their strength, and it is evidenced everywhere, both overseas and in Iran, by the large numbers of supporters the Mojahedin attracts, as opposed to the Fedayan or others. I think Najmabadi is correct when she argues that some Islamic alternative is preferable for most Iranians, rather than a radical, socialist, or communist alternative to Khomeini.

Van Engeland: The Mojahedin is a clandestine movement, it has always been a clandestine movement, and has never had control of its members. Within the Mojahedin movement there are different tendencies and very different people. Within the Mojahedin movement there are royalist militants and extreme leftist militants. So it is absolutely impossible to characterize the Mojahedin from a purely political point of view. You must also notice that the situation of the opposition within Iran is very desperate. When one places a bomb or has to fight for survival, then he doesn't care if he receives help from a monarchist or from a leftist or from a Feda'i. I think that at the moment there are links between the Mojahedin and all the other movements and it is impossible to characterize the Mojahedin and say that they belong to a specific political faction.

Najmabadi: I agree with what has been said about the social base of the Mojahedin. I would argue that their social base is different from all the other opposition currents like the National Front, the Freedom Movement, the Royalists, etc. I do think the Mojahedin have a broad base in what can be loosely called the lower-middle class. There is another base they have, although there is not enough information, but they definitely have more support in the working class than all the other movements do. Of course, now because of very high unemployment and the state of the economy there has been a virtual disintegration of the working class in Iran. But immediately after the new regime came to power when there were all these workers' councils in different factories the Mojahedin were popular. I know this was true at least in factories where there was a high ratio of women workers, because it was in these that I was conducting research in 1979—that is the various pharmaceutical factories around Tehran and the textile and thread factories where the predominant force was women. I had contact with the workers in these factories. The dominant political force in the workers' council was the Mojahedin, not the left, and not supporters of the Islamic fundamentalists who later began to take over these councils. The people who eventually took over the councils were actually workers who were put into factories as part of the IRP political project to take over the councils, but this was a much later development. The initial radicalization of a lot of the workers in the councils was due to the Mojahedin. To this day, I think, they still have a pretty good base there, but because of the economic situation their influence has less significance in the general sociological pattern of the country than before.

Akhavi: I would like to ask Afsaneh Najmabadi about the Mojahedin-e khalq and Taleqani and the cult of Taleqani since his death. Do the Mojahedin still revere Taleqani and how are the differences between Taleqani and Bani Sadr explained since the recent alliance of Rajavi and Bani Sadr? In other words, what is the Taleqani connection right now?

Najmabadi: To the best of my knowledge the Mojahedin still consider Taleqani their theoretical and spiritual father figure, as they have always. Bani Sadr never explicitly brings out his differences with Taleqani, especially not now. It seems to me that the Mojahedin had a lot more serious political differences with Bani Sadr than their connection to Taleqani, but all these differences are being left in silence anyway. I haven't seen anything in the way of a change in their position on Taleqani.

Akhavi: Despite his repudiation of them at the tail end of his life?

Najmabadi: I don't think they ever tried to distance themselves from Taleqani because of that. They have always stressed their continuity, and in a sense, they do have a continuity to Taleqani since they originally came from the Freedom Movement. And for a long time, even though other figures in the Freedom Movement like Bazargan openly disassociated themselves, Taleqani went out of the way to protect the Mojahedin in both political and material ways. So, I think that Taleqani is the only other religious leader who enjoyed very strong popular support, in some ways even stronger than Khomeini. Not so much as a political leader, but as a spiritual father figure of the country so to speak. The Mojahedin, continue to hold on to Taleqani's reputation as part of their image.

Bakhash: I would generally agree with the statements about the weakness of the opposition abroad and the problem of finding support for the opposition at home. But there is a very curious situation because the opposition seems to be very weak, and yet the government rules by suppression. It has to shut down newspapers, break up rival political meetings, shut down party headquarters, and imprison and execute the opposition. I think that one needs to look a little bit at this apparent contradiction. I have a feeling that the answer lies in that while not a single opposition group is strong, as was pointed out, there is a kind of general feeling of opposition, which is vague and undefined and hasn't fully taken shape, but exists. And I think that there is more potential than has been suggested for a post-Khomeini movement that will be opposed to the present structure. This is where we might see developments in the future.

Najmabadi: I don't disagree that there is a lot of dissatisfaction in the country, but I tend to think that dissatisfaction by itself cannot become a political movement unless there is a positive political alternative toward which people can channel that dissatisfaction. I am trying to argue that this is not forthcoming, not in the shape that things exist now, with the forces that exist now.

Rose: I would like to raise a few questions. First, it seems to me that we often forget how difficult it is to organize opposition under conditions of extreme suppression and an organized security apparatus. One has to worry about things like whether one has the proper documents, whether one has safe houses, how does one smuggle one's arms around. That consumes a lot of a person's energy under repressive circumstances. It is a primary survival question for many people in the opposition in Iran which diverts them from political organizing which in turn would reflect a degree of their support in the general populace.

   Secondarily, I wonder whether what we have here is an apparatus of repression that does not reflect the degree of threat to the regime, but rather represents a certain paranoid tendency on the part of the regime. Khomeini genuinely believes in the possibility of a monarchist restoration. I don't think any objective observer thinks there is a foundation in reality for any such fear, but the apparatus of repression has been set up as a reaction to paranoid illusions on the part of senior officials in the IRP. I would suggest as a hypothesis that we have not seen much in the way of a strong political activity on the part of opposition in Iran because the social base for any viable alternative simply does not exist. There is among the opposition, with the possible exception of Moqaddam in Tabriz, no following in the country. Bazargan and Bani Sadr are out of power today because their base of support in Iran packed their bags and left. And I think that is true of the opposition in general. The apparatus of repression has been generated out of paranoid fantasies, illusions.

Van Engeland: Well, I would agree that it is very difficult to organize an opposition movement, and it is especially difficult under the Khomeini regime. It is a regime that has really decided to kill the opposition, and it kills its opponents in a very simple way. It doesn't care about anything; it is not under the pressure of human rights committees all over the world. During the shah's regime, even though the shah was also very authoritarian, he was often under the pressure of international organizations. That is not the case with Khomeini. He doesn't care about the International Red Cross, Amnesty International, or anything, he has just decided to kill to suppress all opposition. That seems to be a very efficient way. The Islamic Republican Party and the mollas have agents everywhere in the country, in every aspect of Iranian life. They have shown an incredible capability for finding information about the opposition. The newspapers almost every day report finding safe-houses. The government has a good intelligence service, and knows how to find people. And there are no more trials. When they find a safe-house, they kill everybody. No trials, no firing squads.

Sick: Khomeini's regime has every reason to be suspicious, justifiably so. If you look at what the Mojahedin have done, launching a challenge in the streets, and the number of coups that have been talked about, some of which must have had a basis in reality, a war on the border, a war with the Kurds, the Qashqa'is in revolt, then it is obvious the government has got problems. It's not as if they were inventing these things. It's not an illusion. And the fact is that they are using repression as their answer, so far their only answer. I agree with Van Engeland that they have been so far very efficient. One doesn't have to like them to realize that they are going to be in power for a while. That, I think, is the distinction. There is a tendency in the West to think that if they aren't likeable, then somehow they are going to fall. I would argue that Hitler and Stalin and a number of other people prove that is not necessarily true. Terror really works sometimes, and this regime has shown a substantial capacity for the use of terror.

That gets back to what we were discussing earlier. We have a thorough survey of the opposition elements, where they are and so forth, but I think the only conclusion that one could come to is that there is no serious opposition. The Mojahedin may have offered that at one point but are not a major challenge now, the way things currently stand.

What does that do to the theory of permanent instability? And where is that instability really coming from, and what are we really talking about? I would like to ask the panelists: where is some future organization or opposition likely to emerge? Would it fundamentally change the nature of the regime, but not the personnel? Is that what we're talking about as instability, a rotation of elites? But what about the regime itself, what it stands for, Khomeinism? What is the threat to that basic concept, a threat likely to overturn it?

Najmabadi: I want to comment about this question of paranoia because I think the regime is paranoid. But in the relationship of their paranoia to reality they are much less paranoid than the shah really was. I think the opposition to the shah was much weaker than the type of repression he unleashed against it. I agree with Gary Sick's comment that people tend to forget past repression. Thus, at least for a while, repression can work. We don't have to go to the extremes of Hitler and Stalin, we have the shah at hand. He worked with the same methods, and there are plenty of regimes in Latin America and other places where repression is the basis on which government works. The repression doesn't have to be at the level of groups that are going to threaten your existence tomorrow. Repression is necessary if you want to eliminate all expressions of dissatisfaction in any form. And there is a lot of dissatisfaction. But if it allows a free press tomorrow, the government won't fall immediately. There will be an outpouring of all kinds of distress and dissatisfaction, which is dangerous. So, I think there is a very real danger, between the state of mind of the population and the level of dissatisfaction. I also think there is an internal, political need for this type of repression in an Islamic government. It is a type of government which cannot tolerate any kind of dissent. It has to be monolithic. Over the past three years, any expression of dissent has been eliminated.

If you have a concept of government providing a body of people who can decide what is good and bad for everybody, then whatever falls outside the limits of that definition will have to be eliminated. This will continue. I think the instability of the regime in material terms has been its failure to provide any kind of positive solution. There is a limit to how long one can turn away people's attention by reference to external threats like the U.S. or the Iraqi war, or to counterrevolutionaries. There is a limit and it will be exhausted sooner or later. They are trying to extend this blame to wherever it will go, but there is a limit to the blame you can put on others before it is directed at yourself for the failure of your project. That is the actual material basis on which this instability will continue. On the political and ideological level I think this instability will continue because of the conformist element within the definition of an Islamic government. It would not be surprising that once Bani Sadr and other secular opponents are eliminated, various factions within the IRP will turn against one another. This type of continuous elimination by the stronger, who know "the truth" and can eliminate the weaker, will continue for a long time to come.

VI

Iran and the Superpowers

WASHINGTON'S ENCOUNTER with the IRANIAN REVOLUTION

Gary Sick

NOBODY IS EVER REALLY READY for a revolution. That certainly applied to the Carter administration, which was particularly unprepared for the Iranian revolution. I think it would be useful to examine some background in order to try to explain why the U.S. government was so poorly prepared for the Iranian revolution.

In 1953, right after the coup or counter-coup that restored the shah to the throne, the first American to visit Iran was Vice President Richard Nixon. He came in December, and was granted an honorary degree at Tehran University. There were some riots at the time, and he met the shah, I believe for the first time. These two men took to each other immediately, and Nixon later wrote a memo to Eisenhower which was very warm and full of praise for the shah.

That attitude became much more important some years later. In 1972, Nixon and Kissinger visited Tehran and discussed a new relationship with Iran, based essentially on the Nixon Doctrine and relying on the shah as a U.S. surrogate in the region. One important outcome of that meeting was the "blank check" given to Iran for military equipment. "Black check" is not too strong an expression, for it was spelled out precisely in a subsequent memorandum to the government that basically said that we would not second-guess the shah, that he would define his own needs for military equipment, and that we would not impose our own views. There were people in the government who opposed that, but they were beaten down rather quickly.

The outcome of this sequence of events was that the United States officially accepted the shah's own view of himself. We saw Iran as the shah and the shah as Iran. In 1972 he was very firmly in power. Ironically, in 1972 both Nixon and the shah were at the apex of their careers; all of their greatest achievements were behind them and it was all downhill from there. In any event, this view of the shah as the center of Iranian politics and society came to be totally institutionalized in the U.S. government. It was built into the bureaucracy and it affected the way people thought. It certainly affected the way the shah thought about himself; he must have appreciated the fact that Henry Kissinger basically confirmed his view of himself as one of the world's great strategists.

One of the results was that the U.S., among other things, dismantled many of its intelligence operations in Iran. This wasn't done consciously. People were not ordered to stop meeting with or reporting on the opposition. Rather, it was recognized that we had very good relations with the shah and we prized those relations; and since the shah showed enormous sensitivity towards anyone peeking under the rug of Iranian society, especially activities of the opposition, such efforts gradually ceased in order to avoid offending him and upsetting the relationship. As a result, the ability to look into Iranian society (apart from the palace) had largely been lost by the time the revolution began to build up.

In many respects, as a result of the Nixon Doctrine and consequent U.S. reliance on the shah for regional security support, the United States in effect became hostage to the shah, to his particular view of the world and in some respects to this concept of Iranian and U.S. interests.

In addition, there was the cultural aspect. Americans knew almost nothing about Iran. That fact applies not only to the body politic, but to U.S. leaders as well. I would say the U.S. government approached the Iranian revolution and events inside Iran from a position of almost unrelieved ignorance.

When the Carter administration took office, there were no alternatives to the Nixon Doctrine or the U.S. reliance on Iran and the shah. Contrary to the popular image that Carter came in and immediately began browbeating the shah about human rights and military sales, very little in fact changed.

People knew that attitudes had changed in Washington, and the shah was, in fact, making changes on human rights, but it was not a major campaign. On the contrary, everybody was aware, and President Carter was certainly aware, that the shah was shocked when Carter was elected and that he was not pleased about this. Washington believed that in order to maintain the kind of relationship that we had had, it was important to reassure the shah that the U.S. relationship would continue. And in fact, during that first year, instead of browbeating the shah, the year was spent reassuring him that the relationship would continue and that he had nothing to be concerned about on that account.

The Carter administration arrived in Washington with a highly programmatic foreign policy. In the first weeks of the administration a document was circulated which identified a number of key foreign policy objectives, including a comprehensive peace in the Middle East, the Panama Canal treaty, the Salt II treaty, and a wide range of other major initiatives. For two years there was no major crisis to interfere with this program, and by the end of 1978 each of these programs had acquired its own momentum, to the point where the Carter administration had, in effect, created a crisis of its own. Consequently, it was extraordinarily difficult to face a new, unanticipated crisis when it arose because of the intense pressures generated by the foreign policy initiatives that had been set in motion and that were all coming to fruition at the same time.

Further, because there had been no major crisis for two years, crisis management machinery existed only on paper. It had never been tested, and until crisis management machinery is actually used you don't know it will perform. In fact, it did not work smoothly when put to the test.

Finally, there were serious divisions within the government about what to do when the revolution began to gather steam. Disagreements found their way into the press, and the leaks simply turned into a torrent. Detailed notes about policy meetings often appeared in the press the day after the meeting. I remember one set of meetings, some of which Hal Saunders chaired, when I joked with him afterwards that I didn't need to take notes at the meeting because I could read it in great detail in the *Washington Post* the next morning.

Part of the problem was that the stakes were extremely high. If this revolution has occurred in Bolivia, the United States would have been much better able to handle it. But because we were so committed, because our interests were so deeply engaged, there was a tendency, a very human one but a dangerous one for a government, to want to deny that it was really happening. Basically we wanted to believe that somehow the shah would get this under control. There was a tendency for wishful thinking.

Also, there was a very real reluctance on the part of the government, again partly because of the high stakes, to "make the call," that is, to say: "The shah is really incompetent; he can't do this." No one wanted to do that. The ambassador in Tehran didn't want to do it, and the people in Washington hesitated to do it. As a result, when people came to the inevitable conclusion that in fact the shah was unable to act effectively, it was long past the point where U.S. policy could have much effect.

Finally, it may be worth noting that the U.S. government is designed like any government, to operate on a chessboard model, where you have an opponent, and competition is structured as a series of moves and countermoves. This was not a chessboard problem. A revolution is more like a hurricane, where you have a very different set of decisions to make: Are you going to run for the basement and hide; are you going to get the hell out of there; is the house going to stand; or is it going to be blown away? Not just the U.S. government, but all governments are not well equipped to deal with questions of that nature.

I'm not going to spend much time on the hostage crisis. First of all I think its importance was badly inflated and distorted in the United States in comparison to the importance of the revolution itself. It was treated primarily as a human-interest story, with great emphasis on the individuals and families involved. It got tremendous play, but really it was an epiphenomenon, a continuation of the effects of the revolution by other means. It obviously had enormous consequences for the U.S. government, but in the overall frame of events its real importance tended to be concealed by its dramatic content.

In the case of the hostage crisis, however, there was crisis machinery in place, well oiled, and in fact it ran very smoothly. There was almost no in-fighting within the government, people worked in tandem very well; but as you can see, it didn't make much difference. We still didn't get the hostages out for a long time.

The key policy choices that the government faced deserve reflection. Should we have downplayed the crisis from the beginning? Should we have used more force? Should we have used less force? Was there any rationale for the rescue mission? I just want to go on record: I supported the rescue attempt at the time, I support it now, and would be happy to argue it with anyone who wants to.

Let me take one brief look at Iran today. At the start, there was the question of whether this new regime would survive at all. It looked very shaky; it was chaotic; it represented a whole series of ideas that we had never seen before. I would argue that as time has gone on, the regime has gradually consolidated itself. It seems to me that the crossroads came with the June, 1981, attack by the Mojahedin, the all-out effort in the streets to bring down the regime—by an Islamic group, not by outsiders or by monarchists. The regime won that test.

That internal challenge was paralleled by the external crisis of the Iraqi invasion. it may be useful to compare the Iranian experience to other revolutions. I would say the French Revolution really began being taken seriously when its neighbors decided to march in and overthrow the revolution. The French assembled a levée en masse, a rag-tag group of people, or at least that is what it was believed to be, and threw them at the European armies that were marching in, defeating them soundly at the battle of Valmy. At that point the Europeans had to admit that, although they didn't like the French Revolution, it just wasn't going to fade away quietly. Similarly in the Russian Revolution, when the Red Army stood off attacks and interventions by internal and external enemies, it again proved that this was not a cream-puff operation. You didn't have to like their politics, but you had to take them seriously.

It seems to me that very much the same kind of watershed was passed in Iran in their ability to put together an effective army in Khuzistan and to make it felt. They have crossed a threshold from being primarily regarded as a weak, shaky organization that is about to fall, to one that one must conclude may well be around for a long, long time.

All revolutions, it seems to me, if they are real revolutions, introduce an idea into their region that is regarded by many of their contemporaries in the region and elsewhere in the world as illegitimate: the French Revolution with its concept of egalitarianism; the Russian Revolution with communism; and so forth. These ideas were regarded as illegitimate by the people of their time, and it was only after a considerable amount of time that one had to conclude—however reluctantly—that a certain amount of legitimacy had been achieved.

I would say that the same thing has happened in Iran. There is a strong tendency to look at the Khomeini regime and say, "This group is illegitimate; it represents an idea that is wrong, that is unacceptable, that is crazy," but that still doesn't mean that it will, necessarily, go away. It seems to me conceivable that this revolution, introducing what is viewed as essentially the "illegitimate" idea of a theocratic state, may have the same kind of effect on its region that the French and Russian revolutions did in Europe and elsewhere. With that gloomy note, I will conclude.

THE POSSIBILITIES of a NEW IRANIAN–UNITED STATES RELATIONSHIP

William Miller

WE ARE SO CLOSE to the emotional immediacy of the continuing Iranian revolution that we cannot profit from histories, no matter how cogent and complete. There is too much controversy about the events themselves. We clearly could use the psychological distance that art can provide to give us the perspective we need. Satire is one such perspective. There have already been feeble attempts to do this. In the absence of persuasive history or of competent satire, and in a time of contentious policy views and great emotion, we perhaps can turn to a successful work of art from the past to see if we can learn at least by analogy.

In the past two decades, the Swiftian image of the helpless giant pinned down by the entangling threads of Lilliputians has been used by political commentators and cartoonists to describe the plight of American power. The nature of the United States predicament, first in Vietnam and later in Iran, suggests an appropriate analogy to the circumstance of Swift's satiric hero, Lemuel Gulliver, shipwrecked and alone on an island in uncharted waters.

The principal points of relevance between an eighteenth-century satire whose moral view was intended, Swift said, "to cure the vices of mankind," and the particular policy dilemmas of the United States and Iran lie in the uses of ironic vision. The main literary devices used by Swift in *Gulliver's Travels* to illuminate the folly, cruelty, deception, destructiveness, pretensions, and corruption of mankind and nations (particularly his own) were intended to change normal perspectives and permit new angles of sharpened moral vision. By shrinking in the realm of Lilliputians, enlarging in the land of Brobdingnagians, and creating a race of talking horses in Houynymland, Swift was able to lay bare, for relatively unobstructed, culturally unencumbered rational scrutiny, the actual practices of the England of his time. In repressive societies satire in the form of cartoons, and a variety of poetic or dramatic devices, is sometimes allowed free rein, even if newspapers and public assembly are harshly controlled. In Pahlavi Iran, Towfiq's savage cartoons were published for a wide audience for years, and devastating criticism of the regime in the form of poetry was allowed despite its clear intent. Even these escape valves were shut off as the regime grew more repressive.

The willing suspension of disbelief that satire or fiction encourages in order to look at the world more clearly, is a much harder task for history. Aside from the very difficult problems of describing facts and events accurately and in proper proportion, we are confronted with conflicting analyses of what those facts or events mean, and what the men and women involved intended. Whether an action was wise or foolish, generously friendly or maliciously manipulative, is hard to determine. As in the case of the overthrow of Mosaddeq, some larger cause or purpose is often used to justify action even if it is vicious and harmful. It is difficult, if not impossible, in the present turmoil to stand aside and look at the complications of history with unbiased vision. This applies particularly to contemporary Iranian history.

I am not the only one who wishes for a writer with the eagle-like acuity of a Jonathan Swift to give a beady-eyed look at the American-Iranian dilemma. Nor do I mean to suggest that it is an impossible task for historians to sort out the distortions of point of view and come up with a faithful and proportioned account of the recent past that many of us have, in some measure, directly experienced or witnessed. However, a judicious accounting and substantial agreement will probably not be possible until passions have diminished and a few more years have passed.

In a Swiftian vein, if we were able to sustain an ironic temper we would, of course, all agree that Kermit Roosevelt's account in his book *Countercoup* of the overthrow of Dr. Mohammad Mosaddeq has found gracious acceptance among the Iranian supporters of the National Front. It would probably be no less clear that the Khomeinist factions of the clergy share the same view as Western diplomats about the sanctity of embassies, or the validity of the various international conventions that have established rules of acceptable diplomatic practice. And there is surely agreement that the purposes of the Iranian revolution are clear, and that there is undivided loyalty to these goals and confidence in all their leaders, just as there is agreement that United States policy has been clear, direct, unchanging and consistent with the constitution and the United Nations charter, and that what we have done in Iran has had universal and uncritical support.

Only in the world of imagination, and in the realms of unsullied rational thought, does this kind of clarity exist. We are actually confronted by a confusing babel of charges and recrimination, a bewildering array of new ideas, slogans, leaders, and purposes. The problems and obstacles before the United States and Iran are legion, but despite the despairing difficulties that face the two nations, every effort must be made to forge a decent relationship between the United States and Iran. The key question is how and when to begin that relationship. A second, only slightly less important, question, is whether the recent past has anything to tell us that would help to create a new relationship based upon mutual respect, shared interests, and trust.

It may seem impossible for some to conceive that a new relationship can be forged based on lofty ideals of mutual respect, shared interests, and trust; certainly, the enormities of past events have created bitterness, hate, despair, and a resultant policy rigidity. The record of the overthrow of Mosaddeq, CIA, SAVAK, military repression, political manipulation, interference in internal affairs, the corruption of individuals and groups all contribute to the elaborate mosaic of the history of United States–Iranian relations since 1945. But so does the defense of Iran by the United States against Soviet aggression in the Azerbaijan crisis, the help given by thousands of Americans and many billions of dollars of aid to better the health, education, housing, and general well being of the Iranian people. Those who were helped directly through these purposes or when earthquakes struck, a famine ravaged, or disease ran rampant have cause to remember American generosity. Tens of thousands of Iranians have studied in the United States and have brought to Iran the benefits of their learning and some of that student group, of course, were spearheads of the revolution.

Mistaken perception lies at the heart of the baffling confusions about United States–Iranian history. Our leaders mistakenly identified the fate of Iran with the shah, the student captors of the American Embassy confused some misguided aspects of United States policy with the overall goals of the United States. It is difficult enough in the clear realms of thought—in the area of logic or mathematics—to get categories straight, but in the rich brew of U.S.–Iranian history false categorical imperatives have led to fatal and cruel mistakes. The outsider, like Lemuel Gulliver in Lilliput or in the country of the Brobdingnagians, looking at the record of U.S. involvement in Iran could easily engage in dialogues about Iran that would be straight out of Jonathan Swift. The confused record of United States–Iranian relations would puzzle, amuse, and dismay the Lilliputian king or the Houyhnhnms just as much as the narrations of European politics given by Lemuel Gulliver to his strange captors.

The Iranian-American relationship is a mixed record of folly and wisdom; mean self-interest and heartfelt generosity; vicious cruelty and caring gentleness. There is betrayal and loyalty; craven behavior and nobility, on the part of both Iranians and Americans. There will be long and continuing arguments by historians about the relative ingredients of the mixtures of good and bad, but there is room on all sides for blame and criticism.

I believe that recent United States–Iranian history reads like a contemporary version of *Gulliver's Travels*. It is hard to comprehend that some of the events that have taken place have indeed happened, and are not just the satiric imaginings of a troubled moralist. Perhaps as Swift has taught us so entertainingly, if we allow ourselves to change points of view, turn assumptions on their heads, and try to see problems from opposing perspectives, we will acquire a valuable sense of humility and perhaps more important, a sense of reality; and perhaps if we escape the insanity of despair, a useful sense of shared humanity will emerge.

The Gulliver-like immobilism of United States policy in the past several years is perhaps the beginning of wisdom. The inability to do anything has forced many to ask why and what can be done about it. The search for explanations of how the United States could have found itself so helplessly pinned down in the aftermath of a revolution, by a much less powerful nation, has led to a spate of "who lost Iran" speculations and the search for scapegoats or heroes. Much more helpful are the accounts of what has happened as the course of the revolution winds on, who its leaders are, their plans, attitudes, and relationships, and the effect of the new leadership of Iran on the urban poor, the bazaari, the tribes, and the villages.

For those interested in United States policy towards Iran, the period of immobilism in the recent past and its accompanying internal emotional fervor has been matched in Iran by the stages of revolutionary fervor identified decades ago by Crane Brinton. Perhaps we are now witnessing the stage of consolidation after rather violent periods of internal struggles for power and influence. Ayatollah Khomeini still rides above the storm of the revolution he led, but the question of who or what group will succeed him remains.

Prophecy is a gift reserved for a specially privileged breed, usually unheeded like Cassandra, even if possessed of foreknowledge, and certainly resented when prophecies come true. I have no predictions to make—only guesses. Most observers of Iran agree that it seems likely that as long as Khomeini lives, the present pattern of rule will continue. Khomeini, although the greatest power in Iran, does not rule like his predecessor, Shah Mohammad Reza Pahlavi. He is far less directly involved. Decisions for the most part are made by a clique of his followers, except when problems are brought to him or he decides for unpredictable reasons to act or make a pronouncement.

The clerical infrastructure, the local religious courts, the network of komitehs and local law enforcers such as the pasdaran have not acted with consistency, cohesion, or under clearly defined rules or guidelines from the top. When Khomeini leaves the scene, it is very possible, even probable, that there will be serious challenges to the present system from those who are not now in the clerical government. It is likely, too, that there will also be a struggle for power and control from various factions within the governing cliques of mollas.

With the sweeping away of the monarchical past and the government structures of the Pahlavi dynasty, one element has remained—and has in fact been strengthened—the idea of the constitution, particularly the 1906 Constitution before it was weakened by later amendments imposed by the Pahlavis. The Khomeini revolution of 1979 is only the latest stage of the Iranian search for cultural equilibrium that began at the end of the nineteenth century. The purity and glory that Iranians saw in the first few months of the Khomeini-led revolution is matched in the Iranian historical memory by the 1906 constitutional movement. In fact, the legitimacy of any government in Iran requires the acceptance and embracing of the framework of ideas of the Constitution of 1906. The cleric-dominated constitutional convention of 1979 found itself enmeshed in an historical context that it could not escape. The idea of constitutionalism—that is, a body of national principle, ethics, and law—is shared by all Iranian political groups. Even the quarreling and divided exile groups are united in their support for a return to the Constitution of 1906 as a place to begin the search for governmental legitimacy. The present Khomeini constitution, of course, departs from the 1906 Constitution in important respects, but even these radical changes lie within the original framework of the 1906 document. In this sense, the Khomeini revolution is a conservative one, and must be viewed as a stage in a large revolutionary movement rather than the whole of the revolution. The twisting path of the Iranian revolution continues and we can expect at least one and perhaps several stages of reactions in the search for a national balance acceptable to the many diverse cultural and political groups that make up Iran.

Because we can expect new stages of political activity, and the certainty that new political alignments will emerge, the United States should make every effort to try to understand what those new alignments are likely to be. Certainly, the present rigidities of clerical rule, compared by some to Savonarola's Florence, will give way to a more open, more securely oriented Iranian government. This more secular Iranian government, like all of its predecessors, will have to base such legitimacy as it may have on the heritage of constitutionalism.

The strong belief among a number of important political groups in the validity of democratic constitutional rule provides a natural basis for a relationship with Iran. The key principles: the acceptance of a pluralistic society made up of many diverse ethnic groups, the professions, the bazaari, the intellectuals, the mollas, the villagers, regional and provincial interests, tribes, and minorities, all of whom have a stake in shared power restrained by the rule of law. The United States should, if the path of events so leads, if asked, and if assistance can be given in legitimate ways, seek to support groups in Iran that uphold these values of democratic constitutionalism.

However, the enormity of the actions taken by the United States in 1953 to assist in the overthrow of the Mosaddeq government, and its complicity in the creation and maintenance of repressive security forces cannot be dismissed by any Iranian political group, not even those groups who believe a closer relationship with the United States is necessary and desirable. These acts did take place, and as we all know, they have helped destroy the good will created by the many generous acts by American individuals, groups, and the American government. In retrospect, our geopolitical concerns about Soviet intentions distorted our perception of Iran, and poisoned what should have continued to be a friendly relationship. While the United States must carry that historical burden, it has, nonetheless, the capacity to learn from mistakes of the past to carry out a more sensible, forthright policy based on mutual trust and respect.

Some students of revolutions, particularly of the French Revolution, are of the view that a strong military leader, a Bonaparte perhaps, will emerge out of a possible post-Khomeini turmoil to establish civil order and to create a new government. The military's role in the war against the Iraqi invasion has given it a legitimacy it never had under the previous regime. The names of various military leaders of the war against Iraq are being mentioned as future heads of government as are those of former generals and colonels now in exile. On the other hand, despite prediction to the contrary, the Islamic Republican Party has managed to maintain considerable popular support and continues to strengthen its hold on the ministries and other organs of government. While there is no certainty that turmoil will in fact occur when Khomeini leaves the scene, the disputes between the various factions of the clergy over the question of how involved in government the clergy should be are already pronounced: it is by no means clear that after Khomeini's departure the clergy will choose to remain so active in the day-to-day functioning of government as they now are. The future roles of the remnants of the Mojahedin and the

Fedayan or the Soviet-supported Tudeh are further uncertainties. It is also possible that the descendents of the old constitutionalist groupings could rise up phoenix-like in the struggle for power.

Where do all these uncertainties place the United States, presently in a hands-off state of immobilism? Should we have any relationships with Iran? How do we begin? What should the nature of the relationship be?

There is very little optimism under present circumstances that there will be any departure from the active hostility of the Khomeini regime to the United States. The United States should continue to try to have normal diplomatic relations with any government that is in power in Iran, because it is in the interest of both Iran and the United States and all the Western democracies. In primitive geopolitical terms, Iran needs the United States as a counterweight to pressures from the Soviet Union which are always present. Further, for any government in Iran to have an independent foreign policy, the United States and the Soviet Union must be in equipoise. There is a necessary mutually beneficial commercial link between the two countries primarily through the sale of oil. The United States' products and technology are needed by Iran, and are vital to its reconstruction, its future growth and development.

Under present circumstances it is likely that commercial ties will come before diplomatic relations begin. In fact, such links are already evident. The sale of military hardware, oil in the spot market, and the settlement of claims now under way, appear to be the crude beginnings of a renewed commercial relationship.

The restoration of formal relations between our two nations is a much more difficult matter. Even though the Khomeini regime has refused to have any relations with America, the United States approach should be to continue to declare openly the desire to have a bilateral relationship based on mutual respect for each other's interests and cultural differences. It is important to emphasize that we should be open and direct and avoid any temptation to establish clandestine arrangements with any group or faction. We should, of course, try to know and to understand as much as possible about the political movements in Iran, but we have to recognize that the open hand of friendship has yet to be grasped by the present government of Iran, nor is it likely to be, and that the memory of United States manipulative efforts in Iran is clear to all Iranian political groups even those who favor close ties to the United States.

Until Khomeini leaves the scene it is unlikely that there will be a shift in political power towards government dominated by secular elements, but even now commercial interests within Iran, in the bazaar and elsewhere, are beginning to press for more ties with the outside world including the United States. The Iranian social structure is a diverse, rich mixture of groups, cultures, and traditions that far exceeds the bounds that the present clericalism of Iran thus far has allowed. It is this cultural richness and diversity that has contributed so much to other civilizations and that will by the sheer weight of its historical past require a change in Iran's present international behavior. Periods of xenophobia are a part of the pattern of the continuing Iranian revolution. Xenophobia and internal turbulence seem to go together. With the prospect of a successful end to the war with Iraq, there is, however, some reason to believe that Iran will once again seek to achieve better relations with other nations including the United States.

The key question is how long the xenophobic, clerically dominated phase will last, and whether historically dominant secular patterns will reassert themselves. If the examples of history offer any answers, it is likely that this violent, turbulent, and authoritarian phase of the revolution will moderate. It is also unfortunately likely that there will be a struggle for power by contending forces when Khomeini leaves the scene. It is at that point that undoubtedly the United States will be asked by some of the contending forces for assistance. One can only hope that the United States government is sufficiently sensitive to the interplay of Iranian politics to help—if it chooses to help—in constructive ways.

There is little doubt that if the opportunity arises, the Soviet Union will actively support Tudeh Party efforts and groups on the extreme left of the Iranian political spectrum. For that reason alone, it will not be possible for the United States to remain in a state of immobilism. Under such circumstances, if the United States does decide to become involved, it should be in an open and direct way and in support of groups that favor democratic constitutionalism.

The extreme clerical right and the Soviet supported Tudeh and the extreme left are hostile to any efforts to restore close relations between Iran and the United States. These authoritarian extremes are also inherently opposed to the broad pluralism explicit in the 1906 constitutional heritage, even though these extreme groups of the right and the left have been forced by the Iranian historical context to accept the framework of constitutionalism. Their actual authoritarian behavior has been antithetical to the development of any pluralistic democracy for reasons which are doctrinally expressed in their writings and actions. The American interest, if it chooses to be involved at all, would be best served by the support of groups which are striving to achieve the fulfillment of the constitutional vision begun in revolution at the end of the nineteenth century, which rose again in the Mosaddeq period, and most recently in the years of violence, culminating in the overthrow of the authoritarian regime of the shah.

In the years that have passed since this conference on the Iranian Revolution and the Islamic Republic was held, the Khomeini regime has strengthened its hold on the government of Iran. At the same time, the continuing stalemate of the Iran-Iraq war with its attendant brutality, horrific loss of life, and destructive inconclusiveness has diminished the seemingly magical power of Khomeini's personal ideological and religious appeal. This is not to say that the emergence of a charismatic leader, religious or secular, who can convince the masses that a fundamental change is necessary, cannot occur again. On the contrary, the kind of fundamentalism evident in the months after the shah was swept from power by the desire and concerted efforts of almost all of the Iranian people, is still a force that can erupt again in Iran.

While the present expression of fundamentalism in Iran, and perhaps elsewhere in the Middle East, is religious in form, and the most forceful and appealing leaders of the Iranian masses are, at the moment, clerics, the roots of fundamentalism go beyond religion. The fundamental desire for a just society, for fair governance at all levels, as indicated from relations between governments, between the state and the individual and family, and personal relationships on a basis of equity and moral decency was clearly and powerfully expressed in the Iranian revolution. The shah's regime was violently uprooted because it was perceived by the Iranian people as rotten and corrupt, and because it failed to meet those fundamental desires. It was destroyed because it aroused the expectations that such desires for a better life could in fact become realities. The impact of tremendous new wealth, the burgeoning economy, better health, housing, education, communication, all served to awaken hopes for a fair and decent society free of corruption in which all would have some share.

Khomeini, on reflection, seems to have offered, at least for a time, both a religious vision and a practical means to achieve those aroused desires. He appealed both to religious and nationalistic impulses and in his person exemplified better than any other leader of 1979, secular or religious, a constancy of resistance to the shah's rule, a regime that was increasingly perceived by all levels of Iranian society as standing in the way of achieving those aspirations for a just and broadly benevolent government.

Almost all Iranians attest to the universal sense of national purity at the moment of the shah's overthrow. Those lofty feelings, those high desires and aspirations which fueled the flames of revolution that destroyed the shah's regime set a standard impossible for Khomeini, or perhaps any ruler, to meet. Almost immediately after Khomeini and the Revolutionary Council rose to leadership, serious criticism emerged lamenting how the revolution was "stolen" by the clerics from the Iranian people and from other groups who had resisted the shah, or how the repressive regime of the shah was replaced by yet another authoritarian regime that is even more repressive. Without question the Khomeini government has lost the aura of purity ascribed to it by so many Iranians, but it has not lost its grip on the instruments of power.

As some scholars have noted, the Khomeini regime has created a parallel system of government which functions side by side with governmental entities and a bureaucracy that existed before. As Shaul Bakhash has written so cogently in his recent book, *The Reign of the Ayatollahs:* "Alongside the state apparatus, the regime created an array of new organizations. These not only duplicated or usurped the functions of the existing bureaucracy; they also constituted a formidable machinery for patronage, mass mobilization, ideological education and a many faceted repression."[1]

The *pasdaran* constitute a second army which operates along with, and sometimes independently of, the regular army. The komitehs function in the same areas as the established police, while Revolutionary Courts make judgments on matters in the jurisdiction of still-existing civil courts. The civil service and new revolutionary organizations vie for a governing role existing "side by side in an uneasy symbiosis." In essence, the regime has produced a new bureaucracy which owes its position to the revolution.

The key issues affecting the future government of Iran are whether integration of the two structures will take place soon enough to prevent dissatisfaction among large segments of the population because the promises of economic improvement and political justice made by the Khomeini regime remain unfulfilled, and whether continued repression and propaganda as the main instruments of control will remain effective.[2]

I am among those who believe that Iran has been in a revolutionary state since the end of the nineteenth century, and that the Khomeini regime is only the latest phase of a continuing struggle by the Iranian people to find a stable national equilibrium. What is significant about the present phase of the continuing Iranian revolution is the spread of political involvement to the entire society: the masses are now aware, politicized, and involved.

The next and possibly final phases of the Iranian revolution will begin when Ayatollah Khomeini leaves the scene. But the value system of the new Iranian society has already been defined and tested by the swings of experiment, reaction, and counterreaction during the major phases of the continuing revolution.

What values have emerged from the experience of the successive upheavals of the Constitutional Movement of 1905–1906, the Reza Shah dictatorship, the era of Mossadeq nationalism, the absolute monarchy of

Mohammad Reza Pahlavi, and the clerical rule of Khomeini's Islamic Republic? Basic individual and family relationships and values have remained unchanged, while social structures, public codes of expression, demeanor, and dress have undergone great swings of change. After eighty-five years, there seems to have been little change in Iranian notions of truth, equity, fairness, kindness, mercy, brutality, piety, faith, or perfidy. The ideals remain, although the institutional means to carry out these ideals have in every phase of the continuing revolution fallen far short of expectation.

In basic business, commercial, and banking practices throughout the period, although physical changes have occurred, the bazaar world has changed the least and has been the least affected by swings of politics and ideology. Western style banks, industries, and businesses have been more seriously affected as legal and commercial codes have alternated between Western and Islamic models.

In many ways the quality of village life has changed and improved, particularly in the areas of health, education, and communications. But basic village structures have been adversely affected by shifting changes in ownership and land tenure patterns caused by successive land distribution schemes and reactions to them.

The most profound changes that have taken place during the twentieth century in Iran have been in Tehran and to a lesser extent in the other major cities of Isfahan, Tabriz, and Mashhad. The tremendous growth of the cities, which has been largely unplanned and uncontrolled, has created great physical, political, economic, social, emotional, and psychological problems for all city dwellers—particularly for the poor, but also the rich. The harsh difficulties of Tehran city life have caused the old courtesies and civilities which made urban life tolerable virtually to disappear.

The proper degree of religious involvement in what was formerly regarded as secular life is still very much at issue. The argument about the proper balance is a cause of contention in the religious establishment as well as in the world outside the mosques. The role of the faqih has aroused great controversy for theological reasons among the contending ayatollahs as well as in the ranks of secular political theorists. The clerics now dominate the government of Iran, but it is highly unlikely that clerical rule will continue in the long run. Yet the strength of religion in Iran so powerfully expressed at several stages in the last eighty-five years—in 1906, in the Mosaddeq period, and most forcefully in the Khomeini revolution—is evidence enough to believe that religious factors will remain important influences in the eventual Iranian national equilibrium.

Iran has rejected absolute monarchical rule; it has experimented twice with constitutional monarchs; it has, however, accepted the value and validity of a framework of governance by constitution. All of the regimes that have risen and fallen in the twentieth century have attempted to legitimate their regimes by constitutions. The idea of constitutionalism, government limited and empowered by a prescribed system of laws, is now a rooted part of the new Iranian national identity. The nature of the laws within a constitution is still very much at issue as the controversy over the role of the faqih indicates. But it is within the scope of the various constitutional frameworks that Iran has already experienced that the final stage of revolution will finally rest. There are considerable differences between the visions of the 1905–1906 constitutionalists, the constitutional monarchists, the Mosaddeqists, and the followers of Khomeini, and these differences suggest that the long-term balance has yet to be found.

From the time of the Constitutional Movement of 1905–1906 and even earlier, a constant theme sounded by Iranian political leaders, whether secular or religious, has been to follow policies which would free the country from foreign domination of any kind. The experience of occupation, partition, war, and exploitation has fostered xenophobia in its most extreme forms, and also a constant effort to balance great contending powers against one another. All of the rulers in the modern era have sought to do this: the Qajars, the Pahlavis, Mosaddeq, and now Khomeini. It is likely that future relationsips with the outside world, even in a post-Khomeini regime, will be designed to prevent domination and undue influence from any quarter.

As indicated earlier, it is likely, therefore, that Iranian foreign policy for a long time to come will attempt to offset the Soviet Union and the United States. The United States will never again have the influence it enjoyed in the period between 1945 and 1979. As bad as relations presently are between the United States and Iran, there is still every reason to expect that relations will be restored, but when they are it will be on a formal and wary basis. Ties between the two countries will be strengthened gradually over time by increased trade, the sale of oil and the natural consequences of travel to the United States for commercial reasons, for study, and for advanced training.

It is also reasonable to expect that Iran's relationship with its neighbors to the east and west and with the Gulf States will moderate as Iran enters the next phases of its turbulent search for political equilibrium. The extent of openness to the outside world will depend in large measure on the degree of peace, stability and popular acceptance that the Iranian government achieves in Iran itself. At the present time none of these three factors has been assured.

NOTES

1. Shaul Bakhash, *The Reign of the Ayatollahs* (New York, Basic Books, 1984), p. 243.

2. Ibid., pp. 245–246.

THE ISLAMIC REPUBLIC and the SOVIET UNION

Muriel Atkin

IN THE WAKE of the Iranian revolution, the leadership of the Islamic Republic and the Soviet Union strove to reestablish the kind of guarded accommodation that had been achieved under the monarchy. In the short run this was accomplished, not because of any fundamentally similar approach to politics by the two sides but rather because of the desire of each to use the other to promote certain objectives. The more time passed following the revolution, the more the grounds for accord were overshadowed by the two countries' conflict of interest over other objectives. What successive groups of revolutionary Iran's leaders have sought from the Soviet Union is diplomatic, economic, and, to a lesser degree, military support against powers Iran opposed, above all the United States and, since 1980, Iraq. The underlying principle of using the northern neighbor for one's own ends has been practiced intermittently by various Iranian public figures since the eighteenth century. The Soviet objective was at least to have a government with which it could deal in Iran. That is, one which did not emphasize hostility towards the Soviet Union and which was willing to allow a certain amount of contact between the two countries in the form of correct diplomatic relations, trade and development aid, and cultural exchanges—in other words, the situation that existed during the last fifteen years of the monarchy. If there should be additional gains, in such areas as greater leeway for leftist groups, especially the pro-Soviet communists, the Tudeh Party, economic reforms directed against large privately owned enterprises, and a foreign policy stance that coincided to a considerable degree with the Soviet Union's, that would be a welcome bonus.

Both Tehran and Moscow were satisfied most with the benefits they derived from each other between late 1979 and early 1982. Even then there were some areas of discord, particularly the quest for political dominance by the clerical advocates of an Islamic republic and their lay allies, the Soviet invasion of Afghanistan, and Soviet neutrality in the Iran-Iraq War. The war proved to have a crucial effect on Soviet-Iranian relations as the Soviets increased their support for Iraq during 1982, when Iranian troops drove most of the Iraqi forces from Iranian soil and then carried the war into Iraq. The mutual recriminations between Tehran and Moscow on this issue created a climate in which all the other disagreements between them assumed new importance. Relations between them continued to deteriorate, symbolized most dramatically by the suppression of the Tudeh Party in 1983, amid accusations that its members spied for the Soviet Union and repeatedly betrayed Iranian national interests. Yet there are still hints of the earlier spirit of accommodation, as both governments maintain an interest in keeping the lines of communication open.

Despite the major problems of Soviet-Iranian relations, Moscow shows no signs of regret that the revolution of 1978–79 occurred. Soviet rhetoric has repeatedly linked that revolution with other revolutions which they welcome, especially in Ethiopia and Afghanistan.[1]

The main reason for this positive Soviet assessment is that the revolution of 1978–79 produced the utter collapse of Iranian-American relations. The two epithets which the Soviets consistently apply to the revolution are "anti-monarchical" and "anti-imperialist." By Soviet reckoning, the United States is the leading imperialist power. While hostility toward the United States was internally generated, Soviet broadcasts to Iran in Persian and other public statements have been designed to intensify this attitude. The predominant theme since 1979 has been that the United States would use every means at its disposal, including military force, to destroy the revolution, and restore the monarchy. The Soviet media have carried alarming reports about menacing United States naval activities in the Indian Ocean and described the American embassy in Tehran as a base of espionage and subversion directed against the new order. The hostage crisis was at the time and in restrospect portrayed sympathetically in Soviet media. From the Soviet perspective, that crisis was a double asset. It brought down the moderate Bazargan government and acutely embarrassed the United States. The Soviets deemed Iran's demands against the United States legitimate. Every American move in the crisis was used to support the Soviet argument about Washington's counter-revolutionary intentions. The April 1980 raid aimed at freeing the hostages and the development of a rapid deployment force were cited as prime examples of America's hostility towards the new regime in Tehran. In 1984, the Soviets published a book by one of their leading commentators on contemporary

Iranian politics, S.L. Agaev, devoted to a negative portrayal of United States policy throughout the hostage crisis.[2]

Moscow has repeatedly contrasted the dismal state of Iranian-American relations with what it portrays as its own supportive policy toward Iran ever since the birth of the Soviet regime. The most important recent event, in this interpretation, was Leonid Brezhnev's declaration on November 19, 1979 that any foreign intervention in Iran would be considered a threat to Soviet security because of the two countries' long common border. Left unstated was the implication that the Soviet Union could use such a perceived threat to invoke the 1921 Soviet-Iranian treaty (subsequently repudiated by the Islamic Republican government) as a justification for sending troops into Iran. In Soviet sources, Brezhnev's declaration is portrayed as the deterrent that has shielded Iran from American aggression.[3]

While some influential figures in post-revolutionary Iran were reputed to be more interested than others in dealing with the Soviet Union when relations between the two countries were at their best, even then many of them were not impressed with their northern neighbor's contribution to the success of the Islamic Revolution. All who were prominent in the new regime (except for the prime minister of the provisional government, Mehdi Bazargan) made criticism of the United States a prominent part of their rhetoric for a variety of reasons, including that it would have been politically ruinous not to do so. However, criticism of the Soviet Union and communism have also been standard themes since the spring of 1979. Another oft-repeated message links the Soviet Union and the United States as the "two superpowers," both of which are imperialist and have been defied by Iran. The Islamic Republicans' slogan of "neither East nor West" is the shorthand expression of this view.[4]

Although Moscow was slow to realize the extent of the clergy's influence or the rallying power of Shi'i Islamic beliefs as the revolution developed during 1978, once it reconsidered its interpretation under the pressure of events, it had little practical alternative to a declaration of support for Ayatollah Khomeini and the Islamic Republic if it hoped to have any prospect of reaching an accommodation with the new regime in Iran. While Khomeini was perceived as cool towards the left, he was also credited with impeccably anti-American credentials.[5] The apparent incongruity of a state with an avowedly atheist ideology supporting an advocate of the primacy of religious values in political affairs did not trouble Moscow unduly. Since the fall of Prime Minister Mohammad Mosaddeq in 1953, the Soviet Union concluded that it missed an excellent opportunity to advance its interests in Iran because it had failed to give him adequate support through the Tudeh Party. The lesson Moscow learned was not to miss another such opportunity to support a staunch nationalist because of a preoccupation with ideological purity.[6]

The Tudeh Party was far too weak to be a major force in politics on its own. A generation of repressive measures directed against it had done considerable damage. By the time the Islamic Revolution opened the prospect of new opportunities, its leaders were men of advanced years, veterans of political struggles long past, who had spent some two decades or more in exile in Eastern Europe. No doubt the ability to function legally or semi-legally under the new regime enabled the Tudeh to improve its position in relative terms but not, as matters developed, to transform it. The Tudeh's greatest weakness, even while it was legal, was the widely held perception in Iran that the Tudeh was a Soviet puppet. It traditionally drew much of its support from the educated and from industrial workers. However, since the 1970s it faced serious competition from other parties for the support of the same constituency. By its own admission, it had little success recruiting among workers. The politically active young have usually preferred rival parties. In any event, the closing of universities and purges of leftists from their staffs deprived it of its main arenas for recruitment. Since before the revolution, the Tudeh was interested in the revolutionary potential of the peasants but was unable to make headway among them before it was crushed in 1983. The majlis elections of 1980 showed the Tudeh finishing a weak third among the parties on the left, behind the Mojahedin-e Khalq and the Fedayan-e Khalq.

The Tudeh's support for Ayatollah Khomeini undercut whatever possibility there might have been for the party to establish a distinctive identity with broadened appeal but temporarily saved it from the repression directed against other, unreconciled leftists and allowed such Tudeh members and sympathizers to occupy a number of civilian and military positions. Such infiltration must have been of limited value since the Tudeh proved unable either to push the government towards the policies it advocated (be it radical economic reforms or a changed stance toward Iraq and Afghanistan) or to prevent the suppression of the party in 1983. After the wave of arrests of Tudeh members, an official Iranian source claimed that the party's infiltration of the military and security forces was small scale, involving only about two hundred people.[7] The only policy uniquely the Tudeh's proved to be no asset: support for the Soviet Union in all things, including the invasion of Afghanistan.

In recognition of its weakness (and Soviet policy), the Tudeh also sought alliances with other leftist groups. In the early post-revolutionary period, it wooed the Mojahedin, the largest leftist group, only to be rebuffed. From that point until the Tudeh itself was in desperate straits, it approved of the Islamic Republicans' war against the Mojahedin and may have lent assistance.[8] Unable to conclude an alliance with the Mojahedin, it made one instead with the self-styled "majority" faction of the now divided Fedayan, whose members the Tudeh's leader had previously denounced as "infantile leftists."[9] The Fedayan was begun in the 1960s by young Marxists disenchanted with what they saw as the Tudeh's unwillingness to engage in revolutionary activity. In the context of the new opportunities created by the Iranian Revolution, the Majority Fedayan did not merely ally itself with the Tudeh but merged with it. By that time the Fedayan were already feeling the effects of the government's repression. Their union with the Tudeh brought the latter increased numbers and may in the long term provide a stronger base for further growth, but in the shorter term did not improve the Tudeh's fortunes.

By far the brightest area in relations between the Islamic Republic and the Soviet Union has been economic—development aid and trade. For the new regime in Iran the central issue was to diversify economic relations, especially because it was no longer desirable or possible for the United States to continue to occupy a position of any importance. For the Soviet Union the crucial consideration was that economic relations were not merely economic in significance. Rather, such dealings provided yet another means for contact between countries and opportunities to build influence, regardless of the state of expressly political relations. Moscow has believed throughout that any contact that can be obtained with Iran is desirable in itself and that economics is the sphere in which agreements are the most feasible.[10] At the same time, economic disputes should not be allowed to interfere with otherwise acceptable political relations or the pursuit of economic cooperation in general. That is why the drop in natural gas deliveries to the Soviet Union in the winter of 1978–79, and their termination in 1980 when Moscow refused to pay the higher price demanded by the new regime in Tehran, had no wider implications in relations between the two governments.

Soviet-Iranian trade increased dramatically over what it had been before the revolution, reaching a peak in 1981. By that time exports from the Soviet Union and other CMEA (Council for Mutual Economic Assistance) countries to Iran rose to about 15 percent of Iran's total imports. The total value of Soviet-Iranian trade in both directions declined about 13 percent in 1982, and rose some 22 percent in 1983, while political relations reached a new low.[11]

In 1983, the Islamic Republic for the first time surpassed Iraq in the total value of its trade with the Soviet Union (exclusive of military items, which are not included in published statistics) but still ranks behind Japan, India, Libya, and Argentina among non-Communist trading partners of the Soviet Union in Asia, Africa, and Latin America.[12] Despite the relative increase in Soviet-Iran trade, it is still far from the dominant element in Iran's foreign economic relations. The truly spectacular increase has come in trade with Turkey, which increased just under ten-fold between 1978 and 1983. Iran continues to trade extensively with Japan, West Germany, Italy, Great Britain, India, Pakistan, Singapore, and a number of other countries, including several CMEA members besides the Soviet Union.[13]

Most of the economic agreements made by the Islamic Republic and the Soviet Union for such things as electrical generating facilities, dams, grain silos, technical training, and the expansion of the big Isfahan steel mill are continuations of projects begun during the monarchy. Among the important post-1979 developments are the improvement of transportation links between northern Iran and transportation hubs on the Soviet side of the border and joint projects for exploiting border rivers for irrigation and, in some cases, hydroelectric power. In both these areas, some projects have been completed and others are under discussion.[14] Although Iran halted natural gas sales to the Soviet Union, it began selling oil.

Iran has sometimes balanced economic relations with the Soviet Union with agreements in related areas with non-Soviet bloc countries. For example, the Soviets were responsible for a number of development projects in Iranian Azerbaijan, including the electrification of the existing rail line from Tabriz to the Trans-Caucasian border and training some of the railway workers. However, Iran bought some of the new locomotives for the line from Sweden, which would also train some railway workers. The showpiece of Soviet development projects in Iran is the steel mill at Isfahan (begun under the monarchy and expanded since). Tehran has also contracted with an Italian and a Japanese company to set up another steel mill near Isfahan.[15]

Among the most significant of the economic agreements made since the Iranian revolution is that of 1980 according Iran transit trade privileges in the Soviet Union and vice versa. This, too, follows a policy established by the shah in 1957. The volume of trade goods bound for Iran by this route tripled between 1978 and 1981 and has remained strong since then, although the sheer volume of traffic has far exceeded the capacity of the Iranian transportation system, resulting in serious delays. The goods which are shipped to Iran by this route come not only from Soviet bloc countries but also from major capitalist states, notably Japan and West Germany. While the relative importance of this trade route has increased by comparison with before the revolution, much more of Iran's trade still travels by other routes, the ports on the southern coast (where additional facilities are being developed) and the overland link to Tur-key.[16]

Even while relations between the Islamic Republic and the Soviet Union were at their best there were a number of points of friction regard-ing Iran's domestic and foreign policy. These problems have retained their importance and in some cases grown considerably more serious with the passage of time. There are three main domestic problem areas: the Islamic Republic's hostility towards leftist parties; its unwillingness to make extensive anti-capitalist reforms; and Soviet interest in ethnic minorities' disputes with the Tehran government. Beginning with the first months of the new regime's existence, when the political power balance was as yet unsettled, there were elements among the conservative Islamic activists who were openly hostile to the Tudeh Party, harassing its members and on occasion occupying party offices.[17] In August 1979 the Provisional Gov-ernment tried to curb what it saw as a challenge to its authority from the left and briefly proscribed the Mojahedin-e Khalq, Fedayan-e Khalq, and the Tudeh (including their publications). However Prime Minister Ba-zargan's government was unable to enforce this policy even before it was essentially forced out of office on the heels of the seizure of the American embassy that November. The Tudeh's newspaper, along with the publica-tions of other groups of varying orientations opposed to the dominance of the Islamic Republican Party (IRP), was banned again for a time beginning in June 1981.[18]

Although Iran's revolutionary regime nationalized some large enterprises, which the Soviets took as a positive sign of movement towards a non-capitalist economic system, further reforms along those lines were discussed but not made. A major disappointment from Moscow's point of view was the failure to carry out land redistribution, which offered the double political attraction of weakening the large landowners, who are presumably conservative, and raising the possibility that Iran's large peas-antry would become radicalized and more susceptible to Tudeh pros-elytizing.

There are two long-standing considerations which underlie Soviet involvement in disputes between Iran's central government and its ethnic minorities. Whenever the central government is weakened, the provinces, including those with concentrations of ethnic minorities, have tradi-tionally sought greater autonomy. When there are problems in Moscow's relations with Tehran, the former shows interest in ethnic minorities' grievances, at the very least as a way of applying pressure on Tehran. For most of the period from 1979 until 1983 the low-keyed Soviet approach towards Iran's ethnic minorities reflected the working relationship be-tween the two states. The general line was that the minorities had a right to autonomy but that Ayatollah Khomeini was sensitive to this issue and should be given a chance to work out a settlement. The source of the minorities' grievances, according to this argument, was the monarchy's oppression, under which the Persians also suffered. Thus the revolution, by ousting the shah, had already solved the basic problem. If the minorities held uncompromisingly to their demands that would only weaken the revolution and thus play into the hands of the counter-revolutionaries.[19]

Moreover, the Soviets had doubts about the potential for nationalism among Iran's ethnic minorities. This reflected both the Soviets' limited ability to exert influence among some of the ethnic groups and the belief that social and economic changes in the last fifteen years of the monarchy had some assimilationist consequences. The groups least affected by those changes were also believed not to have reached the stage of social evolution which favors the development of a nationalist outlook. The result of these pragmatic and theoretical considerations was that the Soviets were quite interested in nationalism among Azerbaijanis and Kurds but only infrequently among Turkmens, Baluchis, or Arabs.[20]

During 1979, Moscow tried to work out an alliance with the Kurdish Democratic Party of Iran (KDP), some of whose leaders had lived in exile in Eastern Europe before the revolution. However, Kurdish politics in general were fragmented, including within the KDP. While the Soviets' overtures found some response, the dominant faction of the KDP was not interested because it remained at odds with the Tehran government over Kurdish autonomy at a time when Moscow's higher priority was good relations with Tehran.[21]

The Azerbaijanis are the Iranian national minority to whom the Soviet Union has devoted the greatest attention, even though they have not been fighting the central government for years, unlike the Kurdish nationalists. Soviet sources do not refer to Iranian Azerbaijan or to the provinces of East and West Azerbaijan but rather to "Southern Azerbaijan" stressing its kinship with the Azerbaijan S.S.R. (which has a smaller population). The Soviet emphasis has been on encouragement for an Azerbaijani linguistic and cultural revival once the monarchy's controls against such developments were swept away. The Azerbaijan S.S.R. has been used as a model and means of influence on co-ethnics south of the border.[22] The Azerbaijan Democratic Party (ADP) also resumed its separate identity. This communist party was founded in 1945 but was subsumed under the Tudeh in 1960. It was predominantly Azerbaijani, as opposed to the Persian-dominated Tudeh. The apparent intent of Soviet attempts to influence Iranian Azerbaijanis has been to use them to affect the central as well as provincial governments to follow policies which the Soviets favored.

Some Soviet Azerbaijani literary figures, especially veterans of the Azerbaijan Republic of 1945–46, have written about the unity of the two Azerbaijans.[23] However, that is for domestic consumption. As long as relations between Moscow and Tehran were acceptable to the former, Soviet international broadcasts in Azerbaijani treated the Tehran government favorably.[24] Haidar Aliev, first secretary of the Communist Party in the Azerbaijan S.S.R. for thirteen years, until his promotion to first deputy premier of the Soviet Union in 1982, has not publicly advocated the union of the two Azerbaijans. Furthermore, there is the question of the extent to which the Iranian Azerbaijanis are receptive to Soviet influence. While they may be dissatisfied because the new regime in Tehran is as unsympathetic to the use of the Azerbaijani language as was the old, that does not mean they see the ADP or the Azerbaijan S.S.R. as the alternative. At least until the Islamic Republicans took steps to break his political power, Ayatollah Mohammad Kazem Shariatmadari, himself an Azerbaijani, had a much stronger following in Iranian Azerbaijan than the ADP.[25] Although a critic of various aspects of the new regime, he focused on the political controversies in the central government rather than preaching Azerbaijani separatism. In addition to the alienation from the center which Azerbaijanis may feel for cultural reasons, the deep roots of Shi'ism in Azerbaijan produce a countervailing pull towards the center. Symbolic of this is the presence of several Azerbaijani ulama among the influential figures of the Islamic Republic. These include Ayatollahs Ali Meshkini and Abdol-Karim Musavi Ardabili, two of the most powerful clerics in the Islamic Republic, and Ayatollah Sadeq Khalkhali, a leading figure in the Islamic Republic's drive to destroy all opponents.

Among the points of Soviet-Iranian friction in international affairs, the existence of a communist regime in Afghanistan and the Soviet invasion of that country were sufficiently serious problems to be the subject of many public pronouncements in Tehran and Moscow but not so serious as to cause either government to abandon the perceived benefits of their accommodation in other areas. All the different factions that have controlled Iran's post-revolutionary government have denounced the communist regime in Kabul and the Soviet invasion begun in December 1979. The Islamic Republic has given a modest amount of support to the anti-communist guerrillas. Ayatollah Khomeini likened the Afghan guerrillas' struggle to the anti-Pahlavi, anti-American struggle in Iran and proclaimed the Afghan guerrillas similarly victorious. At a time when Soviet-Iranian relations were still relatively good, Foreign Minister Ali Akbar

Velayati described the Soviet presence in Afghanistan as the main obstacle to better Soviet-Iranian relations. There are some indications that the Soviet invasion of Afghanistan may have weakened support for the Tudeh in Iran. The Soviet response to Iranian criticism was to argue that the revolutions in Iran and Afghanistan have much in common, being both popular and anti-imperialist.[26]

The war between Iran and Iraq proved to be a much more serious threat to the Soviet-Iranian accommodation. This conflict was naturally a greater concern to Iran's leaders than the one in Afghanistan since Iran was itself a combatant in this war. Iran and the Soviet Union agreed in blaming the war on American machinations. However, that is where the agreement ended. Iran's leaders wanted Soviet diplomatic support and perhaps military supplies both while it was on the defensive and later when it took the offensive. The elimination of the United States as a source of military hardware and the disruption of the Iranian armed forces by the revolution put Iran in desperate need of military imports once Iraq invaded. Tehran sought to buy what it needed from anyone who was willing to sell. This may have included the Soviet Union, certainly North Korea, which became Iran's main source of supply, and Israel, whose existence the new regime in Tehran condemned.[27]

From Moscow's perspective, the Iran-Iraq War could well leave the Soviet Union a loser regardless of which side wins the fighting. Moscow sought a working relationship with both countries and did not want to have to choose one over the other. Eventually the dilemma the Soviets faced here was compared to the setback it encountered when it tried unsuccessfully to maintain good relations with both Ethiopia and Somalia despite their territorial dispute and wound up being repudiated by Somalia for that reason. Moreover, there was the danger that the insecurities raised by the war could give the United States an opportunity to bolster its influence in the Gulf and thus undo some of the damage resulting from the Iranian revolution.[28]

The solution Moscow hoped for was based on two tactics. It repeatedly urged the combatants to cease fighting and resolve their differences through negotiations and at the same time favored whichever combatant was on the defensive. Thus, while Iraq was on the offensive, the Soviet Union withheld direct arms shipments to it while bolstering relations with Iraq's perennial rival, Syria, and, according to rumor, selling some military hardware to Iran. By the summer of 1982, with Iraqi troops driven almost entirely from Iranian soil, Moscow argued that for Iran to continue the war could aid only the United States and Israel. Once Iranian troops crossed into Iraq in July 1982, Moscow clearly favored Iraq. Soviet rhetoric has portrayed Iraq as willing to make peace while Iran obstinately refused. Accusations of Iranian collusion with the imperialists persist. The Soviets resumed direct arms deliveries and in a variety of symbolic gestures demonstrated its preference for Iraq.[29]

There were a number of other foreign policy irritants in Soviet-Iranian relations. The enmity between Iran and Iraq disrupted the Non-Aligned Movement, which in the past had taken stands pleasing to the Soviets on various international issues. In the wake of Israel's 1982 invasion of Lebanon, Iran accused the Soviet Union of collusion with the other superpower and failing to aid the Muslims in opposing Israel.[30] In its dealings with other regional powers, the Islamic Republic has considerably improved its relations with Turkey and Pakistan, to the dismay of Moscow, which is on poor terms with both.

Thus, there were a host of problems in relations between the Islamic Republic and the Soviet Union even before matters came to a head in 1983. The factor which more than any other made the negative aspects of the relationship outweigh the positive in the minds of Iran's leaders was the Soviet tilt towards Iraq in the war, since that was not only an urgent security concern but also an emotion-charged struggle against evil for Ayatollah Khomeini and at least some of his supporters. However, there were other contributing factors as well. The dominant element in the Islamic Republican Partry (IRP) was authoritarian. It was intolerant of diversity and unwilling to share power all along but initially had not been strong enough to enforce conformity with its will. This was not just a matter of politics. The IRP leadership rejected minority nationalities' calls for the right to use their own languages and have some local self-government. It practiced religious intolerance: its policies were offensive to many of the country's Sunni Muslims; it harassed Armenian Christians, persecuted Jews, and attempted the total destruction of the country's Baha'i community. In the political arena, it broke the power of lay nationalists, whether of the Mosaddeq tradition or its own former allies, like Abol-Hasan Bani Sadr and Sadeq Qotzbzadah. It fought the leftist guerrillas, most spectacularly the Mojahedin-e Khalq, as well as others. Once this campaign to enforce homogeneity was well underway, and the more powerful political competitors were broken, the IRP turned against the Tudeh Party. Another factor which may have contributed to the IRP's turn against the Tudeh and Moscow is the information on Soviet espionage in Iran rumored to have been provided the British by KGB defector Vladimir Kuzichkin and passed on to officials in Tehran.[31]

The deteriorating relations between Iran and the Soviet Union during 1982 were marked by a number of unfriendly gestures on both sides. Iran criticized Soviet support for Iraq. It ordered the curtailment of the size of Sovet embassy and consular staffs, denied visas to Soviet journalists, and closed a Soviet-Iranian cultural organization. Tudeh members and sympathizers were purged from the bureaucracy and educational system. Party activities were harassed. The government did not try to prevent Afghans living in Iran from demonstrating against the Soviet Union. The Iranian delegation to Leonid Brezhnev's funeral in November 1982 was lower ranking than protocol required.[32] High ranking Soviet interpreters of the Iranian scene, journalistic sources, and broadcasts to Iran all criticized the clerically-led regime. The clergy's role in the revolution was disparaged. While Khomeini was not yet attacked directly, his supporters were condemned for serving the causes of reaction and imperialism. The keystone of Iran's foreign policy, the rejection of dependence on either the Eastern or Western superpower, was condemned as abetting imperialism. At the same time, the Soviets increased their efforts to convey a favorable picture of their country through radio broadcasts to Iran.[33]

Early in 1983 Iranian authorities arrested more than a thousand members of the Tudeh Party, including its leaders, and cracked down on the Azerbaijan Democratic Party as well. In April and May of that year, Tudeh First Secretary Nureddin Kianuri and other party veterans confessed publicly. The party was banned. Iran expelled eighteen Soviet diplomats for espionage. Trials of several party members, especially in the military, followed in late 1983 and early 1984, ending with the execution of ten of them and the sentencing of eighty-seven others to prison terms.

Other Middle Eastern governments have occasionally cracked down on the local communist party without badly damaging their relations with the Soviet Union. This was the case in Nasser's Egypt, Iraq under the current government, and even Iran in the last fifteen years of the monarchy. However, the 1983 action by the Iranian government was different because it was explicitly linked to criticism of the Soviet Union.

The confessions and trials of Tudeh members propounded a number of lessons that reflected the Iranian leadership's negative views of the Soviet Union: the Sovet model and Marxist ideology are irrelevant to Iran's needs; the Soviet Union supported Iraq in its aggression against Iran; the Tudeh Party put its loyalty to the Soviet Union ahead of its loyalty to Iran, including by spying for the Soviets; the Tudeh collaborated with Kurdish rebels; it was plotting a coup. The same points have been made by the newspaper of the Islamic Republican Party.[34]

Moscow sees Iran's current leadership as being in a strong position, especially in light of the internecine conflict and repression which have afflicted the left.[37] Yet the Soviets hope for a revolution that will bring the left to power. At the same time, they are strikingly contemptuous of the Tudeh. As they have done in the past, they blame the local communists for the failure of a policy Moscow chose for itself, in this case the Tudeh's support for Khomeini until the bitter end. That policy is now blamed for hampering the party's ability to increase its following, which was not large to begin with. There have been several disparaging comments made about the quality of the Tudeh's leaders from 1979 to 1983.[38] Operationally, the Soviets are pinning their hopes on the Majority Fedayan-e Khalq, now returned to the communist fold. At the same time, they regard the Mojahedin as a plausible and desirable alternative to the IRP. The Mojahedin's ideology is praised as the appropriate type of social radicalism for Iranian conditions. Its war against the IRP since mid-1981, although opposed by the Soviets and Tudeh at the time, is now interpreted sympathetically as the revolutionaries' reaction to an oppressive government. Despite the enormous losses they suffered in that losing struggle, they have preserved their organization and have the potential to be an alternative to the incumbent regime. As S. L. Agaev remarked, "No other Iranian opposition political force can by itself be compared in this regard to the Mojahedin."[39]

The Soviets' search for alternatives to the Tehran government also led them to heightened interest in several minority nationalities. Discussion of the Azerbaijanis, already indicative of lively Soviet interest, continued in much the same terms as before. However, discussion of the Kurds became more positive, now that the Soviets had reason to welcome the Kurds' armed opposition to the Tehran regime. Attention to the Turkmens also increased, as reflected by the fact that the Soviet Turkmen Academy of Sciences added to its areas of study in its 1981–85 plan research on the economic, social, and political status of Iran's Turkmens from the 1950s through the 1980s. This area of inquiry was described as having "great significance."[40]

Despite all the problems in relations with Iran, the Soviets have not abandoned their efforts to improve relations with the existing Tehran government. The prerequisite for that is to keep the lines of communication open despite the mutual recriminations. Economic links play a crucial role in this regard. Even after the assault on the Tudeh Party, the Soviets were arguing for the benefit to Iran of economic dealings with the Soviet Union, and the Iranians were interested. Indeed, the existing pattern of agreements has been continued. The Soviets are interested in other contacts when possible, as when they sent a basketball team from Tashkent State University to Iran in early 1984 to participate in games honoring the fifth anniversary of the revolution.[41] Iran has shown that it does not want to eliminate its option of using the Soviet Union for its own benefit. In June 1984, as the United States appeared to be favoring Iraq against Iran, an Iranian delegation went to Moscow for meetings with Foreign Minister Andrei Gromyko.[42]

Opportunism has been more important than ideology in determining the course of Soviet-Iranian relations since the revolution of 1978–79. Ideology influenced Iran's new leaders in the sense that the United States was the object of especially intense hatred. That gave additional importance to the pragmatic tradition of using the Soviet Union (and before that Tsarist Russia) to counter-balance another foreign power involved in Iran's affairs. Yet the ideology of some Iranian revolutionaries, including the dominant faction of Islamic activists, also deemed communism a reprehensible doctrine and faulted the Soviet Union for being just like the Western superpower, concerned only with its own interests and opposed to the interests of Iran and the Muslim world in general. However, this criticism did not by itself undermine the working relationship between the Islamic Republic and the Soviet Union. On the Soviet side of the equation, ideology affected policy towards Iran by causing Soviet analysts to misinterpret political developments there. This compounded the practical limitations on the Soviets' ability to influence Iranian events. As a result, they were reduced to a reactive policy, revising the ideology to take into account the fluctuating opportunities to advance their interests. The accommodation between the Soviet Union and the Islamic Republic ran into difficulty when it ceased to be opportunistic, that is, when the Tehran leadership came to see its major interests as hampered, rather than aided, by the Soviet Union, above all in the Iran-Iraq War. Moscow reacted in a similar spirit. As this occurred, the other problems in relations between the two countries achieved new prominence. Yet at heart, relations between the two countries are still opportunistic. While the balance between the positive and negative has changed to favor the latter, both governments have chosen to keep contacts open and to seek whatever benefits they can still derive from dealing with each other.

NOTES

1. *Pravda,* March 9, 1982, p. 4; A. V. Gordon, "Sovetskaia Vostokovedy i Afrikanisti o protsessakh formirovaniia natsional'nogo i klassovogo soznaniia v osvobodivshikhsia stranakh (1976–80)" (Soviet Orientalists and Africanists on the Processes of The Formation of National and Class Consciousness in Liberated Countries (1976–80), *Narody Azii i Afriki,* 1981, no. 1, pp. 186–87; S. Aliev, "Islam i politika" (Islam and Politics), *Aziia i Afrika segodnia,* December 1981, pp. 5–9; G. Kim, "Sotsial'noe razvitie i ideologicheskaia bor'ba v razvivaiushchikhsia stranakh" (Social Development and the Ideological Struggle in Developing Countries), *Mezhdunarodnaia zhizn',* 1980, no. 3, pp. 72–73; R. A. Ul'ianovskii, "Predislovie" (Introduction), *Iran: rozhdenie respubliki* (Iran: the Birth of the Republic), by S. L. Agaev, (Moscow, 1984), p. 15; K. Brutents, "Osvobodivshiesia strany v nachale 80–kh godov" (Liberated Countries at the Beginning of the '80s), *Kommunist,* 1984, no. 3 (February), p. 113.

2. S. L. Agaev, *Iranskaia revoliutsiia, SShA i mezhdunarodnaia bezopasnost'* (The Iranian Revolution, the U.S.A. and International Security) (Moscow: Nauka, 1984); *Pravda,* January 17, 1982, p. 5, January 22, 1982, p. 5; *Izvestiia,* February 11, 1982, p. 4; *Bakinskii rabochii,* January 8, 1982, p. 4; Baku international radio in Azerbaijani, January 20, 1982, Foreign Broadcast Information Service, *Daily Report. Soviet Union,* January 22, 1982, no. H. p. 4 (henceforth referred to as FBIS, *Soviet Union*); Ul'ianovskii, "Moral'nye printsipy v politike i politika v oblasti morali" (Moral Principles in Politics and Politics in the Sphere of Morals), *Literaturnaia Gazeta,* June 22, 1983, p. 10.

3. Brezhnev's statement was published in *Pravda,* November 19, 1978, p. 5; for further discussion of this theme see *Pravda,* January 13, 1979, p. 5, February 6, 1979, p. 5, March 5, 1979, p. 5, April 24, 1979, p. 5, May 22, 1979, p. 5, March 9, 1982, p. 4; Moscow radio in Persian to Iran, February 6, 1979, March 7, 1979, July 5, 1979, FBIS, *Soviet Union,* February 7, 1979, p. F 2, March 13, 1979, p. F 10, July 6, 1979, p. H 13.

4. Agence France Presse, May 3, 1979, FBIS, *Daily Report. Middle East and North Africa,* May 3, 1979, p. R 3–4 (henceforth referred to as *MENA*); Tehran domestic radio, May 4, 1979, July 6, 1979, FBIS, *MENA,* May 9, 1979, p. R 4, July 9, 1979, p. R 11; Tehran domestic radio, June 5, 1981, October 21, 1981, February 10, 1982, FBIS, *Daily Report South Asia,* June 9, 1981, p. I 9, October 23, 1981, p. I 10, February 11, 1982, p. I 3; (henceforth referred to as *MENA South Asia*), *Keyhan,* April 26, 1981, Joint Publications Research Service, (henceforth referred to as JPRS), no. 77262, pp. 69–70.

5. E. Doroshenko, "Puti i formy vozdeistviia shiitskogo dukhovenstva na obshchestvenno-politicheskuiu zhizn' Irana" (Ways and Forms of the Shi'ite Clergy's Influence on the Socio-Political Life of Iran), *Islam v istorii narodov Vostoka* (Moscow, 1981), p. 80.

6. S. M. Aliev, "Antiimperialisticheskoe i demokraticheskoe dvizhenie 1949–53" (The Anti-Imperialist and Democratic Movement 1949–53), *Iran. Ocherki noveishei istorii,* A. Z. Arabadzhian, ed. (Moscow, 1976), pp. 215, 251; A. I. Demin, "Obshchestvennye preobrazovaniia i osnovye tendentsii sotsial'no-ekonomicheskogo i vnutri-politicheskogo razvitiia Irana", (Social Changes and the Fundamental Tendencies of Iran's Socio-Economic and Internal Political Development), ibid., pp. 403, 406.

7. IRNA, December 6, 1983, FBIS, *South Asia,* December 7, 1983, p. I 4.

8. S. Bakhash, *The Reign of the Ayatollahs* (New York, 1984), p. 238.

9. "Excerpt from Tudeh Leader Kianuri's Interview with *Le Matin* (Paris) November 27, 1979," *MERIP,* no. 86 (March–April 1980), p. 23.

10. *Pravda,* March 9, 1982, p. 4.

11. *Financial Times,* March 10, 1982, p. 5; Ministerstvo Vneshnei Torgovli, *Vneshniaia torgovlia SSSR v 1981 g.* (Foreign Trade of the U.S.S.R. in 1981) (Moscow, 1982), p. 11; idem, *Vneshniaia torgovlia SSSR v 1983 g.* (The Foreign Trade of the U.S.S.R. in 1983) (Moscow, 1984), p. 11; International Monetary Fund, *Direction of Trade Statistics Yearbook* (Washington, D.C., 1984), p. 213.

12. Ministerstvo Vneshnei Torgovli, *Vneshniaia torgovlia SSSR v 1983 g.,* pp. 11, 13, 14, 15.

13. International Monetary Fund, *Direction of Trade Statistics Yearbook,* pp. 212–13; *Middle East Economic Digest,* March 16, 1984, p. 18, July 27, 1984, p. 13, September 28, 1984, p. 13–14.

14. *Middle East Economic Digest,* September 3, 1982, p. 17, May 11, 1984, p. 15; Moscow radio in Persian to Iran, July 10, 1982, FBIS, *Soviet Union,* July 13, 1982, pp. H 9–10; *Ettela'at,* November 2, 1981, Joint Publications Research Service, no. 79654, p. 29; IRNA, October 8, 1983, FBIS, *South Asia,* October 14, 1983, pp. I 2–3.

15. *Middle East Economic Digest,* January 29, 1982, p. 13, April 9, 1982, p. 11, September 3, 1982, p. 12, November 12, 1982, pp. 32, 72, January 28, 1983, p. 16, June 10, 1983, p. 21, June 24, 1983, p. 24; June 29, 1984, p. 10.

16. Izvestiia, February 11, 1982, p. 4; *Burs,* September 9, 1982, JPRS, no. 79439, pp. 39–40; *Financial Times,* March 10, 1982, p. 5; *Middle East Economic Digest,* February 26, 1982, p. 26, April 30, 1982, pp. 6, 8, and February 4, 1983, pp. 16–17; *Middle East Economic Digest,* September 3, 1982, p. 17.

17. N. Kianuri, "Iran: for unity among patriotic forces," *World Marxist Review,* July 1981, p. 19; idem., "The Iranian Revolution: its friends and its enemies," ibid., November 1982, p. 34; *Mardom,* March 3, 1981, JPRS, no. 77874, pp. 4–6; *Ayandegan,* July 24, 1979, FBIS, *MENA,* July 27, 1979, p. R 4; Agence France Presse, May 4, 1981, FBIS, *South Asia,* May 5, 1981, p. I 1.

18. Tehran domestic radio, June 7, 1981, FBIS, *South Asia,* June 8, 1981, p. I 6.

19. "The Revolutionary and Counter-Revolutionary Forces in Iran," *Information Bulletin* (of the *World Marxist Review*), 1979, no. 14, p. 22; *Pravda,* August 20, 1979, p. 5, August 25, 1979, p. 5, October 16, 1979, p. 5; Moscow radio in Persian to Iran, April 3, 1979, Moscow domestic radio, November 20, 1979, FBIS, *Soviet Union,* April 5, 1979, p. H 8, November 21, 1979, pp. H 3–6; National Voice of Iran in Azerbaijani to Iran, March 25, 1979, April 24, 1979, FBIS, *MENA,* March 27, 1979, p. R 20, April 27, 1979, pp. R 7–8; A. Sella, "Soviet Iranian Relations from the Fall of the Shah to the Iran-Iraq War," *The Soviet Union and the Middle East* supplement 2, 1980, p. 2; A. Kiva, "Natsional'no-osvoboditel'noe dvizhenie" (The National Liberation Movement), *Aziia i Afrika segodnia,* 1979, no. 12 (Dec.), p. 3. A discussion of national liberation by the influential Soviet official R. A. Ul'ianovskii gave considerable attention to the Iranian revolution but conspicuously ignored the question of national minorities, stressing instead the revolution's anti-imperialist character. ("O natsional'noi osvobozhdenii i natsionalizme" (On National Liberation and Nationalism), *Aziia i Afrika segodnia,* 1980, no. 10 (October), p. 6.

20. G. F. Kim et al., *Zarubezhnyi Vostok i sovremennost'* (The Foreign East and Modern Times), vol. 2 (Moscow, 1980, pp. 249–50, 252–53, 256; V. V. Trubetskoi, "K voprosu o vliianii burzhuaznykh reform 60–kh—pervoi poliviny 70–kh godov na natsional'nye protsessy v Irane" (On the question of the Influence of Bourgeois Reforms of the '60s—First Half of the '70s on National Processes in Iran), *Natsional'nye problemy sovremennogo Vostoka* (Moscow, 1977), pp. 82, 83, 85–91, 94–95, 106, 108–109, 112; M. Lazarev, "Sovremennyi etap natsional'nogo razvitiia stran zarubezhnogo Vostoka" (The Contemporary Stage of National Development of Countries of the Foreign East), *Aziia i Afrika segodnia,* 1979, no. 12 (December), p. 23.

21. Sella, "Soviet Iranian Relations," p. 2; *Pravda,* August 20, 1979, p. 5, October 26, 1979, p. 5; "Statement of Central Committee of the People's Party of Iran (Tudeh) August 11, 1979," *Information Bulletin* (of the *World Marxist Review*), 1979, nos. 21–22, pp. 70–71.

22. G. Kim, *Zarubezhnyi Vostok i sovremennost',* vol. 2, p. 257; *Azerbaijan,* 1981, no. 5, JPRS, no. 79497, p. 33; *Adabiyyat va injasanat,* September 5, 1980, May 1, 1981, May 29, 1981, September 18, 1981, March 14, 1982, May 21, 1982, February 10, 1984, March 30, 1984, JPRS, no. 77230, pp. 61–63, no. 78786, pp. 43–44, 50–53, no. 79847, p. 49, no. 81845, pp. 4–5, no. 81843, pp. 4–5, no. UPS–84–973, pp. 11, 13, no. UPS–84–059, p. 9; *Kommunist,* May 7, 1981, JPRS, no. 78786, p. 45; Moscow Radio in Persian to Iran, March 8, 1983, FBIS, *Soviet Union,* March 9, 1983, pp. H 7–8.

23. See the translations from *Adabiyyat va injasanat* cited in note 22.

24. Baku international in Azerbaijani, February 15, 1982, April 3, 1982, FBIS, *Soviet Union,* February 16, 1982, pp. H 4–5, April 6, 1982, p. H 1.

25. A. Faroughy, "Le Pouvoir islamique face aux aspirations autonomistes en Iran," February 1980, p. 9; *Frankfurter Rundschau,* January 9, 1980, JPRS, no. 75106, pp. 38, 39–40.

26. Tehran international radio in Arabic, November 6, 1981, Tehran domestic radio, February 3, 1982, *Jang,* February 4, 1982, FBIS, *South Asia,* November 10, 1981, pp. I 10–11, February 4, 1982, p. I 3, February 17, 1982, p. I 5; Tehran domestic radio, December 29, 1979, FBIS, *MENA,* December 31, 1979 (supplement), pp. 19–20; *Ettela'at,* January 1, 1981, JPRS, no. 77324, pp. 9–11; Faroughy, "L'U.R.S.S. et la revolution iranienne," *Le Monde diplomatique,* July 29, 1980, p. 12; *Pravda,* March 9, 1982, p. 4; Moscow radio in Persian to Iran, January 1, 1982, FBIS, *Soviet Union,* January 5, 1982, p. D 1.

27. *Christian Science Monitor,* October 7, 1982, p. 5; *Washington Post,* May 28, 1982, p. 1.

28. Iu. Alimov, "Dvizhenie nepresoedineniia na vazhnom rubezhe" (The Non-Aligned Movement at an Important Juncture), *Kommunist,* 1983, no. 7 (May), p. 101; M. Atkin, "Moscow's Disenchantment with Iran," *Survey,* vol. 27, no. 118–119 (Autumn-Winter 1983), pp. 252–53.

29. *Pravda,* May 31, 1982, p. 6; *Krasnaia zvezda,* June 8, 1982, p. 3; Atkin, "Moscow's Disenchantment," p. 253.

30. Atkin, "Moscow's Disenchantment," p. 250.

31. Bakhash, *The Reign of the Ayatollahs,* p. 239; *The Economist,* October 30, 1982, p. 54; *Time,* November 8, 1982, p. 51.

32. *Pravda,* March 9, 1982, p. 4, TASS, February 10, 1982, FBIS, *Soviet Union,* February 11, 1982, p. H 1; National Voice of Iran radio (henceforth referred to as NVOI) in Persian to Iran, March 16, 1982, April 16, 1982, FBIS, *South Asia,* March 18, 1982, pp. I 7–8, April 20, 1982, p. I 11; Atkin, "Moscow's Disenchantment," p. 251.

33. Atkin, "Moscow's Disenchantment," pp. 249–50, 254–55, 258–59; NVOI in Persian to Iran, January 21, 1982, FBIS, *South Asia,* January 25, 1982, p. I 16; Moscow radio in Persian to Iran, July 6, 1982, August 12, 1982, August 19, 1982, August 26, 1982, August 27, 1982, September 2, 1982, September 16, 1982, October 1, 1982, FBIS, *Soviet Union,* July 8, 1982, p. H 19, August 16, 1982, p. H 15, August 24, 1982, pp. H 9–11, August 31, pp. H 6–8, September 1, 1982, p. H 10, September 8, 1982, pp. H 17–18, October 5, 1982, p. H 10.

34. Atkin, "Moscow's Disenchantment," p. 251; *Jomhuri-ye eslami,* October 25, 1983 and November 29, 1983, JPRS, no. NEA–84–001, pp. 79–82, FBIS, *South Asia,* December 23, 1983, pp. I 5–6.

35. Brutents, "Osvobodivshiesia strany," p. 104; Ul'ianovskii, "Moral'nye printsipy," p. 10; both authors are deputy chiefs of the International Department of the Central Committee of the Soviet Communist Party.

36. *Izvestiia,* August 3, 1983, p. 5; Ul'ianovskii, "Predislovie" (Introduction), *Iran: Padenie shakhskogo rezhima* (Iran: the Fall of the Shah's Regime), by A. B. Reznikov (Moscow, 1983), pp. 11–12; idem., "Predislovie" (to *Iran: rozhdenie respubliki*), pp. 7–13; idem., "Moral'nye printsipy," p. 10; S. L. Agaev, "Levyi radikalizm, revoliutsionnyi demokratizm, i nauchnyi sotsializm v strankakh Vostoka" (Left Radicalism, Revolutionary Democratism, and Scientific Socialism in the countries of the East), *Rabochii klass i sovremennyi*

mir, 1984, no. 3 (May–June), pp. 135, 139, 140; Moscow radio in Persian to Iran, May 10, 1983, FBIS, *Soviet Union,* May 17, 1983, pp. H 1–2.

37. Ul'ianovskii, "Predislovie" (to *Iran: rozhdenie respubliki*), p. 9; Agaev, "Levyi radikalizm," pp. 141, 142; L. S. Skliarov, "Stanovlenie noyvkh organov vlasti v Irane (1978–81)" (The Establishment of New Organs of Power in Iran (1978–81)), *Iran: Istoriia i sovremennost'* (Moscow, 1983), pp. 197–201, 203, 206–208, 210–11; Atkin, "Moscow's Disenchantment," p. 257.

38. Ul'ianovskii, "Predislovie" (to *Iran: rozhdenie respubliki*), p. 7; Agaev, "Levyi radikalizm," pp. 134, 140, 141–42, 143; Atkin, "Moscow's Disenchantment," p. 258.

39. Agaev, "Levyi radikalizm," p. 144, see also pp. 134, 135–37, 145, 146, and Ul'ianovskii, "Moral'nye printsipy," p. 10; Atkin, "Moscow's Disenchantment," pp. 257–58.

40. Kh.A. Ataev, "Sektor istorii zarubezhnogo Vostoka pri Institut istorii im Sh. Batyrova AN" (The Sector of the History of the Foreign East of the Sh. Batyrov Institute of History of the Academy of Sciences of the Turkmen S.S.R.), *Narody Azii i Afriki,* 1984, no. 1, p. 111; O. I. Zhigalina, "Rol' islama v razvitii ideologii kurdskogo natsional'nogo dvizheniia v Irane" (The Role of Islam in the Development of the Ideology of the Kurdish Nationalist Movement in Iran), *Islam v strankah Blizhnego i Srednego Vostoka* (Moscow, 1982), pp. 123–25; Agaev, "Levyi radikalizm," p. 142.

41. Moscow radio in Persian to Iran, March 11, 1983, April 8, 1983, May 23, 1983, July 11, 1983, FBIS, *Soviet Union,* March 16, 1983, pp. H 3–4, April 11, 1983, p. H 1, May 24, 1983, p. H 8, July 14, 1983, pp. H 3–4; Tashkent domestic radio, February 15, 1984, FBIS, *Soviet Union,* February 21, 1984, p. H 9; IRNA, in English, October 8, 1983, FBIS, *South Asia,* October 14, 1983, pp. I 2–3; Atkin, "Moscow's Disenchantment," p. 259.

42. TASS, in English, June 6, 1984, Tehran domestic radio, June 7, 1984, FBIS, *Soviet Union,* June 7, 1984, p. H 1, June 8, 1984, p. H 1.

DISCUSSANT'S REMARKS

Richard Cottam

I THINK THAT THE BASIC ASSUMPTIONS that really divide us Americans in debates on foreign policy are two: what are Soviet intentions; and how powerful is the United States, how far can we extend our influence? I think we differ very substantially on these. Iran plays a very critical role in those differences. Obviously Iran is in the twilight zone of anybody's definition of our power capabilities. And taking the Carter Administration, Gary Sick said that it came with a lot of programs, but I think it also became very divided on the two points I'm talking about.

People ranged from Brzezinski, who saw the Iranian revolution as

Soviet orchestrated, to Andrew Young, who saw very little threat from the Soviet Union and also saw a United States with very clear limitations to its power. The Regan administration, as Gary says, is unprogrammatic, but it is unified in terms of its world view. That is not to say that the bureaucrats who live under it are unified, but the administration is. It knows. And it knows that the Soviet Union is evil and is ineluctably aggressive, and clearly thinks that we have great power to do something about this.

Iran has given us a couple of real shocks, and I disagree very much with Gary on one point. The hostage issue was not epiphenomenal for me; it was center core. I think the two shocks were the fall of the shah, which we tried our best to prevent, and the hostage crisis going on for a year. We couldn't release fifty people. We are a superpower. The shock, therefore, is in terms of American power.

What are the lessons of Iran? They are still unlearned, but the U.S. was over-extended, irremediably over-extended.

An absolute reassessment of U.S. policy towards Iran and towards the area is now required. It also tells a fair amount about Soviet intentions, because as Muriel Atkin related, the Soviet Union had really good relations with Iran, under the shah, right up to the day when it was obvious that he was not going to survive. Then they shifted and had relations with the new regime. They didn't take much more advantage of our embarrassment on the hostage case than to gloat about it, as Atkin says.

The other great shock, that went right along with the first, is Afghanistan. Afghanistan was a situation in which the Soviet Union behaved in a way that the unreconstructed cold-warriors always thought she would behave. She did behave that way, and when she did we had a month in which we really did ask ourselves the question: what can we do about this and what can we do if the Soviet Union invades a really important country like Iran? The answers were honest for a brief moment—we cannot do much. Maybe the nuclear option was there, but who wanted to use that? Apparently some people did.

In any case these shocks were extraordinary as far as people who hold the view of the Reagan administration are concerned. Afghanistan was such a confirmation to them, that as Carl Gershman said in *Commentary* magazine after describing these two views of reality, "Anyone that argues, today, that the Soviet Union is not ineluctably aggressive, does not have the moral right to express his or her opinion." He is now the aide to Jeane Kirkpatrick, who is a fellow traveler in this viewpoint.

Gary Sick's point about the non-programmatic part of the present administration is a critical one. Given its very strong world view, it has a clear, abstract strategy, and that strategy is to contain the devil. And how do you do that? You do that by creating a cordon sanitaire around him, and we are busily trying to do that. That causes some troubles, because people like Jesse Helms and even Ronald Reagan take seriously the contention that we're engaged in an anti-communist crusade, forgetting about Yugoslavia. The problem with this cordon sanitaire is that a major anchor for it must be China. And that is hard for Jesse Helms to swallow and, as we see, hard for Ronald Reagan to swallow. When you get to the Middle East, it's even harder to work out a program to deal with this.

It is worth saying that Iran has to be seen in the context of its region, that American policy makes no sense seen in isolation. It is within the region that the danger and probable course of action of American policy is going to take shape. I think we have no policy towards Iran right now.

I'm going to recite the three obvious points of what American policy objectives are in this region in order of importance. One: to contain the Soviet Union. Second: to work for the security of Israel, which is a major foreign policy objective, not because she's democratic, but because there is a strong pressure group working for this. Third: to secure the flow of oil.

Obviously we have to reconcile those three, and anyone who thinks that's easy, not only is not a practitioner, but hasn't even looked at the problem very closely. But as you look at fumbling attempts by this administration to work it out, you can look at AWACS. The main theme of AWACS is the cordon sanitaire. Reconciling this with our interest in Israel was something we just plain didn't do. We finally went to the crunch with her on it and caused all kinds of trouble on that point.

This is adding up to a point which is extremely dangerous: we really don't have a policy because we can't figure it out. How do we translate this vague general strategy into tactics, or even a little higher degree of strategy? The result is that we're drifting, and if we drift (as I believe the Soviet Union is drifting) the danger is that we lose control of a situation, which can produce confrontation between us.

What are the dynamics operating in the area that are likely to give definition to the United States? Inadvertently, we are going to be sucked into the Middle East because of the lack of a policy. There are very strong crystallizing tendencies in the Arab world, with a Libyan-Algerian-PLO-Syrian alliance, and hostility toward Saudi Arabia, Iraq, and Jordan growing, not declining. As these things intensify, they are sitting ducks for a horrible incident that could occur, like an Israeli invasion of Lebanon. That act, which is out of our control apparently, is the kind of thing which can produce a genuine crystallization. The reason this is particularly important now is that two other actors in this case, Egypt and Iran, are inclined towards opposite sides in this but haven't really joined them yet.

As for Iran, if you read its statements across the board now on foreign policy, you will see an increasing identification with Syria and its group, and increasing absorption in hostilities towards Israel, and an insistence that as soon as it is over its embarrassment with Iraq, Iran will begin fighting Israel. I'm inclined to think that they mean that, as of this moment. The possibility of this crystallizing into an alliance with Syria is indicated by a major Iranian foreign policy decision (and I don't believe they have made many): to attack the Ikhwan (Muslim Brethren) after their Hama insurrection in Syria. That was gratuitous. It was certainly pleasing to Assad, but for a regime that has announced that it is in favor of showing the way to Islam and avoiding the classification of being Shi'i, this is a major pragmatic move indicating that Iran is moving in a pragmatic direction, but one that is going to take it towards the polarization in the area. Mubarak shows more talent and has not indicated clearly where he is going to go, but he is inclined to move into this Saudi Arabian-Jordanian-Iraqi side. It's interesting to read what those in opposition to him are saying: for heaven's sake, the last thing we should do is to identify ourselves with the conservative Arabs; Egypt should go back to the Arab world, but it should go back to the Arab world as a whole. My contention is that the one thing the U.S. and the U.S.S.R. should do is to try to prevent this polarization from occurring and to do their best to reduce it, now. We don't have much power in the area, but we do have influence in several states, Egypt and Saudi Arabia included, and what I would call for is to try to use what influence we have to try to prevent a clearly identifiable danger.

I want just to speak briefly about Bill Miller's paper. He has a marvelous sense of the absurd that fits today's world into it. Somebody was asking me this morning about the Falkland Islands and how absurd that was and I said that it was no more absurd than the main show. At the same time Bill has great values and he is one of the few Americans, I think, who would like to crusade for democracy. I really say few, and I don't believe that that is in the cards and I guess if it came right down to it, even if we had power, I wouldn't favor it. But in any case, I believe that even though Bill did mention that we were paranoid about the Soviet Union, he continued in his paper with an interventionist thesis, intervening on the side of the good guys, of course. But I don't want to see somebody define good guys again. We did it in the past, in 1953, and we are still paying the price for that definition of the good guys as it came through.

As far as Muriel Atkins' paper was concerned, I thought it was an extremely careful and extremely accurate picture of Soviet policy. My complaint about it is only in the area of caution. I think it was too cautious. A point worth noting is that right in the middle of our terrible embarrassment with the hostages, the Iranians led the fight in Islamabad against the Soviet takeover of Afghanistan—a little country attacking two superpowers at the same time. How come the Soviets sat back and accepted that? I mean, we're 9,000 miles away, they're right there. And the question I would like to have seen her address is, why aren't the Soviets invading? Given General Haig's picture of reality, they should have some time ago. The point she did make, and made very well, is the failure of the Soviets to deal with the minorities seriously; even the Azerbaijan matter seems to be a question of rhetoric; no political action involved in it— indicating that here is a much less risky way of playing with Iran.

Third, her picture of Tudeh was accurate. And if the picture of Tudeh as making mistake after mistake is correct, it hardly fits a picture of a Soviet Union that is diabolical in its cleaverness, which is the view of the other side.

GENERAL DISCUSSION

Miller: I want to clarify the subject of interventions. I don't think we should intervene in any way that resembles 1953. Any engagement we have should be open and direct. I do think that there are kinds of regimes that are easier for us to deal with, and I have preferences—I suspect we all do—but in the diplomatic world, at least, there ought to be a minimum of formal relationships to carry on the normal business of nations.

Any special relationship, and we seem to have special relationships in the world for a whole assortment of reasons, ought to be based on openly declared principles. I hope we have learned from our experience with Iran in the past, but I would dissociate myself from the kind of interventionism that was mentioned.

Sick: I would like to comment on intervention because I think that it is a fundamentally critical point. In looking at the history of U.S. foreign policy in these last two crises, the fall of the shah, and the hostage taking, the one fact that seems to come through as the underlying factor is that, although the use of force and U.S. direct intervention in Iran was offered to the President and was presented to him as an option at a variety of different stages and in a variety of different ways, he refused to accept those recommendations. The history of American foreign policy during that four-year period was one of non-intervention. Now there are people who claim that was what was wrong with U.S. foreign policy, that if only we had intervened we could have solved these problems and American interests would have been preserved. Now at the other end of the spectrum, which is just as common, you hear people say, "you used too much force, you got too much involved, there should be no use of force or even consideration of intervention in Iran." Despite those two perspectives. I personally believe that when the history of this sequence of events is written, not next week or next month, but ten, twenty, even one hundred years from now, the key element that will emerge will be the fact that the United States did not in fact associate itself with direct intervention. This may turn out to be quite important for the future of U.S.-Iranian relations.

Question: I have two questions. One is for Muriel Atkin, and that question is, to what degree do you think Soviet restraint in Iran is a function of believing that things will come into their hands, or that an alternative plan may develop? And the other question is for Bill Miller. I like his idea that the U.S. should be poised and alert to opportunities, and I wish he would explain that a little more.

Atkin: The question to me was how I explain Soviet restraint in Iran. Is it because they are hoping that eventually things will take a much more favorable turn for them? . . . I think there are several possible explanations of which that is one, but even more than the long-range question is the more immediate question: aren't there gains the way things are now? I think in many ways the current situation, poor though it is, has enough in it for the Soviet Union to think that those gains outweigh the cost of outright intervention. And they also have had other distractions which seem much more pressing, not that these exhaust the Soviet Union's enormous military means, but that would lead to the Soviet Union not wanting the burden of getting into a mess in Iran such as the Vietnam-Cambodia fighting and the situation in Afghanistan. In many ways that was a more pressing issue because there was already a pro-Moscow Communist government in Kabul that was in danger of falling, and now the business in Poland. The Soviet Union has the troops to spare if it wants to use them but the costs would far outweigh the benefits.

Also, given the fact that there is so much hostility to the Soviet Union as an imperialist power, the evident weakness of the Tudeh, the difficulty in winning allies, it would not be an easy thing to walk into Iran right now. So, all of those reasons influence Soviet decisions, and they are also still trying to figure out what is going on there. You can see that in the publications of the people in the think tanks, the advisors to the Kremlin on Iran, the Academy of Sciences, Oriental Institute, are trying to rethink and say, "Well what does this mean and where is it leading?"

Miller: What I meant by being prepared in the first instance is to have a solid understanding of who's who and who's doing what to whom, what the interplay of politics is in Iran and abroad. That's a primitive place to begin, but then it seems there are a number of possible ways that the U.S. might want to be involved or that it might find itself enmeshed and to be ready for those circumstances. The simplest and most benign, of course, is if the present regime decides we're not satans and wants to have a formal relationship. We'd be prepared to do that. Certainly the attitude of the Carter administration was that we would like to have a relationship and I assume that the present administration, under certain circumstances, would want to have a relationship, at least on a informal basis. It just makes life easier and certainly would resolve a lot of potential questions.

But looking to a possible post-Khomeini era, there's a whole range of possibilities and perhaps one will emerge. There may not be an orderly succession. It's possible, in my view, that there might be a struggle for power. No one knows what the combinations of factions would be and what the results would be, but it is conceivable there will be a very precarious and sensitive situation in which there is a vying of forces and the emergence of powerful groups supported by the Soviet Union; this would put the United States in a difficult situation. What kind of assistance should the U.S. extend given these circumstances? It seems to me being prepared means if a government comes into power and has problems of reconstruction, its economy is in a difficult stage, there is a shortage of food for heating oil or something of this sort, then these are events we ought to be prepared to help resolve quickly. I myself would be very wary of any military intervention, nor do I think we have the necessary capacity at the present time for this, nor do I think that's very desirable. But the kind of things I worry about are where we have a possible role to play in a fragile period in the era after Khomeini and where we could certainly be of assistance in making life more tolerable for the people of that country. I think we've learned from other instances of intervention that while they may be short-term successes, they can have long-term disastrous consequences. I really don't have a computer printout that says under condition "A" you could do such and such. I don't think it's possible, it never works that way even if you have the computer printout; it really depends on the immediate circumstance. I would say in the process of preparation that this really involves working on alternatives now, in sessions like this.

I'm delighted to see State Department people here as part of their work. They're very good at it, and, one would hope, in the White House and in other areas of the government that there is the same kind of engagement with the issues, so that, even though it will be a surprise whatever occurs, we're at least acquainted with some of the actors and have some ideas about what we can usefully do to help.

Rose: I fear I must take issue with Prof. Atkin on the question of the role and strength of the Tudeh with respect to the current Iran government.

It seems to me, while I don't want to be incautious and overestimate the problem that Tudeh presents, that you have been too cautious. For example, there is increasing concern which can be read in a number of ways on the part of a number of significant cadres in the Islamic Republican Party about the problem of Tudeh and the Fedayan-e Khalq (Majority) supporters, within not so much the party apparatus but within the security apparatus and the komitehs, particularly in the north of the country although this problem is also of concern in such places as Isfahan and Shiraz. This is reflected both in the *khutba* [Friday sermon] delivered by the Imam's representatives in major cities, in internal party publications and occasionally in the open party press. People returning from Iran who have had an opportunity to be in the north of the country, say that in Lahijan the flag of the Fedayan Majority, not the flag of the Islamic Republic, flies over the komiteh headquarters. Signs like that frankly terrify some people in the leadership. Ali Meshkini, for example, two weeks ago devoted his first khutba in Qom on the problem of sympathies on the part of officials in the Islamic Republican Party toward the Tudeh. There is such a configuration within the Tudeh; it's a group that configures around people like Nabavi, Ali Akbar Parvaresh, Mahmud Ruhani, who are for the most part relatively younger, western-educated individuals whose ideological perspective gives them the idea that some sort of anti-imperialist united front could be built with the Tudeh. This scares the average molla in the IRP and a lot of the people in the security apparatus. There have been purges of Fedayan and Tudeh within the pasdaran and the local komitehs. In at least two cases, people who were accused of Tudeh sympathies were unmasked as pseudo-clergymen who were involved in the revolutionary judiciary. So there is an appreciation on the part of the current government of some significant danger there, and I suspect they may overestimate the strength of the Tudeh, but at the same time there are clearly localities in Iran, particularly in the northern parts of the country, where they represent a genuine threat to the basic security of the Islamic Republican Party.

Atkin: I was not arguing that the Tudeh has no support anywhere; obviously it does in some places, particularly in certain pockets. But, first of all, if there are purges going on, that means Tudeh strength is being hurt. In a number of places these have been going on for quite some time, not just now. A second point to remember is that in the polemical rhetoric of a very heated, multi-sided political dispute, a lot of people get called a lot of names. Sometimes some anti-Khomeini emigres say Khomeini and Nabavi and others are linked to the commmunists and the American imperialists, simultaneously, and are all dirty. And the IRP's occasionally broad attacks on communists includes everyone who is vaguely left of center.

Also, I think that some weight should be given to the clandestine broadcasts of the Tudeh in which they complain about their problems. Now this is obviously propaganda, but the Tudeh has learned from experience that they don't look good when they are talking about how weak they are. They complain about being purged from the educational system and the government offices, that workers are being misled and are not following the Tudeh, and that peasants and many of the poor in the cities are too much under the influence of mollas. I think all that information needs to be balanced against the fact that the Tudeh is doing various things in various places and has some influence with some people. It is very hard to say with any degree of certainty, but I at least don't see their strength as nearly as great as your question implied.

Question: I would like to ask Gary Sick a question in regard to one intervention that *did* take place, namely the Iraqi military aggression. Now I happen to think that it was entirely an Iraqi project, but at the same time I remember in the summer of 1980 some very curious dispatches datelined from Washington, London, and Brussels about the disarray of the Iranian armed forces and so on. I remember seeing Mr. Brzezinski on television with his eyebrows arched warning Tehran to keep its eye on the western border, and in fact an article in the *Armed Forces Journal International* some months back by a pseudonymous State Department author claiming that they had direct contact between Iraqi and U.S. military intelligence on that. Could you comment on what the U.S. policy was?

Sick: I don't know how to deal with your question precisely. If you mean to say, was there evidence noticed by the United States that there was trouble brewing on that border, yes. From February on, people in the U.S. government were quite aware that there were difficulties on that border. There was a threat and that threat became more obvious as time went on.

If you are asking did the U.S. somehow put Iraq up to this, the answer is no. We didn't have any contact with them and didn't have any particular interest in launching a war on that front. In terms of the U.S. response to it, there is something else. There was a very dangerous moment, right after the beginning of the war, when I think the U.S. government deeply felt that there was a chance that the war would widen throughout the Gulf, and that, in fact, the whole area could go up in flames. I do not think that was a mistake, a misjudgment, I think it was real. It didn't happen, and it really didn't even get much publicity after the fact, which is maybe evidence that people really were scared. There weren't a lot of people running out to tell their favorite correspondent what had happened.

I'm not sure if I've answered your question?

Question: The question really is, was there any indirect, informal encouragement of the Iraqis?

Sick: No.

Salehi: My question is to Dick Cottam. When I read the private writings and public statements of both policy advisers and policy makers, I'm horrified at what seems to me to be a complete ignorance of the real facts of any given situation in Iran. They don't seem to reflect an acceptance of the information provided by those who they, themselves, acknowledge as experts in Iranian affairs, scholars who have spent years living and working in Iran, who care for and understand the people of Iran and see it from a much more insightful perspective. Is there any hope for U.S. foreign policy when top advisers make statements such as, "If we had just given the shah a free hand, he could have subdued internal rebellions," or "If the shah had just arrested 500 key people, the revolution would have collapsed?" These statements reflect a total misunderstanding, and ignorance of the truth of the situation in Iran in 1978–79. Don't State Department people coming to these conferences just reinforce their own preconceptions by selectively choosing data supplied here? Is this effective in altering policy?

Cottam: Well, I hate the question. I believe that State Department people and academics see reality very differently. And I think that the feeling you have toward them is paralleled by their feeling toward you. My own complaint is a different one I guess. When it comes down to immersion in detail and understanding of detail, in involvement in the day-to-day, then we have nothing to offer them at all. They know personalities better, they know a great deal about a million things that we will never know because of the range of sources they have.

On the other hand, I always fault them on not looking much above the day-to-day, at the longer term, and, now that you have forced me to say this, I don't believe that there is any possibility of our saying this to them and having them take any account of it. But everybody else wants to respond to this.

Sick: To prove the validity of what Dick Cottam just said, I would simply like to point out that in the course of doing my book I'm going back through the writings of a lot of academics writing during the course of the revolution. Although I'm sure it applies to no one in this room (everyone here obviously knew exactly what was going to happen and had it figured out all along), there were a few people even in the academic community, with fairly decent credentials, who didn't have it all figured out, and who in fact were giving us some advice, which had we followed it would have led to worse results. For instance, let me give you an example: I will not mention any names, but there was a suggestion in December of 1978 that we really should have had a free election in Iran with the shah running as president. That that would have been a way out of the problem.

But more serious than that, there was a very large body of opinion represented by a number of authors, some of whom may be in this room, which said unequivocally (or were thinking it privately) that there was no possibility that the clergy would end up ruling in Iran. The expert opinion was that the clergy had no business in politics, they didn't know how to run a country, and they would never involve themselves. They would come back and turn it over to these lovely people in the National Front. I'm afraid there was a real pro-National Front bias in the expert community that tended to cloud judgment as well.

All I would say is when it comes to crystal balls the academic community doesn't have to commit itself in action. It can think what it wants to and then denounce that later on if it feels comfortable doing so. People don't go back and hold them to account by reading what they were saying at the time. Secondly, the academic community tends to be as confused as anybody else. I was trying to be honest about the confusion in the government and I have no apologies for it. It was real, but I don't think you can pretend the academic community doesn't have the same problems.

Miller: I really don't see the division of cultures as valid. If there is any value in the process of teaching and learning, and I assume there is, it has to have some effect at least on some people at some time. There are a lot of people in the Foreign Service who have had a pretty impressive record of being right on questions, who have inquiring minds, skeptical attitudes, they read the scholarly literature, they would be first-class scholars in the academic world if they chose to do that. There is a useful back-and-forth between the two worlds, and I would think that for a country like ours it is very important to have that back-and-forth. We should do everything possible to break down that sense of division, that cleavage. That's why I think it is so helpful to have sessions like this, to try and get areas of understanding and appreciation of different ways of looking at the world and new techniques. In defense of my former colleagues in the State Department, I think they have done very good work. If there are problems with our country it is a collective problem. You have a leadership at the top which, by the nature of decision making, has to be smaller than the group that has scholarly or practical wisdom, and sometimes it doesn't get through. But I would urge you to make the effort to spread the word to those who don't have the perceptions that you have.

Keddie: I don't really think it's the job of the academics to provide the State Department with predictions. Now there may be some who want to do so, but I don't think that's the real point. I think rather, if there is any point to the interchange, it's of the level of Dick Cottam's presentation today, of basic perceptions of what U.S. interest possibilities are, of what Soviet interest possibilities are, and whether they are being perceived correctly, in terms of the reality of the world, by our government. Some of us may make predictions, but I agree with Gary Sick that these predictions should not be taken any more seriously than anyone else's. I think that if we can provide something in the nature of a background on Iranian society, of how US foreign policy conceives of itself in more broad terms, what are the things we think are more possible, what are the Soviet aims, these are the kinds of things which are important.

 Also, to throw in briefly a theme I'm developing at much greater length elsewhere, I think there is altogether too much of a tendency to conceive of the Iran situation and other situations where we go wrong, in terms of individual mistakes. What did we do wrong in 1972 in the Nixon Doctrine? What did we do wrong in 1973? We do that sort of thing rather than look at really major overall interests. For example, should we be giving a green light to our business interests? Should be be putting so much emphasis on restoring our balance of payments by promoting the kinds of economic projects overseas which in fact are not the healthiest economic projects for those countries even though we may kid ourselves that they are? At that level I think academics also can have an input.

Helfgott: I'd like to make a comment. No matter how nice the people in the room are right now, and how nice the people in the State Department are, when we look at the history of the American relations with Iran since 1953, it's been a history of intervention. It's been the history of helping to establish, train, and maintain the secret police. It's been the history of encouraging the establishment of a whole series of enterprises in Iran that probably in the long run did not work to better Iranian society. It's been the bolstering up and support again and again of an incredibly brutal political system and of a royal family that didn't, as suggested before, have the support of the mass population. And what seems to be said is, "well these were all mistakes, they are not part of a consistent policy, and you academics should accept that those were the bad guys, they made mistakes, but we're the good guys right now, so listen to us, and talk to us, and we won't make mistakes anymore." I don't think it is so simple.

Question: On a different subject, Muriel Atkin mentioned yesterday that she had heard Soviet transport officials were invited to Iran. We also discussed the *Time* magazine account of listening posts in Baluchistan. I was wondering if she would assess the Soviet direct and indirect influence in Baluchistan, and whether it is a cause for alarm.

Atkin: What is being done covertly, I don't know, but one interesting barometer of what may be going on is the broad sort of propaganda broadcasts that the Soviet Union beams to Iran. What they say on Baluchistan and the Turkmen is very different from what they said for a while about the Kurds, before things deteriorated there, or even about the Azerbaijanis. The Soviet propaganda line on the Baluchis is that they are Afghan drug smugglers, bandits and whatever, supporters of the Pakistani military dictatorship, and, of course, the U.S. and the stock cast of villains who work there. In that sense it would be a little surprising if they were really cooking up something in Baluchistan to be putting forth such a negative propaganda stream on that particular subject. In contrast, when they were wooing the Kurdish Democratic Party for example, they were putting forth a very different line. In Azerbaijan where they have some people trying to build some support, with questionable success, they are putting forth a very different line. So that's really the main indicator I've got to go on.

Miller: I want to go back to a previous point. I really think it is very important to accept what Leonard Helfgott had to say about Iran. Intervention is part of the record, but as I tried to say in my paper and many of us would agree, the United States record in Iran is a very mixed one. It's one of confused motives, some of which fit the description which was given. But more completely, it seems to me, there were other motives that were at cross purposes. The real question, given this strange amalgam of good and bad, depending on where you stand on the moral question, is to try and understand how that confusion of policy happened. It seems that there are explanations. For example, the very different world views of successive administrations, the degree of experience of the national leadership about these questions which complicate the issue, and events elsewhere in the world. This is not to excuse policy, but only to try to understand and explain it. It seems to me if there are any lessons from Iran it is that Iran is a rich example of how the United States has performed in the world. It would be useful for those who are interested in having the most successful foreign policy that we can, to learn from that experience; it is a mixed bag. There are a lot of good things that were done. There are lots of mistakes, and we are all aware of those, but I would argue for looking at that with a sense of completeness and some purpose of trying to do a better job.

Question: I get the impression from our panelists that the United States needs to be doing something to improve our relationship with Iran. Is it really fair to say that it is up to the United States to define the relationship, almost in isolation? In fact, I think the U.S. did define its relationship with Iran when it accepted the revolution. It kept its embassy there for a good deal of time and tried to establish a relationship with the revolutionary forces that were there. What happened in the aftermath indicates that it is the Iranian regime that must give a definition to the relationship. We have staked out our attitude toward Iran. I think what we need is to wait, to see what the Iranian regime is going to look like and what it will determine as its interests. It's sort of a combination: it takes two to tango. I would fear that too activist an approach by the United States, particularly at this time, could very well set back any latent movements by this regime or whatever follows it, to move toward more normal relationships.

Miller: I'm not advocating anything more than expressing the desirability of having formal diplomatic relations. There is in fact some business between the nations; why not do it according to the rules of the game, or at least discuss the rules to see how a relationship can be arranged? You don't have to plunge in up to your armpits to have a relationship. There are differences between something which is formal and correct, and being in lockstep with a country in a complex of ways. I don't think immobilism is a desirable policy. I don't think having such a cleavage between the two countries is a desirable situation for either party. You as a diplomat believe in the proposition that there are ways that nations can benefit from one another. It's just a way of doing business in the world. That seems to be the first step that we ought to achieve. That's not a radical step, nor does it involve intervention; it's just the beginnings of discussions.

Sick: I was one of those who, along with Dick Cottam, strongly supported Bill Miller as ambassador to Iran. I still support him in that capacity and obviously he is still working for that. But seriously, establishing formal, diplomatic relations with Iran is not in the cards until Iran re-defines the issues and has a set of circumstances that makes it possible. There is no way that we can go in. If we walked in tomorrow and said let's have formal diplomatic relations, no matter how we said it, formally, privately, publicly, they would dismiss the idea out of hand. It just isn't going to work. And it isn't going to work until enough things have developed in other areas that make it either necessary or possible politically.

Miller: I would agree with that.

Question: I'm very much persuaded by most of what I've heard here that there is neither a very good case for or prospect of any Iranian-American relationship in the foreseeable future, certainly in the next few years. And I don't think this is necessarily too regrettable. I'm not inclined as much as many people here to be consumed by feelings of guilt by the American relationship, because that is based on the assumption that we are perfect in the world and also responsible for the world at large, which is a delusion which we fall victim to, both on the right and on the left in American thinking too often. But I would like people to comment on something that hasn't been mentioned at all. That is, that Iran and the United States don't exist alone in this world.

There is the Soviet Union looking down on the Iranian border from up there to the north. Iran has relations with a lot of people and the implications of the Iranian revolution for much of the rest of the world are at least as great or greater than they are for us. The Iranian economic relations in the future are going to turn much more on relationships with Europe, the Middle East, and Japan than they are on relations with us. This is the way it ought to be. The implications of the Islamic revolution for other Islamic countries are enormous. Iran's relations are developing very interestingly in certain directions at this time with countries such as Turkey. Iran's relationship with Europe is a very interesting question and topic, and, I think, it is very much in our interests as Americans to stay in the background but to encourage a very wide range of other nations, friends of ours, to have relations with Iran. I don't hear a bit of comment on that.

Sick: Just one brief point. This relates to what Muriel Atkin was saying earlier, a point that bears pulling out a little bit more. Although Iran did continue a number of relations with the Soviet Union and has expanded some of those, the one that they haven't continued is the gas pipeline, and the Soviets really wanted that badly. It hurt them that first year; it was very painful for them. The Soviets had to divert gas from other areas, cut down a lucrative transit market. The Iranians have held very firm on this. Even when they were pushed hard by the Soviets they refused to restore natural gas deliveries to the U.S.S.R. They have now gone ahead with the idea of a gas pipeline across Turkey, which I take seriously. I think they really mean it and that they are going to market their own gas in Europe. I take that as the death knell for their major gas relationship with the Soviet Union. This was the core of the economic relationship, and even kind of a mutual dependence. I take this as a response to the idea that the Soviets are really building up a powerful influence and presence in Iran. On the contrary, I would say that the Iranians are very definitely keeping them at arm's length.

Iran is having some fascinating discussions with the UAE and trying to open up some relations with the Gulf Cooperation Council, which I think are terribly important in the long run. Iran is showing signs of moderation in a variety of areas, which I think is healthy. In fact, the Soviets seem very worried about the fact that Iran is opening up to Turkey and Pakistan. The Soviets say "How can you do this? These are countries both of whom are aligned with the United States and this is contrary to the objectives of the revolution." They are being quite strong in their propaganda currently against the opening to Turkey and Pakistan. But I don't think that it is going to be the millenium that is going to change the politics of U.S.–Iran relations. If in fact the situation does arrive where we can begin to have a relationship with Iran again, I think it will be because of the relationship with intermediate countries which will then lead to other things. That strikes me as a very healthy recent development.

Hooglund: I'd like to bring something up that may tie some of these themes together and has implications for broader U.S. foreign policy. If U.S. foreign policy continues to be based on a perspective whereby relationships with all countries are seen through a prism of U.S.–Soviet relations, how can we develop effective policies with countries which may view the U.S.–Soviet rivalry as secondary to their own concerns? I think Iran is a clear example where the whole relationship with the shah was built up as part of a containment policy against the Soviet Union, however that containment was defined, whether it goes through periods of cold war tension or detente and so forth. It was always from the perspective that whatever was happening in Iran was related to the Soviet Union. In several other countries in the Middle East it is the same. And as long as that continues to happen, as long as U.S.–Soviet rivalry is the overriding perspective, how is it ever possible within the policy-making apparatus to take recognition of what is going on domestically, especially when domestic politics may have nothing to do with the conflict between the superpowers? But these same politics may have significant consequences for U.S. Mid-East policy.

I mean, the revolution in Iran was an internal matter, and yet you can pick up the newspapers and the news weeklies all through 1978 and read that the clerics were somehow Islamic-Marxists. There was an inability, after so many years of conditioning, to see that anything could be internally motivated, and it's not just Iran where this happens. I guess what I find disturbing about this is that as long as policy is always seen through that prism, how can we have policies which serve, in the long term, the interests of the United States? We can have short-term policies, but in the long term by not having any recognition of what's going on internally, we risk alienating those domestic groups, especially those that are opposition forces to authoritarian governments which are allied to the U.S. In the end we are going to run into not just one disaster like Iran, but one right after the other. In the long run, is that serving U.S. interests?

Sick: Well everyone in the government, of course, is intensely aware of the problem you are talking about. It has different names: the globalists versus the regionalists, the top-down versus the bottom-up view, a whole range of things. My understanding of the problem is this: there is a constant balancing of priorities. Where do you put your first priority? On, say, domestic affairs in Iran? As the United States government, do you place your primary long-term interests on the domestic welfare of Iranians? Or do you place it on the constellations of U.S.-Soviet relations? Now you can be ludicrous about this in the extremes. For example, the case where you care only about whether the people of Iran are happy and satisfied, so you spend all your time worried about 150 countries in the world, all of whom should be happy and satisfied with their governments. We should be doing everything we can to help them; if we do that, it will serve our long-term interests. That really isn't a realistic policy, but it is an extreme. The other extreme is to care nothing about regional affairs, nothing about the realities of current political regimes, only the relationship between the U.S. and the Soviet Union, and nothing else. Both of those approaches are dead wrong. The people in the government, especially senior policymakers, tend to fall towards the globalists' side of the game and don't know much about domestic affairs. To be fair, however, the people who are most concerned, the genuine experts in the region, tend to get so involved in the regional or domestic affairs that they fail to see that there really is a global dimension that involves U.S. interests.

There has to be a balance between those two. There's going to be a constant tension, but that is a place in fact, as I think Nikki Keddie just said, where the academic community can help. It can help to establish where our real interests are in terms of this tension that is constantly pulling decision makers a variety of different ways. There is no answer to the question. The tension is always going to be there, but I think the academic community does have something of offer.

Question: I want to ask Gary Sick a question on the crisis-management aspect of the Iranian revolution. You mentioned that at least for the hostage crisis the management worked very well. But the American crisis-management machinery for the revolution failed. Could you elaborate on that?

Sick: This is a very technical subject and I'll be very brief, because I don't think everyone is interested in the details about how the government does its business. Basically, the difference was that when the hostage crisis occurred a task force was formed almost immediately at the State Department. Almost instantly there was a group at the National Security Council level that began meeting almost daily. This was at the cabinet level for the most part, and it met generally at nine o'clock in the morning. Every day there was a high-level discussion. Issues were formally examined from all different points of view; different opinions were discussed; summaries were relayed to the president the same day for comment; and his answers and guidance were taken up the next day. It was a constant, ongoing event, with tremendous communication within the government and also with great security. There were almost no leaks, for instance, from this process. Everyone knew that people's lives were at stake, and that had a sobering effect on the usual fun-and-games that are played in Washington.

   That didn't happen at all during the fall of the shah. There were sporadic high-level meetings, but nothing of a continuing basis, nothing that really forced the issues to be raised, identified, refined, argued out, and carried back and forth to the president on a regular basis. The NSC was playing its game and the State Department was playing its own game. Everybody had their own back-channel to Ambassador Sullivan in Tehran. Everybody was playing the game their own way, with very little communication and nobody trusting anybody. Partly that was the nature of the crisis. The hostage crisis was one that united the American people and the government around an issue; the fall of the shah was not. So in a sense it was not just the machinery, but the machinery could have helped a great deal in illuminating the issues. One of the amazing things that has been obvious to me in reviewing that whole period is that there were unbelievably few—you could count them on one hand—policy meetings that were held to examine those issues. Although there were a lot of discussions going on, a lot of telephone calls, a lot of bureaus and papers and things of the sort, systematic, high-level discussions of the really critical issues tended to be avoided. I don't know if it would have changed our policy a bit, I don't know if we would have come out at any different place, but I do know that we would have felt better about it and would have more fully understood what we were doing, if those meetings had taken place.

Cottam: Why didn't they?

Sick: Well, the problem is not a simple one. First of all I think it is true that the machinery had never been tested so that it wasn't an automatic reflex reaction. Secondly, I just can't stress enough how thin the Near East bureaucracy is, and has been, in Washington. The number of people involved is really very small. The day Jaleh Square occurred President Carter was at Camp David with Begin and Sadat on the second day of their discussions, and he was really preoccupied and so was virtually everybody else in the Middle East bureaucracy, across the board. In the State Department, the Defense Department, the NSC, everybody was focused on Camp David, on the Egyptian-Israeli treaty. It took almost the entire manpower of the U.S. government on the Middle East question to focus in on that and meet the kind of tremendous day-by-day, hour-by-hour needs that were going on. It's impossible for people outside to appreciate just what those pressures can really be, when the President is personally engaged and you have a rapidly moving situation. So Iran was not the top of the priority list. Later on people could look back and say, "Oh, my God, the things we should have been doing. We should have done this. . . ." But Iran got shoved aside, and I think that that contributed heavily to the wishful thinking process that was going on. I don't say that is a good thing, it's just a fact.

IRAN and SOVIET-AMERICAN RELATIONS

Richard Cottam

SINCE THE RELEASE OF THE AMERICAN HOSTAGES on the day of President Reagan's inauguration, Iran has played very little part in the American media coverage of world events. Also confined to an occasional back page story is the Soviet occupation of Afghanistan. And so the public memory is beginning to fade of three great shocks administered American foreign policy during the Carter years: the inability to prevent the collapse of America's chief surrogate in South Asia, the regime of the shah of Iran; the inability to free fifty Americans held hostage for over a year in Iran; and the helplessness with which the government watched Afghanistan overrun by Soviet troops. These events were of sufficient importance to challenge the very basis of American strategic thinking regarding South Asia and the Middle East. They should surely have led to a reexamination of the basic assumptions on which American strategy in this part of the world rests. But, in fact, with the passing of the immediate crisis, American attention has turned elsewhere, and the meaning of these events remains unexamined.

Most fundamental of the assumptions which provide the underlay for competing American foreign policy preferences are estimates of Soviet foreign policy intentions, and estimates of American capability to play a preeminent foreign policy role in areas many thousands of miles distant from the North American continent. There are those who see a Soviet Union dedicated to bringing communism to the rest of the world and hence are committed to a policy that is ineluctably expansionist. Others, no more attracted to the Soviet form of government, see a Soviet leadership that is motivated more by fear of the USA and the PRC than by a desire to spread communism and are committed to a defensive, ultimately status quo policy. There are those who see an America fully capable of fulfilling its commitments in the eastern hemisphere if it is able to garner the necessary will and determination to do so. Others believe the American resource base can no longer support an activist foreign policy quite literally on the other side of the world. Obviously, the individual who sees a Soviet Union with a strongly imperialist policy and an America that has the resource base for containing it but has lacked the will to do so, and the individual who sees the Soviet Union with an essentially status quo policy and an America already overextended in relation to its resource base are operating within sharply different world views. Just as obviously the two will advocate sharply different general strategies and only rarely—and for different reasons—can agree on specific strategies and tactics. It follows that there is no task more important than that of assessing the case for these differing assumptions. And the events in Iran and Afghanistan in 1979 were of such a magnitude of importance that they should have told us much about these most basic assumptions.

When, in November 1979, Ayatollah Ruhollah Khomeini made the decision to retain as hostages Americans taken captive when the American embassy in Tehran was overrun by a mob of student "followers of the line of the Imam," his purpose was to humiliate the USA and to demonstrate to Americans and Iranians that the USA was indeed impotent. Khomeini saw as one of his major missions demonstrating to the oppressor states of the world—we call it the North—that they no longer had the ability to impose their wills on the oppressed—the South. America, he felt, should have learned this lesson from the shah's fall. But apparently, more shocks would be necessary to make the United States understand.[1] Nor did Khomeini ignore the other great oppressor, the Soviet Union. It was entirely congruent with his thinking that he should have authorized his foreign minister, Sadeq Qotbzadeh, to take the lead at an Islamic conference at Islamabad in April 1980 in denouncing the Soviet invasion of Afghanistan. It was one thing to seek to humiliate a superpower nine thousand miles away, but it was quite another to antagonize the other superpower simultaneously, especially since Iran shared a twelve hundred-mile border with that superpower. Khomeini was determined to prove his thesis, apparently unconcerned with the risks involved.

Could the United States have saved the shah and released the hostages shortly after they were taken? Anyone answering "yes," and many do, should develop their answer with detailed scenarios incorporating the tactical plans that could have achieved these ends. But, in fact, those answering in the affirmative make their argument at a much higher level of generality. The American failure, they insist, was largely a failure of will. The remedy is to restore a sense of determination and to demonstrate that determination by an expanded military preparedness program. Could an America, fiercely determined and optimally prepared, have saved the shah? The question is never seriously addressed. The United States had interfered successfully in Iran a generation and a half before, why not again? But in 1953 the mass of the Iranian people were politically dormant. In 1979, they were politically alive and overwhelmingly in support of revolution. There is indeed every reason to question American ability to stand against a popular revolution in a third-world state in the eastern hemisphere. Those American failures in Iran really should lead to an examination of the proposition that, in this new era in which mass politics characterize much of the third world, the American stability to interfere in the internal affairs of those states, in the manner of the 1950s, has come to an end.

For those who are convinced of the ineluctable aggressive purpose of Soviet foreign policy, the Soviet invasion of Afghanistan was seen as one more irrefutable piece of evidence. Carl Gershman, a member of Jeane Kirkpatrick's United Nations staff, for example, said after Afghanistan, those who question Soviet aggressive intent "no longer deserve to be listened to."[2] But how do the totally convinced explain Soviet policy toward Iran? Why, when Iran's military was in a state of collapse and several ethnic groups in Iran with which the Soviet government has easy access were opposing the reestablishment of central control did the Soviet Union behave so passively? Why accept the world's opprobrium and Carter's enmity by invading Afghanistan when Iran, an infinitely more valuable prize, was so available? If the Soviets feared the United States might exercise its nuclear option in the face of a direct invasion, why not throw support to Kurdish, Turkmen, Baluchi, and Arab separatists and bring about Iran's disintegration with little risk of ultimate confrontation with the United States? Again, these questions were simply not asked. Soviet passivity and the support of the revolutionary religious element of the Khomeini regime by the pro-Moscow Tudeh Party were explained as part of a devious ingratiating and infiltrating plot. For those utterly convinced of Soviet aggressive intent, actual Soviet behavior, even when it appears passive, cooperative, and peaceful, is apparently never seen as falsifying the basic assumptions.

Seen from the perspective of these two base assumptional positions, the Carter and Reagan policies in the Middle East have had very different manifestations. Carter, in foreign and domestic policy, was inclined to be strongly programmatic. But the often very talented individuals who prepared the programs for the Middle East ranged broadly on a scale between these assumptional poles. Foreign security adviser Brzezinski was of the ineluctably aggressive Soviet Union, American activist school, whereas Secretary of State Vance, and even more the American United

Nations representative, Andrew Young, approached the Soviet status quo pole. Programs therefore tended to be compartmented. In areas where Brzezinski's views prevailed, as in the policy toward the Iranian revolution in the shah's last months, the program was designed to oppose Soviet aggression. The revolution was treated as Soviet-orchestrated, and American opposition to it approached the absolute. Then, when Vance's views prevailed, as in the months following the revolution in Iran, the program was one of virtually ignoring any Soviet subversive threat and concentrating on establishing close relations with and using what influence the United States retained to attempt to strengthen the Bazargan liberal element of Khomeini's regime. What was inevitably missing in a policy consisting of a set of diverse and often contradictory discrete programs was overall strategy. Should strategy be directed toward containing the Soviet Union or toward regional detente with the Soviet Union? Given the fundamental differences among members of the administration, no decision at this level could be made. It is fair to say that Carter had discrete policies in the Middle East but no general strategy.

In sharp contrast, the Reagan administration has a fairly clear general strategy which embraces basic policy in the Middle East but has very few programmatic translations. It is easy to identify basic strategic objectives of the administration but impossible to identify lower level strategic and tactical plans. This reflects an administration in which there is broad world view consensus. Seen in terms of the two basic assumptions, the Reagan administration is without any self doubts. The Soviet Union is ineluctably aggressive, and American capability is potentially fully sufficient to contain that aggressiveness in South Asia and the Middle East. Strategy obviously calls for constructing a cordon sanitaire stretching from Japan to Great Britain that will keep the Soviet Union in its lair. To be sure, there are some terrible problems as yet not fully resolved, even at this level. Is the enemy communism or the Soviet Union? If the former, then surely Taiwan must be supported against a communist PRC. If the latter, then surely the PRC must be one of the most critical links in the containment chain. The Reagan administration is having difficulty choosing.

But at a lower level, the problems are far greater. How does one deal with a Khomeini who is bitterly hostile to one great oppressor state, the Soviet Union with its millions of oppressed Moslem citizens and in occupation of Islamic Afghanistan, but who is possibly even more hostile to the other great oppressor state, the United States? Should a patient, careful policy of rapprochement with Khomeini be devised, or should the United States give its backing to anti-Khomeini, anti-Soviet Iranian exiles who could be as friendly to the United States as the shah was but who might have great difficulty attracting any popular support? Fortunately, the passive quality of Soviet behavior in Iran, however devious the administration considers its long-term purpose, reduces the urgency of addressing this question, and negative evidence suggests it is not addressed. There is, in fact, no discernible American strategy toward Iran.

Nevertheless, Iran cannot be ignored. The Middle East and South Asia are critical arenas for American containment strategy, and Iran is deeply involved in regional affairs. But this involvement is strangely contradictory from the Reagan administration's point of view. The regime has reasonably friendly relations with Turkey and Pakistan, allies of the United States. And anti-Soviet Afghan refugees are receiving Iranian support and conducting operations against the Soviet-dependent Afghan regime from Iran. But Iran's primary preoccupation has been her war with Iraq and, in this great drama, Arab regimes friendly with the United States are supporting Iraq, and those friendly with the Soviet Union are supporting Iran. To add to the confusion, the Soviet Union has sold arms to both Iran and Iraq, and America's closest regional friend, Israel, has engaged in at least small-scale arms sales to Iran.

Beyond this, the Khomeini regime is openly interested in seeing the great Islamic revolution which has embraced Iran spread to other areas of Islam. Governmental rhetoric indicates that the Iranian Islamic Republic should serve as example to others and denies any intent to interfere in the internal affairs of other states. However, radio broadcasts from Iran do encourage revolution in many areas of Islam, and Tehran is a willing host to revolution-minded Moslems from a broad range of countries. Indeed, there is scarcely a regime in the Islamic world, friendly or unfriendly to Iran, that does not fear the possible destabilizing effects of the Islamic revolution in Iran. For Americans concerned with containing the Soviet Union, instability in areas of strategic importance has always been seen as a major opportunity for Soviet expansion. On these grounds, surely the Iranian regime should be seen as posing a major problem for the achievement of American strategic objectives.

As long as confronting the Soviet Union in South Asia is a central strategic concern for the American government, Iran must be a preoccupation of American policymakers. Its strategic location and its vast oil resources make this inevitable. Since the Reagan administration is at least as committed to containment as any of its predecessors, the current indecision regarding Iran cannot long persist. But an administration that views the world in a Cold War perspective will have difficulty understanding how to deal with Iran. Rejecting both the East and the West, the Khomeini government is, in effect, offering a third model for the "oppressed" nations, and, in particular, oppressed Islamic nations, to emulate. That model has lost some, possibly much, of its attraction as the reality of the Khomeini government program becomes clear. Offsetting the appeal of an Islamic ideology is the fact of a stagnating economy, programmatic indecision, and brutality toward those who do not share its ideology. But significant appeal remains especially for the large poor and lower-middle classes.

Iran's foreign policy operates not at all within a Cold War perspective. Iranian policy is designed to do what is necessary in the external arena to secure the health and vitality of the Islamic revolution. At times, this leads to specific policies the United States government can approve of, as with Turkey, Pakistan, and Afghanistan. At other times, it leads to discomfort, as with Iran's alliance with Syria, Libya and the PLO. And its revolutionary messianism, since the areas most vulnerable are Arab territories near or bordering the Persian Gulf, is clearly perceived as very dangerous. For an administration whose perceptual blinders are almost exclusively those of the Cold War, Iranian policy is bewildering and other worldly and a response to it has yet to be formulated.

What do the South Asia–Middle East links in the cordon sanitaire chain look like? Turkey and Pakistan are clearly vital links. A decision on Iran can be deferred for the time being. But what about the Arab world and Israel? Surely the ideal arrangement in that area would be that proposed by Senator Henry Jackson. By his proposal, the three vital links would be Egypt, Israel, and Saudi Arabia. With such an alliance system, obstreperous regimes, such as those of Syria, Libya, and South Yemen, could be isolated and quite possibly overturned. Furthermore, the proposal would marry the central American objective, that is, to contain the Soviet Union in the area, with two other vital objectives; preserving Israel's security and independence and assuring the flow of Middle and Eastern oil to Western economies. Unfortunately, though, from the Administration's point of view, Arab nationalism is too strong a force for Saudi leaders to dare to consider such a plan. Only peripheral regimes lacking any real legitimacy and therefore needing external support, such as that of Sultan Qabus of Oman, would be willing to associate with Egypt in a de facto alliance with Israel.

Nevertheless, the administration proceeded with its policy of constructing a cordon sanitaire across the Arab world as if it had received the agreement to do so from central Arab actors. But the decision to make the AWACs sale to Saudi Arabia brought the contradiction in this policy to a head. The Saudi Arabian government wanted the sophisticated radar warning system but, as its spokesmen made only too clear, the scenarios for its use the Saudis had in mind involved first Israel and second a militant Iran. Thus the AWACs sale was seen as threatening first to Israel, to whose defense the United States was committed, and second to Iran, concerning which American policy had yet to be formulated.

Furthermore, the assumption that Egyptian-Israeli harmony could continue to prevail—and this is the central assumption for the Jackson proposal and indeed implicitly for any administration plan for extending the cordon sanitaire through the Middle East—is unduly optimistic. Mubarak's Egypt has been sounding increasingly serious about its determination to avoid becoming embroiled in superpower conflicts in the Middle East. Whereas Sadat appeared to solicit an American surrogate role, even at times to offer to act as America's Cuba in the African-West Asian arena, Mubarak has made clear his wish to return to the Arab world. Any such return for Egypt would necessitate an Egyptian acceptance of a leadership role in compelling Israel to grant Palestinians a minimally acceptable form of self determination. It certainly precludes being America's surrogate in the area.

At the same time, Israel, for her part, has shown no inclination to grant Palestinians an autonomy that goes beyond the simple administrative level. This position plus what Arabs see as the inexcusably brutal June 1982 invasion of Lebanon makes any further success for the Camp David approach for settling the Arab-Israeli conflict problematic at the very best. The primary alternative to Camp David that has been proposed is the Geneva Conference model by which the United States and the USSR act jointly to encourage a settlement. The terms of such a settlement, it is generally understood, would adhere to a formula that has been advanced with minor variations since shortly after the 1967 war. The formula includes a formal Arab recognition of an Israel incorporating essentially the pre-June 1967 de facto boundaries. Israel, for its part, would agree to the creation of a Palestinian entity which, whatever its form, would be truly independent of Israel. The formula includes an international guarantee of these borders that would not incorporate an increased Soviet-American presence. Whereas this model would be attractive for those who, seeing a defensively inclined Soviet Union, are favorably disposed toward ventures that offer the possibility of developing political detente with the Soviet Union, it is hardly attractive to an American administration which sees a Soviet Union yearning for greater influence in the Middle East. The Reagan administration advanced its own plan, the so-called Reagan Plan, which inclines toward the settlement terms of the formula but excludes the Soviets as either mediator or guarantor. However, when this plan was quickly rejected by the Israeli government, the administration in effect acquiesced in its demise and was left with no plan for settling the Arab-Israeli dispute.

Stated baldly, the Reagan administration's policy in the Middle

East is clear only at the highest strategic objectives level: halting any Soviet expansionist schemes. But none of the multitudinous, complex and interacting conflicts in the Middle East is obviously Soviet-inspired. Indeed, Soviet policy is remarkably parallel to American policy. Both superpowers supply arms to their friends; neither has a clearly formulated policy toward Iran; neither appears able to help settle any of the disputes that define conflict in the area. The result is quite simply that the two superpowers are deeply involved in the Middle East and yet are unable to exercise any real control over the dynamics of conflict in the area. This loss of control carries with it the very real danger of inadvertent superpower confrontation. American policy toward Iran, it follows, must be viewed in this regional context. The particular shape it ultimately takes in all likelihood will be determined by the dynamics of developments in the region—dynamics operating largely independently of the United States or the Soviet Union.

Actual conflict in the Middle East has three major foci: the Arab-Israeli conflict over the future of the Palestinian people, the Iraq-Iran conflict involving more broad resistance to the appeal of Islamic revolution, and a complex of inter-Arab conflicts. Since these conflicts interact, the overall regional conflict picture is a maze filled with gross contradictions and ironies. Yet there are discernible, within this maze, emerging trends that neither the United States nor the Soviet Union appears to be noting but around which patterns of future conflict are likely to crystallize.

The strongest crystallizing tendencies until 1982 emanated from the inter-Arab conflict. The roots of that conflict lie deep within opposing responses to the forces of rapid change in the region: traditional elites struggling to accommodate change while holding onto power, opposed by a variety of counterelites seeking to overturn the traditional elite structure. But the conflict picture is not simply one of traditional versus modernizing regimes. At its core since 1978 has been the Iraq-Syria conflict in which the opposing governing elites closely resembled one another. Both regimes have been vigorous proponents of Arab nationalism and rapid modernization. Both have been emphatic advocates of a Palestinian state and bitter opponents of the Camp David approach. Both have inclined toward the Soviet Union in the superpower conflict. Yet the Syrian-Iraqi conflict, until Israel's invasion of Lebanon, was the generic conflict in the Middle East—the one that gave definition to the polarizing tendencies in the area. In 1978 Saddam Hussein of Iraq, charging external involvement in a plot against him, broke off what had seemed to be promising negotiations with Syria for a move toward unity. Shortly thereafter, he made a radical shift in alliance toward traditionally based Arab regimes—Jordan, Saudi Arabia, and much of the Arabian peninsula and Morocco. In doing so, he demonstrated an almost casual disdain for the Soviet Union, which viewed his new allies as American client states. He almost equally casually offended Arab nationalist orthodoxy which denied the nationalist legitimacy of these new allies. And at the same time he carried out acts of brutal repression against Shi'ite leaders, thus demonstrating disdain as well for the radical Islamic movement focusing on the Shi'ite community of Iran.

When Iraq invaded Iran in 1980, Saddam Hussein made his intention clear to use his expected easy victory as a means for achieving personal preeminence in the Arab world. But his efforts to picture the conflict as Arab-Iranian found little receptivity with those Arabs allied with Syria, who saw Saddam Hussein's alliance with pro-American Arab regimes as a betrayal of the Arab nation, and implicit cooperation with Israel. To counter this view, the Iraqis made much of reports of Iranian purchases of military supplies from agents of the Israeli government. Israel's sale of arms to Iran was a natural act of taking advantage of the acute embarrassment of one of its most intransigent enemies, Iraq. But that small degree of Iranian-Israeli cooperation was always counterpoint to the main Iranian theme, which was one of irreconcilable opposition to Israel. The Islamic leadership of Iran in its rhetoric has been the equal of the most dedicated Palestinian nationalist in its attacks on Israel. Syrian and PLO leaders therefore could reasonably describe the Iraqi invasion of Iran as an act that threatened to deprive the Arabs of a potentially powerful ally in its struggle with Israel. When Iran launched its successful campaign to liberate Khorramshahr, it gave the campaign the code name of "Operation Jerusalem." After the campaign achieved its final success, Radio Tehran spelled out in no uncertain terms Iran's determination to continue with Operation Jerusalem until not only the liberation of Jerusalem but the complete elimination of Israel.[3] And this was before the Israeli invasion of Lebanon.

The governments of Syria and its allies were a far cry from the model of an Islamic republic that the Imam Khomeini had in mind. But the policies of those regimes were, in the opinion of the Iranian government, consistent with the demands of dignity and self confidence that Khomeini has called for from regimes of the "oppressed" peoples. In marked contrast, the Iranians saw Iraq and its allies as agent regimes of the great oppressor, the United States. Therefore, the Iranian attraction to the Syrian alliance was very strong. Just how strong was made clear by the Iranian response to the Muslim Brotherhood challenge to the Syrian government. Foreign Minister Ali Akbar Velayati denounced the Muslim Brotherhood as having, in effect, become an agent of Israel and its mentor, the United States.[4] Since the Iranian leadership has been making every effort to depict its revolution as Islamic and not simply Shi'ite and since the Muslim Brotherhood is Sunni in membership and has been favorably inclined toward Khomeini, this attack on the Muslim Brotherhood was of major significance. It appeared on the surface to be a major indicator of a pragmatic turn in Iranian foreign policy.

But if Iran was associating with the Syrian pole, the pull on Egypt was in the opposite direction. Arab regimes allied with Iraq were openly calling for the end of Egypt's isolation in the Arab world. With Iraq's setbacks in its war with Iran, the attraction of the idea of bringing Egypt into the conservative block was irresistible. Egyptian opposition leaders, who have been surprisingly able to express a dissenting view, argued strongly in favor of an Egyptian return to the Arab world but to all the Arabs, not just the conservative bloc.[5] However, Husni Mubarak had sided strongly with Iraq in the Iran-Iraq war and had established close and friendly relations with both Oman and the Sudan, strong antagonists of the Syrian alliance. In 1982, the dynamics appeared to be on the side of Egypt's becoming a bloc leader.

The situation in the summer of 1982 prior to the Israeli invasion of Lebanon could be described as precrystallization. The dynamics of interacting regional conflict were producing strong tendencies toward a polarization, one consequence of which would have been almost certainly an emerging hostile American policy toward Iran. At this point, an incident, such as an Islamic coup in Bahrain, could have produced two hostile blocs, each with its superpower ally and a serious danger of superpower confrontation.

The incident that did occur, the Israeli invasion of Lebanon, was a shockingly dramatic demonstration of superpower loss of control. Indeed, the most palpable change that has occurred in the period following the Israeli invasion has been an altering view of the capabilities of various actors.

Most obviously affected has been the Palestine Liberation Organization. The military performance of the PLO in the war revealed a commitment and a technical proficiency beyond expectations. But the inability of the PLO to persuade any Arab regime to come to its support beyond the symbolic level made clear an extraordinarily weak bargaining position. Yasir Arafat appeared to seek to counter this weakness by ingratiating himself with friends of the United States, in particular Egypt and Jordan, and included kind words for the Israeli peace movement. This tactic risked tarnishing his own legitimacy and led to serious splits in Fatah and a loss of support from the ranks of political Islam. The Khomeini regime, for example, viewed Arafat as having followed the path of Sadat and Saddam Hussein in betraying the Arab nation, Islam, and the oppressed peoples generally. Arafat's tactic was the one strong factor working after the invasion for a deepening polarization. But other developments countered this tendency, and the early movement toward a crystallization into sharply separated poles, each with its great power mentor, quickly reversed.

A major reason for this reversal was the altering view of superpower capability in the area. Israel's disregard of any possibility of a serious Soviet response to the defeat and humiliation of her PLO and Syrian friends proved to be fully justified. This was in the pattern of Iraq's having paid no serious price by having allied with American friends in the area, by condemning the Soviet invasion of Afghanistan and by persecuting Iraqi communists. Similarly, Iran saw no particular risk in expelling Soviet diplomats and in arresting and prosecuting Tudeh Party leaders. These episodes, combined with the Soviet embarrassment in Afghanistan, produced a view of Soviet functional capability in the region that was in sharp decline.

The alteration in the view of American capability was significantly more dramatic than that of the Soviet Union. An initially vigorous American diplomacy following the Israeli invasion accented by a symbolic military presence gave the impression of exceptional powerfulness. Indeed, the fact that even Syria acquiesced for a time in America's taking the diplomatic lead gave the impression of a power assymetry that reflected the decisive defeat of one of the poles in a polarized conflict. For the great power mentor of victorious Israel to be negotiating peace terms suggested more than anything else a graceful capitulation of the Syrian alliance. Yet within a few months the American presence was challenged, at first tentatively and then decisively, by indigenous forces. The withdrawal first of the marines and then of the offshore fleet had an even greater symbolic impact than had their arrival. The American hegemonic moment was a brief one.

The view of Israel's capability altered as well and in a direction that Ariel Sharon had not foreseen.[6] To be sure, Israel's military superiority over any combination of her immediate neighbors remained unquestioned, particularly with regard to the air force. But the expected easy, twenty-four-hour victory over the PLO and the Syrian forces in Lebanon did not occur. Even more important, the price of occupying southern and west central Lebanon for an extended period of time was clearly much too high. Two years after the invasion of Lebanon, the image of Israeli relative capability was a diminished one. As a consequence, Israeli policy was less determining of the regional dynamics than it had been.

Nor were the forces of Arab nationalism the beneficiaries of this great power and Israeli decline. Syria, whose leaders claim the mantle of Arab nationalist orthodoxy, did indeed profit from the capability changes.

But Israel's discomfort in southern Lebanon was far more the product of an extraordinarily rapidly developing Shi'ite political activism than of Syrian policy. Indeed, Syrian policy lends itself to the interpretation of being primarily concerned with regime survival. For a great many Lebanese, and not only Lebanese Moslems, the Syrian regime was far less the focus of Arab nationalism than a refuge for the small Alawite minority which had been dominating the Sunnite majority of Syria.

The real beneficiary of apparent alterations in capability was political Islam, beginning with Iran. The Islamic Republic of Iran was diplomatically isolated. The Soviet Union, France, the United States, Egypt, and the Arab traditional alliance were all determined that Iraq not be defeated militarily by Iran. Still, with all this support, Iraq appeared to be striving for no more militarily than a stalemate. Given the dimensions of the support Iraq was receiving and given Iran's denial of essential military equipment, Iran's ability not only to stand firm but also to pose a serious threat to Iraq was impressive. And the Iranian regime was only one manifestation of the force of political Islam. From Pakistan to Morocco, every regime was being forced to adapt to its increasing presence. Since political Islam was following diverse paths across the region and since adaptation strategies of regimes varied widely, political Islam remained largely inchoate. Here again an incident, such as an Iranian breakthrough in Basra or the replacement of a secular regime with a clerical-dominated government, could produce some crystallizing tendencies. But even in this unformed state, political Islam more than any other factor is in control of regional dynamics.

There are, as a consequence, many anomalies appearing. The Reagan administration, preoccupied as it is with containing a perceived Soviet threat in the area, became the de facto ally of the Soviet Union in opposing the Iranian pressure against Iraq. However, relations between Iran and the Soviet Union are far better than those of Iran and the United States. The Soviet Union, despite many rebuffs from Iran and Iranian support for some Afghan rebels, has made serious efforts to effect improved relations with the Iranian revolutionary regime. With regard to Afghanistan, however, the American government is supporting rebel groups that look to the Iranian government as a model. In the Arab world, Soviet and American policies toward Islamic political forces tend to be derivative of the Soviet and American attitudes toward the particular regime in question. Thus, when Islamic forces appear to be destabilizing an unfriendly regime, the attitude toward that force is positive. And, of course, the converse also holds.

In sum, even though the force of political Islam is a major, if not the primary, determinant of interactional dynamics in the Middle Eastern region, neither the United States nor the Soviet government has developed a strategy for dealing with it. They continue to react on an ad hoc basis to tactical moves of Islamic forces, and the governing basis of the reaction is the impact of the particular tactical move on regimes with which they have a historical relationship of friendship or enmity. The exception to this pattern occurs especially with respect to the United States when American citizens or interests are the target of violent attack. When this occurs, the attackers are described as "terrorists," and there is an apparently natural tendency to associate the "terrorists," clearly enemies of the United States, with an aging but still operating picture of a Soviet-connected alliance system. Libya and Syria thus are seen as probably culpable and behind them is the hidden orchestrator, the Soviet Union. Iran, as a friend of Syria and an enemy of Israel and of friendly Arab regimes, is viewed also as probably culpable. The fact of Iranian enmity toward the Soviet Union is conveniently overlooked.

The tendency, therefore, is a strong one for the Americans to see political Islam in the Arab world, the perpetrator of terrorism and the tormentor of friendly regimes, as not only in alliance with, but actively manipulated by, the Soviet Union, but Iran too is actively manipulating political Islam in the region, in the American view, and yet the Americans and Soviets are both engaged in an effort to contain perceived Iranian messianic expansionism. In Afghanistan, where Iranian involvement with selected rebel groups is overt, American and Iranian policy is strongly opposed to the Soviet presence. The contradictions implicit here are too serious to persist over time. Their resolution, however, is likely to occur as a consequence of a serious incident; and Soviet-American loss of control of the situation is such that the crystallizing incident, should one occur, is likely to be the product of forces acting independently of either of the so called superpowers. In terms of probabilities, these determining forces are most likely to be Islamic. The United States government could regain some control over the direction of developments in the region only if it were to formulate strategies to deal with actual areas of conflict in the Middle East rather than simply worrying about containing the Soviet Union. Since this is unlikely, the formulation of an American policy toward Iran must wait until new regional conflict patterns emerge.

NOTES

1. Khomeini gave me his basic picture of his role in bringing to the oppressed people the consciousness of having the power to resist the oppressors in an interview in

France, December, 1978. His explanation for his sanctioning the taking of hostages was reported to me by the then foreign minister, Sadeq Qotbzadeh, and the then UN ambassador, Mansur Farhang, in a series of interviews in the winter of 1979–80.

2. Carl Gershman, "The Rise and Fall of the New Foreign Policy Establishment," *Commentary,* July 1980, p. 24.

3. *FBIS,* May 25, 1982.

4. See *Ettelaat,* March 4, 1982 as reported in the *FBIS,* March 23, 1982.

5. For an articulate expression of opposition thinking, see the interviews of Mohammad Haykal, *Monday Morning,* Beirut, March 22–28, 1982. *FBIS,* March 26, 1982.

6. For an excellent journalistic account of Sharon's thinking and decisional role, see Ze'ev Schiff and Ehud Ya'ari, *Israel's Lebanon War,* (New York: Simon and Schuster, 1984).

INDEX

THE IRANIAN REVOLUTION AND THE ISLAMIC REPUBLIC

was composed in 10-point Mergenthaler Linotron 202 Sabon and leaded 2 points
by Coghill Book Typesetting Co.;
with display type in Ryter Bold by Rochester Mono/Headliners;
and ornaments provided by Jōb Litho Services;
printed sheet-fed offset on 55-pound, acid-free Glatfelter Antique Cream,
Smyth-sewn and bound over binder's boards in Joanna Arrestox B
by Maple-Vail Book Manufacturing Group, Inc.;
with dust jackets printed in 2 colors by Philips Offset Company, Inc.;
and published by

SYRACUSE UNIVERSITY PRESS
SYRACUSE, NEW YORK 13244-5160